≫≮

STILL REBELS, STILL YANKEES
And Other Essays

STILL REBELS, STILL YANKEES

and other essays

BY DONALD DAVIDSON

Wood Engraving by Theresa Sherrer Davidson

LOUISIANA STATE UNIVERSITY PRESS

Library of Congress Catalogue Card Number: 57-7495
Copyright 1957 by Louisiana State University Press.
The essay "Theme and Method in *So Red the Rose*"
was first printed as part of the introduction to Stark
Young's *So Red the Rose* (copyright 1953 by Charles
Scribner's Sons and used with their permission).

idson, **Donald.** Still Rebels, still
kees, and other essays. Wood en-
ving by Theresa Sherrer Davidson.
. 284p. illus. Louisiana State Univ.,
0.

ys by a Southern critic, poet, and pro-
or which center on the conflict between
ition and antitradition in modern litera-
and society. A central, recurrent theme
at the South, deeply rooted in folklore,
stral ties, and a sense of the past, has
ined tradition, while many other areas
he U.S. have, in the name of progress,
ived themselves of the past's rich her-
. His articulate, if one-sided comments
ace relations, the Southern literary ren-
nce, and the outlook of the contemporary
th are variations on the primary motif.
e of the essays have appeared in the
anee Review, Kenyon Review, and other
odicals.

4 American literature—Hist. & crit.   57-7495

tely

fes-

Vell

o a

nd RICHARD E. DODD

rgia

d Admiration

s *viget*

ACKNOWLEDGMENTS

THE ESSAYS and articles chosen for this book are mostly concerned with the impact of the modern regime upon the great vital continuum of human experience to which we apply the inadequate term "tradition"; and no less with the response of tradition to that impact, in the arts and in society. The Southern scene, past and present, naturally affords examples of the clash between tradition and antitradition, but the conflict is all-pervasive, though its manifestations are often disguised. The conflict, wherever it occurs, is what gives this book occasion for being. Two of the essays ("Poetry as Tradition" and "The Tradition of Irreverence") have not been previously published. Others have appeared in periodicals or books over the last twenty years or more. My thanks are due to the copyright owners who have kindly given their permission to reprint.

The following essays have appeared in periodicals: "Yeats and the Centaur," "The Traditional Basis of Thomas Hardy's Fiction," and "Mr. Cash and the Proto-Dorian South," in the *Southern Review;* "In Memory of John Gould Fletcher," in *Poetry;* "The Sacred Harp in the Land of Eden," in the *Virginia Quarterly Review;* "In Justice to So Fine a Country," in the *Sewanee Review;* "Some Day, in Old Charleston," in the *Georgia Review;* "Futurism and Archaism in Toynbee and Hardy," in the *Conservative Review;* "Origins of Our Heroes" in the *Kenyon Review.*

"Theme and Method in *So Red the Rose,*" is a part of the introduction to Stark Young's novel, *So Red the Rose,* copyright 1953 by Charles Scribner's Sons, and is here reprinted by their special permission. In this shortened, slightly modified form it also was published in the *Hopkins Review.*

vii

"Current Attitudes toward Folklore" was read as a paper at an annual meeting of the Tennessee Folklore Society and in this first form was published in the *Bulletin of the Tennessee Folklore Society,* December, 1940.

"Why the Modern South Has a Great Literature" was given as an address at the annual meeting of the Southern Literary Festival, Mississippi State College, 1950, and was subsequently published in *Vanderbilt Studies in the Humanities,* Vol. I. It is reprinted by permission of Vanderbilt University Press.

"Poetry As Tradition" was given as an address before the Alpha of Tennessee Chapter of Phi Beta Kappa in 1956.

Three of the essays appeared in this author's *The Attack on Leviathan* (Chapel Hill, 1938), long out of print. These are: "Still Rebels, Still Yankees," "New York and the Hinterland," and "Regionalism and Nationalism in American Literature."

D. D.

CONTENTS

Part V

REGIONALISM AND NATIONALISM

Part I

TRADITION AND EXPERIMENT
IN MODERN POETRY

POETRY AS TRADITION

LOOKING BACK over a hundred years of poetry, from Poe and Baudelaire to Eliot, Yeats, Frost, Ransom, and Tate, we can easily distinguish certain features that mark off the poetry we call "modern" from the poetry that preceded it. The sharp dissociation of the poet from society, the low valuation put by society upon poetry as an art, and the rise of experimental modes of poetry, accompanied by a parallel development of an enormous body of criticism—these are the features whose history must be traced, whose causes must be probed, if poetry, as we commonly say, is to be "understood" in modern terms.

These phenomena are of course interrelated. The dissociation of the poet from society, already in definite prospect in the sixteenth century, has become more painfully apparent as society has accepted the dominance of science and consequently has become indisposed to accept poetry as truth. If poetry comes to be regarded as a trifling fiction, of no use as compared with the dicta of physical science, the gap between the poet and society widens to a chasm. The experimentalism of the modern poets may represent a conscious or unconscious effort, in one group of tendencies, to bridge the chasm by making the style and subject matter of poetry conform to the fluid, highly unstable social regime created by the rule of science—a regime in which popular fashions must change in step with the changing hypotheses of science and the accompanying economic figurations that are the response of applied science. Or, by countertendency, the chasm is accepted as permanent, and experimentalism becomes the celebrated ivory tower to which the poet retires. In other terms, poetry becomes a specialty, one among the many specialties forced upon society by the modern regime. Then it can be practiced and understood only by specialists, who are only too likely to be college professors and critics.

Meanwhile, poetry has to be defended, and it is chiefly in his role as defender of his art that the poet becomes literary critic. The task is inescapable, and it cannot be left to the scholar and the nonpoet critic if the true role of the poet and the meaning of his art are to be asserted with sufficiently compelling force. From Sidney's defense, on through Wordsworth's *Preface to Lyrical Ballads* and Coleridge's *Biographia Literaria,* and down to Eliot's essays, Yeats's reminiscences, the discourses of Frost at his poetry readings, and the prose works of Ransom, Brooks, Warren, and Tate, the defense of poetry has been steadily and brilliantly waged. It necessarily becomes more broadly expository and philosophical as the common ground of understanding between the poet and his audiences approaches zero as a limit.

And the poets themselves, or the poet-critics, become almost the sole defenders. No help comes from the physical scientist, the social scientist, or the businessman, who has become their too-willing ally. The professional world of education, now committed to antihumanism and firmly indentured to the service of science, is not interested. The clergy, who in the Middle Ages were often the friends and preservers, if also the censors, of poetry, have gone over to the enemy. This is a notable defection and heresy. To the promulgators of secular and socialized religion, poetry has ceased to have much meaning. With dismay we can observe how the modern cleric, explaining to his flock that the Scriptures at certain cardinal points are merely symbolic, is in this way asserting that they are mere poetry, and *therefore* not Truth.

It is not surprising, then, that the criticism of poetry, increasing vastly in our time, sometimes explanatory, more often polemical, is nearly always in principle a defense of poetry, conducted by the poet and his last remaining allies, the critics, against a regime hostile or indifferent to poetry. Nor is it sur-

prising that the defense often takes the form of direct counterattack upon the regime itself. In this phase of operations the
poet may well become an outright traditionalist in religion,
politics, and economics. He examines the defects of modern
civilization. He develops a sense of catastrophe. With an insight far more accurate than the forecasts of professional social
philosophers, he begins to plot the lines of stress and strain
along which disaster will erupt. He predicts the ruin of modern secularized society and makes offers of salvation. These
are unheard or unheeded. Then upon the deaf ears and face-
less bodies of modern society he invokes the poet's curse.

In form, this curse may be as deceptively facetious as the
famous last sentence of Sidney's apology: "That while you
live you live in love, and never get favor for lacking skill of
a sonnet; and when you die, your memory die from the earth
for want of an epitaph." Or as Eliot's "This is the way the world
ends/Not with a bang but with a whimper." Or it may be
Allen Tate's more explicit

> *All are born Yankees of the race of men*
> *And this, too, now the country of the damned.*

Or, in another vein, the curse may proliferate into broader
indictment, containing a positive as well as a negative, such
as may be found in the desperately voluminous prose works
of Richard Wagner in the nineteenth century or the restrained
vehemence of the symposia of the Southern "Agrarians" of the
twentieth century.

However framed, the poet's curse cannot be dismissed as
a trifling eccentricity. The historical record will show that it
has seldom, if ever, failed to work. A civilization that says to
the poet, "Go up, thou baldhead!" by that act proves itself
ripe for comminatory sentence. Rejection of poetry is the
sign that the civilization is preparing its own doom. And after
the catastrophe, whether sudden or only a decline and fall,
all that survives is the rejected poetry, the religion if any, and
whatever else, being immaterial tradition, is not subject to

physical destruction. The rest is nothing but ruins to be picked
over by archaeologist and historian.

II

But if such, in epitome, is the history of modern poetry, it
does not seem encouraging. It would be unrealistic not to re-
examine the grounds on which the modern defense of poetry
is being offered. If it is a valid defense, why does not poetry
gain in currency and influence rather than diminish as it obviously is diminishing?

The Elizabethan defense of poetry was a highly successful
defense, for it may be said to have created, or helped to create,
not only a new poetry but also a new audience for poetry.
Wordsworth and Coleridge, who rode in the whirlwind and
directed the storm of English romanticism, repeated the success
of the Elizabethans, though not until after they had suffered
some initial defeats—as generally happened to romantic experimentalists. Our more modern poets have succeeded in only
one phase of the battle. They have created a new poetry—or
poetries—and their defense, working in critical reflex, has undoubtedly aided the perfection of their art. But they have not
created a new audience. On the contrary, they have lost most
of the audience that existed for poetry a hundred years ago.
That audience, which as late even as fifty years ago, was attending in large numbers the performance of Tennyson and
Browning, or at least of the Fitzgerald who found his way in
limp leather to many a parlor table, has abruptly dwindled
to a faithful, well-schooled few. The show is financially on the
rocks; the poet-author-actors would starve if not supported
by Guggenheim fellowships and lectureships in creative writing.

Obscurity of style and meaning is most often mentioned as
the chief cause of the exit of the audience. To this the poets
retort that they are no more obscure than Donne or Milton
or Dante and indeed are much more clear and explicit than,

say, the intolerably vague Shelley or the intolerably verbose Browning. And they are right. More serious might be the charge that they are eclectic, as Stark Young defines eclectic. In their poetry there is often a good deal of the "lustre of the artist" without a perfectly equivalent illumination of the subject. In much of their poetry—and this is true of many poems of apparently innocent simplicity, as in the poems of Frost— we cannot get at the subject until we master the style in all its intricate implications. Comprehension of the style is the condition on which we get the subject, which is not to be abstracted as an element separate from the poem in its absolute totality. For such poetry, what Joseph Conrad makes Marlow say about a story may well apply: the meaning of the poem is not a kernel lying at its center, but is in the wrappings that must be unfolded one by one as much as it is in the center.

The style has the distortion peculiar to modern art. The metrical system is shattered into dissonance or avoided altogether. "Prose effects" are deliberately cultivated. In some extreme instances typographical oddities are used to accent the pattern of dissonance, of divergence from the traditional. "Poeticisms" and "clichés" are avoided. Metaphor becomes intricately symbolic; and its closely woven inferential and referential scheme, worked into both the texture and the structure of the poem, puts a severe tax upon the most devoted reader's attention. The poem must be pondered like a problem; it is not made to be read aloud, but must be studied in secluded contemplation.

The total result is what may be called the "guarded style" —guarded, that is, against any suspicion of romanticism or sentimentality, and in this way made objective truth. Much of the New Criticism, particularly that part of it which has been elaborated in the essays of John Crowe Ransom, is concerned with the necessity of purging poetry of any betrayers of the art who weaken the cause by mere repetition of past conventions, or by assuming that prettiness of language, ef-

florescence of rhetoric, or loud assertion of laudable sentiments is enough to make poetry valid. At the heart of Mr.
Ransom's statement of the case is his apprehension that science
—or at least the scientific mind—is only too ready to point to
poetic rhetoric as affectation and to seize upon it as evidence
that poetry, as compared with science, is mere pretense and
that therefore poets cannot be trusted to pronounce on the
serious business of life. The style of poetry, then, must be
made impregnable against such attack.

But the impregnable or guarded style, whether it precedes
or follows defensive criticism, does not increase the general
currency of poetry and is not intended to. The aesthetic argument does not reach a wide public. Mainly it reaches only the
literary elite of poets, critics, professors of English, and the
students who are electing certain courses and have to submit
to it. The general public does not know that science is hostile
to poetry, and furthermore harbors a suspicion, inherited
from some old rumors about the behavior of Byron or Poe,
that poets are queer. The guarded style does nothing to dispel
the suspicion. A Virginian or Mississippian may faintly remember his Shakespeare and somewhat uncertainly essay to
quote Shakespeare. He may carry in his head some distant
echo of Pinckney's "I fill this cup to one made up /Of loveliness alone"; but, unless specially schooled, he may feel himself becoming a stranger to poetry when his son returns from
studying under Ransom at Kenyon or Brooks at Yale and tells
him that "The Dry Salvages" and "Sailing to Byzantium" are
great poems, and that the following lines, also from a great
poem, deal with the predicament of a young man, a modern,
who is musing beside a Confederate graveyard as Gray once
mused in an English country churchyard:

> *Night is the beginning and the end*
> *And in between the ends of distraction*
> *Waits mute speculation, the patient curse*
> *That stones the eyes, or like the jaguar leaps*
> *For his own image in a jungle pool, his victim.*

The father at this point is likely to remember only that poets are queer. His ancestors, a hundred years ago, may have indulged Mr. Poe, even though Mr. Poe was queer. But the arrangements of our time will give him little opportunity to indulge Mr. Allen Tate, whom he will probably never meet, and whose "Ode to the Confederate Dead" will not be bound in limp leather to ornament his parlor table. In fact he will have no parlor; his new dwelling is of the ranch-house design.

This same father—who must be drafted here to represent the hypothetical audience of the modern poets—may also have an uneasy apprehension, if he attempts to read the books that his son brings back from Kenyon or Yale, that Messrs. Eliot, Yeats, Ransom, Tate, *et al.* are disagreeably reproachful toward the regime that he, the father, is committed to uphold and that he derives revenue from.

The apprehension, which somehow filters through the barrier of the obscure, guarded style, is certainly justified. Much more definitely than the Elizabethans and the Romantics, the modern poets are Ishmaelitish dissenters toward the society that they must as contemporaries inhabit. A hundred years ago John Stuart Mill took comfort from the poetry of William Wordsworth and openly confessed the fact that Wordsworth had made a new man of him. This result could hardly have been achieved by Wordsworth's verbal eloquence alone. There must have been—and indeed there was—some common metaphysical ground between Wordsworth the poet and Mill the political economist. Between the modern political economists and the modern poets there is no such common ground. Every serious poem by Messrs. Eliot, Yeats, Frost, Tate, and their most able contemporaries is in fact a reproach, direct or implied, against the modern political economists— that is to say, the social scientists in general. It is difficult to imagine a member of the Academy of Political and Social Science as turning to these poets for restoration of spirits. The social scientists know the poets are not on their side. And even when a poet does appear on their side—as Mr.

Archibald MacLeish has done—they would almost rather he wouldn't. What will people think if they have a poet in their ranks volleying verses instead of surveys?

Thus the modern defenders of poetry have lost a resource that their predecessors enjoyed. They cannot do much proselyting for poetry and cannot enlarge the area that they defend. Sometimes, frankly admitting the limitation, they are content to say that the role of poetry is now minor and that they must therefore devote themselves to the perfection of the minor poem. But in any case, they do not cease to compose poetry or to defend it. This display of valor is as necessary as it is admirable. Yet meanwhile the audience, or the age in general, flows around them and goes on about its concerns, very much as the mass armies of World War I flowed around the "strong points" of the famous Western Front, leaving them to be slowly reduced to rubble by artillery and mortar fire from the rear, or else simply to "wither on the vine."

Whether the strong points occupied by the modern poets can be held long enough to be relieved by a general counter-offensive, I would not undertake to say. But, to carry the military figure further, I would argue that the defense of poetry has been made on too narrow a front and lacks a real defense in depth.

III

The modern defense of poetry is a defense of poetry in its literary character only. It refers to the poetry of the printed page, or even more definitely to the poetry composed *for* the printed page, the poetry received by the solitary, silent reader who ponders it in voiceless seclusion. It is a defense of poetry as a literary tradition, not of poetry as a tradition that includes, with much else, a literary tradition.

Poetry of the strictly literary tradition is a fairly new phenomenon, uncertainly developed amid the shifting hazards of post-Renaissance culture, a rare specialty that has tended to become ever more rare and more special.

In the great tradition of poetry, the fact of publication, whether in manuscript books or printed books, is an incidental result, not a determining cause, of the public authority of poetry. But to the modern poets the printed page has become a determinant. This unacknowledged factor has had much to do with the form and style of modern poetry. Failure to reckon with it has caused modern poets, turned critics, to direct their defense to what is really but one small segment of the great tradition which they constantly invoke.

It is splendid for T. S. Eliot to argue that the poetry of Western civilization from Homer to the present is one continuous body of tradition into which the modern poet should strive to incorporate his own art, even if, to do so, he has to use the dubious, revolutionary means of dislocating language, syntax, and grammar. But the implied contention that *The Wasteland* extends the tradition of Homer and Dante is not valid unless the *Iliad, Odyssey,* and *Divine Comedy* are to be taken as published books, just as *The Wasteland* is a published book. But the fact that Homer's and Dante's works have been repeatedly printed does not reduce them to the status of mere books. They are much more. The essential Homer lies outside the tradition that we think of as literary, nor does the existence of manuscripts and vast libraries of annotated editions, made for practical purposes of record and study, convert the poetry of Homer into a literary poetry. Whether it was in any sense a written poetry is something of a moot question. The important thing is that the Homeric epics were composed for oral performance and that the rhapsodes memorized them and for centuries recited, declaimed, or chanted them from memory.

The epic of the great tradition is not a book in the post-Renaissance sense. The epic of Dante, standing as it does in a critical period of the Middle Ages, is more of a book than the Homeric epics are; but a purely literary tradition could not have begotten *The Divine Comedy.* Of the three great masters to whom Eliot professes close allegiance—Dante, Donne, and Baudelaire—only Baudelaire belongs wholly to the purely literary tradition and wrote books of poetry rather than composed poems. John Donne is a learned poet, but both Elizabethan drama, as a spoken medium, and Elizabethan song strongly affect his composition. He was not published as a poet in his lifetime. Shakespeare was the author of stage plays, and published no books except the minor experimental poems, *Venus and Adonis* and *The Rape of Lucrece*. His sonnets were published, but in a pirated edition, not with his consent. Chaucer may be claimed as a literary poet, but his style, so far as it actually is literary, is the style of an age that, as to poetry, was strongly influenced by nonliterary elements. A manuscript book of Chaucer's poems, like the manuscript books of classic Greece and imperial Rome, was a very different affair from a modern printed book. It can hardly be said that the form and style of Chaucer or any other pre-Renaissance poet were determined by the book as a medium of publication. All such poetry in a sense is preliterary, for it stems from a culture in which the literary art is not yet severable from its associations with oral narrative and practical song.

This poetry is not only the poetry of tradition. It is tradition itself. If the Bible is approached as a mere book, even though it be called the Good Book, it is continually in danger of becoming only "literature." The Bible as "the Word of God" is a different thing entirely—the sacred though tangible and convenient instrument of Divine Revelation handed down as truth, and therefore in the highest sense tradition. The difference between Catholic and Protestant as to the merit of Biblical authority as such occurs, we should note, at the period when book-publication of the Bible is facilitated by the advance of printing, and this is also the period when poets, sometimes hesitantly, sometimes with only disguised reluctance, begin to write books of poetry.

The separation of poetry as literature from poetry as a tradition embodying both literary and nonliterary features begins, that is, in the late sixteenth century, when printer and publisher appear as entrepreneurs between the poet and his audience. That the separation was definitely beginning by 1557 we know from the complaint voiced by Richard Tottel in his preface to the first printed anthology of English lyric poetry: "It resteth now (gentle reder) that thou thinke it not evill doon, to publish, to the honor of the English tong, and for the profit of the studious of Englishe eloquence, those workes which the ungentle horders up of such treasure have heretofore envied thee." Mr. Hyder Rollins takes this as Tottel's complaint against the "anti-publication complex" of the Tudor poets who were courtiers or affected the manners of courtiers. But Tottel could just as well have been apologizing to the public for his impudence in printing in book form the "songs and sonnets" which everyone knew were intended for singing or for private circulation in manuscript.

The great triumphs of Elizabethan lyric poetry were the songs composed for actual performance as songs during the Golden Age of English vocal music. To recover the original texts of most of these songs, we must go either to the numerous songbooks of the period and disentangle the words, as Canon Fellowes has done, from their dispersed positions among the vocal parts; or else, with less difficulty, edit them from the songbooks of the lutanist school or from the fairly late printed editions of stage plays, masks, and interludes. The so-called antipublication complex of the poets was so firmly established that poets generally refrained from any published collection of their lyric and dramatic verses. The temptation to publish was nevertheless there, and we know that Ben Jonson, for one, yielded to it and was joked about it, if the evidence of Sir John Suckling's "A Session of the Poets," published in 1646, is to be credited:

> *The first that broke silence was good old Ben,*
> *Prepared before with Canary wine,*
> *And he told them plainly he deserved the bays,*
> *For his were called Works, where others were but Plays.*

"Works" is a literary title; "Plays" is nonliterary.

So far as literary poetry is concerned, we can trace the two tendencies, really counter to one another, yet intermingled, in the lists of songbooks and miscellanies published from 1557 to the beginning of the Puritan revolution. The songbooks, beginning in 1588 with William Byrd's *Psalms, Sonnets, and Songs,* and ending, say, with Bateson's *Second Set of Madrigals,* 1618, give us lyric poetry allied with music, in its oral, non-literary character. But the miscellanies, which contain songs without tunes, emphasize the literary character and are definitely books of poems.

It would be reasonable to assume that poetry took no great harm at first from its appearance in that great novelty, the printed book. At first the relationship of book to poem was not very different from the relationship of manuscript to poem during the previous centuries. It was a relationship of pure convenience. The printed book offered greater convenience than the manuscript and naturally had its appeal both to poet and to audience. Easy reproduction of copies by the printer's press meant extension of audience and ultimately made the poetry book an article of commerce, profitable both to author and to printer.

By the time we reach Pope, the relationship between book and poem is beginning to change. Pope was, no doubt, the first real best seller among the poets, and therefore the first to achieve financial independence through publication. From Pope's time to ours the book becomes more and more a determinant of the poetry, with other causes of course intermingling to sequester poetry as a purely literary art. From this time on there is hardly any survival of poetry as a nonliterary or even half-literary art. Only ballad and folk song survive at the oral level to remind us that genuine poetry can flourish without benefit of publication.

It seems obvious that if the whole tradition of poetry is to be taken into account, the modern defense of poetry is very unenterprising in developing a critical strategy that serves very well to defend Dryden or Coleridge or Eliot, but that ignores the vast resources poetry had at command during the preliterary centuries and that cannot adequately defend or even fully explain the poetry which made use of those resources. In the former centuries, not only did music and sweet poetry agree, but poetry was all-penetrative, and prose was a poor second or worse in the grand competition.

In our own bookish, entirely literary age the gains of poetry are relatively small, perhaps, in proportion to its losses. The gains are chiefly in flexibility of style, and they occur mainly in the province of the short or quasi-lyrical poem, of which, from Donne to Dylan Thomas, we have a great number. This poetry now accepts the printed page as its essential medium, and it is not otherwise accessible or approachable. It is seldom quoted except in critical essays. It is all but incapable of oral dissemination. Only on the printed page can it be pondered, grasped, and absorbed. It cannot flourish widely, and in fact has no large-scale circulation now except in school and college textbooks. Therefore, it does not filter down from the highest cultural levels to the lowest, as the preliterary poetry did, nor can it, like that earlier poetry, recruit its strength by drawing upon a deep-rooted folk culture.

The losses of poetry, under the literary regime, are in fact spectacular and disheartening.

We have lost the epic entirely. In the three centuries since the appearance of Milton's *Paradise Lost* Western civilization has not produced a single great epic poem. We have had long poetical works of epical dimensions, like Goethe's *Faust,* Wordsworth's *Prelude,* Hardy's *The Dynasts,* Bridges' *The Testament of Beauty,* but not one of these is a true epic. These long poems, and all others of their character, are books that happen to be written in verse. They are distinctly literary works, quasi-dramas, quasi-essays, which project a poet's highly personal and subjective interpretation of experience. They have no capacity for existing independent of the printed page. They could not survive the tests which Homer, Vergil, and Dante have successfully endured.

Whether Milton can survive may now be doubtful. His

epic, it is true, uses a highly developed literary style. Yet it is much more than a purely literary venture. If Milton, like T. S. Eliot, had had only the context of a literary tradition to support him, his epic could never have been composed. It would have been an extended verse-essay like *The Testament of Beauty* or an extended quasi-lyric like *The Wasteland.* Milton, a belated Elizabethan, was farther away from the non-literary tradition of narrative poetry than Dante, but he still felt its influence. *Paradise Lost* carries the implication of spoken performance. It was in fact first conceived as drama, and it still bears the marks of dramatic intention in its declamatory idiom—the famous "Miltonic blank verse"—and in the structure of its "scenes." Milton as music-lover also felt the alliance of poetry with its sister art, and some of his peculiar metrical practices, as Mr. William Hunter has shown, are best understood in the light of Milton's habituation to the seventeenth-century style of rendering psalms and hymns. Furthermore, since Milton the epic poet, like the Homer of fable, was blind, he dictated rather than wrote his epic.

But beyond all these considerations, which link Milton with the poetry of preliterary tradition, his epic is tradition itself in its content and impact. From it, the eighteenth-century poets abstracted some remnants of the Miltonic style—and nothing more. They failed to understand and accept it as tradition. The cause of their failure is implied in Pope's *Rape of the Lock,* the cartoon of an epic which tells us that British society was cultivating formality but losing all sense of form, with the implication now clear to us, if not to that society, that to repudiate tradition is to lose the sense of form. On the other hand, at a wider cultural level Milton's epic had the impact of tradition in giving Protestantism a certain power of visualization that austere Calvinism utterly lacked and could never impart by doctrinal means. The Heaven and Hell of Protestant England and America for some centuries have been at least as much Miltonic as scriptural in their visualized images. That the debt to Milton is unconscious is all the more a tribute to the power of genuine epic. The all-penetrative though somewhat strange compound—classical, Hebraic, Christian, and occult—of Milton's vision substitutes its own εἴδωλα for the images of "Papist" tradition that Puritan fanaticism discarded. And so the enemies of "mythology" accept, without realizing it, an Adam and Eve, a Satan, a Michael, that Milton may almost be said to have invented. No purely literary work of the last three centuries has achieved comparable results.

In losing the epic, we have also lost narrative poetry in general. This loss has occurred gradually, but it is now definite. The short story is now the preferred vehicle for minor narratives, the novel for major narratives. Both of these rejoice in the printed book and periodical, without which they could never have developed or even come into existence.

We have lost poetic drama. Prose rather than verse has long been the accepted medium for the stage play. In its rise it exactly parallels the preference for realism and naturalism on the stage. Poetry dare not show its face in the theater except in opera—which must generally be in an Italian, French, or German libretto—or in revivals of plays composed as Shakespeare's were, when verse was the accepted medium and when drama and poetry were inseparable.

This loss of poetry as a dramatic medium begins in England, significantly, just about at the time when poetry was passing over from its preliterary period into its literary development. The perfection of dramatic verse by Shakespeare and his contemporaries is approximately coincident with the beginning of the decline of dramatic verse or, one can almost say, its abrupt extinction.

But there would seem to be no good reason to blame this attainment of perfection as itself the cause of the decline. Literary historians are not very convincing in their explanations of the shift from dramatic verse to dramatic prose; in fact they do not seem to exhibit sufficient concern over the phenomenon. In particular, they fail to note that the identification of poetry with book publication, which is definite by the time of Cowley, dissociates the art of poetry from spoken performance, and therefore from stage use. From this time on, the capacity to write verse for the stage diminishes as the capacity to write literary or bookish verse increases. Verse dramas no longer succeed on the stage. Even as literary pieces they tend to become tour de forces, and may have thin claims to merit on either literary or dramatic grounds.

In our own time, it is true, there have been some notable attempts to recover the stage for poetry. But Eliot's *Murder in the Cathedral,* for one instance, is far better as a book than as a play. Its merits are literary rather than dramatic. At a performance one is quickly aware that the poet's capacity in literary composition, concededly impressive, is interfering with rather than assisting the dramatic action. It is a patch-work of soliloquies and splendid "imaginary conversations" that offers the semblance but not the dramatic reality of a play.

Finally, we have all but completely lost the alliance of poetry with music. Poetry as practical song no longer is composed at the higher levels of art, except in grand opera. The tradition of poetry as song survives only in our heritage of folk song, secular and sacred, of the centuries past when no cultural gulf separated the true poet from the good musician, and when there was not, as now, one audience for poetry, another for music. Robert Herrick's "Advice to Virgins to Make Much of Time," said to have been the most popular song of the seventeenth century, is a last convincing example of a good lyric by a sophisticated poet which is also a good song, current as song and not merely "read" as poetry. The period when a lyric by Sidney or Shakespeare or even Donne might, as a matter of course, be set by musicians as fine as Morley, Will-bye, or Alfonso Ferrabosco was ending, of course, before Herrick's arrival. The songs of Robert Burns, more than a century later, are a recrudescence of an earlier tradition, lingering in Scotland and Ireland, but rather thoroughly stifled in England by the rise of science, commerce, industrialism, and abstraction.

By the nineteenth century the alliance between music and poetry tapers to a thin sentimental vein, as in the romantic effusions of Thomas Moore. Some of Tennyson's lyrics have had music forced upon them, but they do not "set" well. The death of the alliance is marked as certain by the emergence of the comic operas of Gilbert and Sullivan, in which parody and burlesque dominate. The songs of *Pinafore* or *The Mikado* are a far cry from any of those that Shakespeare wrote for his plays or that appear, for example, in Nash's *Summer's Last Will and Testament*. We can see that the only medium in which the English-speaking public will accept a union of the talents of Gilbert and Sullivan is a bantering, humorous, satirical medium. The old tradition must put on the mask of light comedy if it is to be accepted at all. Beyond this stage of degeneration lies only, as we know, the steady descent into vulgarization, sentimentality, and finally outright bawdry and obscenity that mark popular song in our own century.

The vogue of Schubert's *lieder* may be cited as an exception to the general tendency. But a moment's reflection shows that this vogue represents a triumph of music as music rather than of music and poetry as sister arts. Heine's *Die Grenadiere* and Goethe's *Erlkönig* require the technical genius of a Schumann-Heink, accompanied by a virtuoso pianist, for full realization as art songs, and are then essentially music. They are not very accessible to amateurs; they do not survive on the popular tongue. They have had no enduring influence upon our general culture, which has been steadily drifting away from *lieder*. Goethe's lyrics, true enough, could be set as songs by a great musician, but they are actually literary exploitations of a traditional form, not poetry as tradition itself. As poems they lead a book existence quite dissociated from their occasional musical performance.

Today there are hardly any poets of merit who can or will write a literary ballad or would even consider composing a song lyric. It is unimaginable to readers of Eliot or Tate that those poets would be caught composing lyrics that actually could be used in a Rogers and Hammerstein type of Broadway musical. The distance between the literary poet of today and the jukebox might have to be measured in astronomical light-years, but it would be a fair measure of the cultural distance between the finest poetry of the twentieth century and the general audience. That is what we mean when we say our culture is falling apart.

IV

Whether the gains achieved by modern literary poetry, with its extraordinary command over nuances and hidden implications and its quality of absolute self-containment, overbalance the losses that I have enumerated, I do not undertake to say. The defense of this poetry has been well argued by Eliot, Ransom, Tate, Brooks, and other able poets and critics. Within the terms of the argument as it has been conducted for the past three decades or more, it is as conclusive as a defense can be.

There remains the question: What next?

The possibilities of poetry as a literary art seem now to have been as thoroughly explored and exploited as we could expect them to be. In that direction there are no more fields to conquer. There are no literary techniques that the modern poets do not already have at their command. In fact we may have now reached the point of diminishing returns for literary techniques as such. The poetry of the book may have reached its limit and finished its term. The publishers of books seem to take that for granted; they no longer welcome the poets to their lists. The admission of modern poetry to the textbooks of school and college classes may be, in a sense, as much an entombment as a triumph. This is for poetry a kind of death-in-life, to exist only on the printed page, not on the lips of men, not be carried by their voices and therefore almost never carried in their memories, rarely in their hearts.

In its submission to the printed page poetry is taking the greatest risk it has ever taken—the risk of extinction. Books as instruments of record and convenience have their legitimate use, but it is of a relative nature; they are a means, not an end. As instruments of such relative character, books are highly perishable. What is imperishable in them is what passes over into human life, unconsciously retained or consciously, even devoutly, treasured in memory and handed on from one memory to another.

The poet is not in the plight of the encyclopedist, who must be provided with his set of alphabetized volumes, periodically brought up to date in new editions, or else fail to exist. Nor is the poet in the plight of the novelist. Divorced from the book, prose fiction cannot flourish or even exist in the literary form wrought by the author; so divorced, it can survive only as a told story, which is a very different thing. What story could be remembered and told out of the printed pages of Dostoevski, James, Proust, Joyce, or Hemingway? But poetry, like its sister arts of drama and music, can always reduce the book to its true function as an instrument of convenience and exist, even flourish, as an oral art, or as an art combining oral and literary features. The long persistence of meter, rhyme, and other formal elements of verse are the strongest parts of the proof of this great capacity. They ally poetry with memory; they are the marks of poetry that not only derives from tradition but is tradition. It is not surprising that modern poets, habituating themselves to the printed page, have often discarded entirely the formal elements of verse, or else so irregularized them that they are hardly recognizable as formal elements. But thus to bind the great art of poetry to typography is to surrender the major part of the once vast province of poetry in favor of the dubious security of the library.

A poetry that puts itself in a position not to be recited, not to be sung, hardly ever to be read aloud from the page where it stands, and almost never to be memorized, is nearing the danger edge of absurdity. It not only cannot become tradi-

tion in the large sense. It is risking the loss of the literary tradition which it now too hopefully magnifies.

In his *Idea of a Theatre* Francis Fergusson says:

> A drama, as distinguished from a lyric, is not primarily
> a composition in the verbal medium; the words result, as one
> might put it, from the underlying structure of incident and
> character. As Aristotle remarks, "the poet, or *maker,* should
> be the maker of plots rather than of verses, since he is a poet
> because he imitates and what he imitates are actions."

I would amend this profound observation at one point and
make it read "A drama, as distinguished from a *merely literary lyric. . . .*" For the spoken or sung poem actually has
many of the properties that Mr. Fergusson, following Aris-
totle, ascribes to drama.

There is no place for poetry to go next unless it reasserts its
old independence of the book and finds a way to restore some
of its former oral character. That such independence may be
very difficult to regain is conceded. But that is a problem for
our civilization no less than for our poetry. A civilization cannot feed and flourish upon perishable things. Only imperishable things at its center can give it life. Nothing is more imperishable than poetry. In comparison, the material works of
science and industry are but fleeting trifles. No civilization
of the past has ever lived without poetry. Our civilization can
hardly be an exception.

YEATS AND THE CENTAUR

THE LATER YEATS, writing his memories of the years between 1887 and 1891, records that the early Yeats thought "that all art should be a Centaur finding in the popular lore its back and strong legs." It is a striking utterance, and it has often been quoted to define Yeats's relation as poet to the Ireland of tradition. This intellectual poet, the quoters seem to say, had his back and strong legs in the lore of his people. The artist Yeats, who was of the Rhymers Club, and wrote "Sailing to Byzantium," and edited William Blake, nevertheless spent his summers in Sligo, with the fox-hunting Pollexfens. The ancient Irish myths, the later popular superstitions, perhaps even the lilt of Irish folk song somehow merge into a complex idiom that even the most advanced moderns can accept. And, furthermore, the conception of unity between art and life is everywhere in Yeats's works—sometimes positively, as in "The Trembling of the Veil," where he says, "I had begun to hope, or to half hope, that we might be the first in Europe to seek unity as deliberately as it had been sought by theologian, poet, sculptor, architect, from the eleventh to the thirteenth century"; but more often negatively, as in his typical modern poems, where he bewails the lack of unity, the disintegration of arts and of society itself.

This general view of Yeats's poetry is accepted, I suppose, by all except the Marxist critics, who are determined to convict him of escapism, on one ground or another. But to talk of unity, even as well as Yeats talks, whether in poem or prose, is not to achieve it. The question of Yeats's relation, as artist, to the popular lore, remains unsettled, and indeed almost unexamined. Perhaps it cannot be settled very easily. We know a great deal about the technique of poetry; and for some time we have been very seriously engaged in discussing the relation of the poet to his tradition—meaning, especially, his literary tradition and all that goes with it. But we know almost nothing about the proper relation between the poet and popular lore. Our critics are discreetly mum on that topic. They know a great deal about *The Golden Bough;* but that is anthropology, and only obscures the question of what the poet will do with popular lore if he *has* it, as old Scotsmen and Irishmen used to *have* the Gaelic. I do not presume to offer any conclusive answers, but it does seem possible to clear away a few wrong assumptions and to establish a context within which discussion might develop.

To begin with Yeats's figure of the centaur, it seems a little unfortunate. Ixion, king of the Lapithae, was the father of the race of centaurs. He begot them of a phantom sent by Zeus to represent Hera, with whom Ixion was presumptuously infatuated. Later, Ixion was punished by being bound to the famous wheel, eternally revolving. The subsequent history of the centaurs is none too encouraging. They fought the Lapithae at the marriage feast of Pirithoüs, and were in general rowdy and turbulent, if not treacherous. The centaur Nessus gave Deianira the poisoned shirt, which put an end to Heracles. Among the centaurs, only Chiron seems to have a good reputation. He taught, among the Greek heroes, Jason and the Argonauts, yet evidently did not teach them enough, at that, to save them from a rather empty quest.

But aside from the Greek myth, which does not seem to put centaurs in very great honor, the figure of art as a centaur does not offer quite the proper respect either to art or to popular lore. If art grows out of popular lore and derives a certain animal strength from it, surely the union between the two deserves a less monstrous representation. Is art a hybrid, with its intelligence of one species and its solid substance of another? A tree would be a better image, if we must have an image. For its boughs and fruit make no uncouth junction with trunk and roots, but are the upward proliferation of the original germ, from which the dark, earthseated parts are a corresponding downward proliferation. Between the upward and downward parts, the relation is organic and reciprocal; the one cannot do without the other. And yet—if one wishes to indulge in homily and pursue the image further—it is perfectly true that the stump of a tree will flourish for awhile and put out suckers when the top has been cut away, while trunk and branches perish forthwith when deprived of a root system, or survive only as sawed lumber.

I suspect that the later Yeats did not think too well of the young Yeats who could conceive art as a centaur. The context in which the famous figure is set is a little deprecatory. "I did not foresee," he adds presently, "not having the courage of my own thought, the growing murderousness of the world." And he proceeds to quote the first two stanzas of "The Second Coming." There could be no excellent unity, he perceived, between art and popular lore (let us say intelligence and vitality) in a society where

> *The best lack all conviction, while the worst*
> *Are full of passionate intensity.*

And the beast of this later vision is also a hybrid—a lion body and the head of a man—but he has become ominous and apocalyptic.

The figure of the centaur will not do to characterize the ideal relationship between art and popular lore, though, unfortunately, it may describe adequately enough the false conceptions that have long troubled and misled the poets, perhaps Yeats among others.

It is easy to say what the ideal relationship should be—as easy as it is to draw any other ideal picture. The popular lore ought to pass readily and naturally into the art; it ought not to have to be sought out by specialists in special corners, collected, edited, published, and reviewed; and then, perhaps only through some accident of taste or fashion, be appropri-

ated, at long range, by a very literary poet. The reverse of
the process ought also to work naturally and not at a forbidding long range. The art ought to pass readily into the popular
lore, and not remain eternally aloof and difficult. Unless both
processes continue in mutual interchange, society as well as
art is in a bad state of health; but the bad health of society is
a cause, not a result, of this unfavorable relationship.

For further clarification, the terms need to be given a more
precise content. By "art" I think Yeats would mean "high
art"—the art of the greatest poems, plays, novels, paintings;
by "popular lore" I conceive that he would mean not merely
the beliefs, whether religious, superstitious, mythical, or historical, of the common people, but also the embodiment of
these in arts and crafts. Thus, if the epic or drama is "high
art," the folk song, ballad, or folk tale is "low art"—a term
not used, of course, in derogation.

When the "high art" and the "low art" of a nation or a
society are out of proper relationship to each other, the "high
art" becomes too "arty," and the "low art" too "low." It was
this condition that Yeats saw in Ireland. Along with other
poets and patriots of the Celtic Renaissance, he sought to correct it while it was still not too late for correction to take hold.
"We might be the *first* in Europe to seek unity," he wrote, for
Ireland, out of its "backwardness," if for no other reason, was
not yet too deeply committed to the specializations and the
dissociations prevailing in England and elsewhere. Ireland
could not yet be said to have a "high art" at all, of a modern
kind; and its "low art" was not yet too low, was indeed deep-
seated, native, abundant, and not quite perverted in its expression. And perhaps Ireland might once more, as in former
ages, lead Europe in the arts, high and low. But Yeats did not
foresee how murderous Western civilization had become. I
do not think Yeats meant to suggest that his labors were tragically interrupted by World War I. Long before 1914 the gaps
were there, between the best and worst, between high and
low art. Even in peace, these gaps were murderous.

The question evidently takes us far beyond the range of any purely literary issues, but I must be content here with limiting it to more or less literary issues, as they become apparent in the works of our notable example.

The early Yeats wrote ballads, like the "Ballad of the Fox-hunter" and the "Ballad of Father Gilligan," and folk songs, or quasi–folk songs, like "Down by the Salley Gardens." He also wrote "The Wanderings of Usheen," a semiepical poem, and composed lyrics and plays that utilized the ancient Irish myths. He edited a collection of genuine Irish folk tales, and in *The Celtic Twilight* he brought together prose tales and sketches in which he put the gleanings of popular lore that he got from Mary Battle, his uncle's servant, and from his own wanderings about the countryside in Sligo. Then, after a time, the poetry ceases to be narrative or in any way "folkish." The myths and popular lore become occasional references, or they become, in the modern sense, symbols, which are merged into the larger "frame of reference" established by the private mythology explained in *A Vision*. Yeats has become a modern poet, indistinguishable from other modern poets except in his subject matter, which is unique, and in a superior grace of idiom, which we can never cease admiring, the more because his contemporaries fail so badly in comparison, for they rarely attain both grace of idiom and seriousness.

Does this poetry, then, have its strong back and legs in the popular lore? Probably not, so far as Yeats deliberately intended to build it upon popular lore. But probably yes, so far as he did *not* deliberately so intend.

It would not be easy to classify the poems on such a basis, but I think it is possible to discuss a principle. A popular lore is essentially a subject matter, and its reality, to the people among whom it is communicated, is the reality of fact, not the reality of art, as we define it in our lofty discussions. Furthermore, a popular lore is of course a subject matter which is looking for an art—that is, a ready means of emphatic communication and preservation. The art of popular lore therefore is art in the old, and perhaps philosophic, sense of contrivance or artifice. It has much about it of the utilitarian and purely functional. And for this reason it must be a conventional art, with clearly marked patterns.

On the other hand, our literature, or art in the sophisticated sense, has become the other thing: an art looking for a subject matter, and rather heedless of what the subject matter is, so long as it sets the art to working.

So far as Yeats, therefore, already had, by birthright and direct, naïve acquaintance, a hold on popular lore as a subject matter, and went looking for an art to communicate it, he may be said to have built his poetry upon the popular lore, in a way which by implication is desirable. But when he began to think of himself primarily as an artist, and went looking for a subject matter, and decided that he must have a strong back and legs in the popular lore, he did not stem from the popular lore any longer, but merely appropriated it, as he would appropriate any other subject matter, or a metaphor, or a rhyme. The unity of the popular lore and the high art cannot be obtained in this manner. And the proof is (if my statement of the ideal condition is at all tenable) that the process does not work reciprocally. Thus Yeats might appropriate the matter or even the manner of the street ballad singer of Dublin, but the Dublin ballad singer could not make any use of the art of Yeats; and in fact the art of Yeats remains accessible only to a relatively small group of persons: the high art has become unquestionably very high, very distant from the low art.

In the collection of stories entitled *The Secret Rose* is a tale called "The Old Men of the Twilight," in which Yeats tells of an old smuggler who, to his surprise, saw a long line of herons flying over the sea toward the land, from an unaccustomed direction. He took his gun to hunt them, and found them standing in shallow water among the rushes.

> But when he looked along the barrel the heron was gone, and, to his wonder and terror, a man that seemed of an in-

finitely great age stood in its place. He lowered the gun, and once more the heron stood there with bent head and motionless feathers. He raised the gun, and no sooner did he look along the barrel than the old man was again before him, only to vanish when he lowered the gun for the second time.

It was enchantment, of course. The herons were artists of the druid time, who had been cursed by St. Patrick because the click of their knives, writing their thoughts on ogham tablets, disturbed him.

Yeats is like the old smuggler. He sees the popular lore only when his gun barrel is leveled to bring it down. Without the weapon of the artist, he does not see it; nor do we in general see it, except as hunters. Only then does it become a subject matter that can be used.

As for the difference between popular art, as contrivance, and sophisticated art, as being almost an end in itself, another experience of Yeats's will serve as an illustration. He heard John F. Taylor, the Irish orator, speak and recite verses, and the experience gave him "a conviction of how great might be the effect of verse, spoken by a man almost rhythm-drunk, at some moment of intensity, the apex of long mounting thought. Verses that seemed when one saw them on the page flat and empty caught from that voice, whose beauty was half in its harsh strangeness, nobility and style." Rhythm and rhyme are intended, in folk poetry, to do exactly what Yeats describes them as doing. They are instruments of performance, really enacted. But on the printed page, the very fiction of performance has now gone, and we have the delicate nuances of modern art, to be enjoyed for themselves, no longer functional.

The inevitable conclusion, it would seem, is that Yeats, like other great romantic poets, has found a subject matter for his art in the popular lore, and that it serves to develop the literary effects, but does not, except through occasional imitation, of itself produce the literary effects. There has been little more real fusion between the popular lore and the advanced art than between Keats's medieval lore and his art.

Yet perhaps this is too broad a generalization. What Yeats had natively, he must have carried along, without the act of romanticizing. But it would be hard to identify the poems or passages of which this may be truly said.

Nobody would deny, of course—and least of all would I —that Yeats's use of the popular lore is in any sense illegitimate or shallow, according to our standards, or that it serves in any other way than to enrich his art. But to use popular lore is not enough in itself, if a unity such as Yeats describes is to be attained. When the subject matter of the popular lore belongs natively to those who make the high art, as much as to the people, and does not need to be hunted or reclaimed; and when the high art is not too subtle and complex to serve as a functional instrument for the popular lore—in that time we shall approach the ideal condition. At one moment, in the eighteenth century, when the high art became conventional, we began to approach that condition, perhaps, and folk song caught up a little of the manner of the high art of the time. But the moment quickly passed, and it has not come again, in poetry.

IN MEMORY OF JOHN GOULD FLETCHER

WHAT FILLS my mind, as I think of John Gould Fletcher, is the image of the man as I saw him not long ago in his Arkansas home, on a steep, pine-covered ridge near Little Rock. On a bright April day we walked among his pines, and, following the pointing of his finger, picked out the faraway glint of the Arkansas River in a cleft of the mountainous ridges. Below us the slope fell away precipitously toward the river. It was so steep, Fletcher said, that he had not yet made bold to walk the boundary of his own land in that direction. Some day he intended to.

Around us the wild bird's-foot violets were blooming, strawberries were fruiting, and iris and shrubs, set by Fletcher and his wife, Charlie May Simon, were in flower. Their pleasant and beautiful house, built from stone quarried on the place, stood on the level top of the ridge, well-sited, overhung by old pine trees that had been cleared only enough to accent its repose and make it, too, seem rooted in the ridge. As we sat on the porch, a lively small bird sang on a pine branch that brushed the wire screen. "A Carolina wren," Fletcher said. Beyond the distant gate at the end of the narrow, winding driveway, we knew that modern traffic sped on the paved road; but the Fletchers' house was like a place in the wilderness, quiet and removed as a pioneer homestead. A poet could have wished for no better retreat. There was no thought in my mind but of admiration and satisfaction that Fletcher, who in his time had been one of the most restless of wanderers, had found this spot in his own country, where he might spend in happiness the many years one hoped God would still grant him.

Our talk on these April days and evenings was often of the historic past, and now and then of the immediate present, but hardly at all of Fletcher's personal past, though reminders of that past were all around us—the books of the French symbolists and many other garnerings of his days in England and France, ranked from ceiling to floor around three walls of the living-room; ornaments and furnishings from the American Southwest; rugs from Mexico and the Orient; a single brilliant painting of an Arkansas scene above the fireplace. Fletcher was busy arranging material for an anthology of Southern poetry that he was commissioned to edit. He talked much of that. We discussed, among other things, the contemporary pertinence of William Grayson's pre–Civil War poem, "The Hireling and the Slave," a rare copy of which Fletcher brought from his study to show me. Together, we speculated on what sources would be helpful for use in a new historical work on which Fletcher and Charlie May planned to collaborate as soon as the Southern anthology was out of the way.

The Bollingen Award to Ezra Pound somehow came into the conversation, and Fletcher said, without bitterness but a little sadly, that he felt the great controversy over this award definitely marked the end of a period of art—the period of the primacy of art above all else that had dominated his own generation of poets. But mostly Fletcher spoke of the Arkansas past—partly out of his own intense absorption in it, partly by way of courteously instructing his visiting friends; and under his quiet guidance, in company with Charlie May, we went to see the restoration of the old territorial capitol of Arkansas, then the state capitol, and finally the Pike mansion —the "old house" of his boyhood and certain of his poems. At every point of the journey Fletcher had tale after tale to tell. In the evening, some of his young friends dropped in for a visit; and Fletcher discoursed on the culture of the rice country that we would traverse next day, traced on a geological survey map the strange topographical features of the country between Little Rock and Memphis, and called our attention to a remarkable cypress lake that we must be sure to notice.

When we told him good-by next morning, I did not dream it was for the last time. But the darkness against which he often fought valiantly was pressing him hard, although I did not know it. Two weeks later it conquered finally, and took him. And now, though the memory of the John Gould Fletcher of that last meeting is still warm in my mind, and is the happiest of many fine recollections that I have of him, I must leave the mortal image, which cannot survive our personal memories, and seek the meaning of the immortal part that the poet in his works has made truly memorable.

A score of notable works, from his *Irradiations—Sand and Spray,* published in 1915, to his *Arkansas,* a history of his native state, contain in poetry and prose the distinguished record of John Gould Fletcher's tireless and passionate devotion to the art that he, like others of his generation of poets, put first among all considerations. Yet, despite Fletcher's avowed allegiance to art as a supreme and all-determining goal, in that same score of books there is evidence that, almost from the beginning of his career, he was no art-for-art's-sake aesthete, but a man of broadest intellectual capacity and intense moral purpose. At heart he was much more of a traditionalist than he intended to be or would have been willing to acknowledge during the rebellious early stage of his career.

At first only a faint undercurrent in his poetry, his return to tradition finally became dominant in *Branches of Adam,* a semiepic and by far his most ambitious and weighty poem. In this work, begun apparently in 1921 and published in England in 1925, yet still little known in America, Fletcher dealt boldly with the metaphysical and religious problem forced on him by the pressure of events. Shocked by the collapse in World War I of the European society to which he had fled in order to practice his youthful religion of art, he had written Amy Lowell in 1917, as he records in his autobiography: "Since 1916 I have wanted with all my heart to write about humanity—not about landscapes. . . . As you say, the War has certainly brought this about in me—it has produced a tremendous clash between my imagination and the reality—and the results of that clash will change me, have already changed me tremendously."

Although Fletcher never completely abandoned his earlier style, from as early as 1921 he strove tremendously to realize his new ideal, "to uphold man's search for God as the theme of all great poetry," even though he was, in his words, "committing myself to an anachronism, greater even than the anachronism I had committed myself by becoming primarily a poet." He regarded his *Parables* and *Branches of Adam* as a "counterblast" to the naturalistic realism of James Joyce, whose pessimistic representation of humanity, however honest and courageous, Fletcher could not accept.

Increasingly, too, Fletcher turned his eyes, almost desperately, to the America and finally to the South from which he had once deliberately exiled himself. By 1920 he was ready to ally himself with the most thoroughgoing traditionalists in the Western world, the "Southern Agrarian" group, with some of whom, in their earlier phase as "Fugitive" poets, he had become acquainted during his 1926 visit to the United States, and with whom, too, he had maintained a fairly regular correspondence. When the Agrarian symposium, *I'll Take My Stand,* appeared in 1930, Fletcher was represented, not by an essay on art or poetry, but by a formidable study of education, in which he took a sternly argued conservative position. In 1933, after an exile of twenty-four years, he returned to the United States and to residence in his native Arkansas. In this, the happiest phase of his long career, Fletcher seemed to feel the need of paying a debt of affection to the state and region he had once forsaken. His creative energy went largely into historical works, and he gave much time to the encouragement of young writers and to fostering cultural enterprises in his own region.

But this later Fletcher is almost completely unknown to the
literary public of 1950. His early reputation as "Imagist"
fixed upon him a label that he could not live down. Although
Fletcher's close friendship with Amy Lowell brought him
what he afterwards called the "scandalous success" of publication as one of the Imagist group, in the long run he probably
lost as much as he gained through Amy Lowell's overenthusiastic championship. For, with very little amendment,
critics, reviewers, and anthologists have followed Amy Lowell's emphasis and ignored the poet and man of letters who
in *Branches of Adam* reversed his earlier position and who
even at the outset was probably more a symbolist than an
Imagist. The belated award of the Pulitzer prize to Fletcher's
Selected Poems (1938) evidently honored the supposed "Imagist" rather than the poet who had resolved to grapple with
metaphysical reality and epic magnitudes. It must be granted
that the choice of material in the *Selected Poems*—the only
available collected edition of his poems—invites a false emphasis. This volume draws chiefly upon his early work: *Irradiations* (1915); *Goblins and Pagodas* (1916); *The Tree of
Life* (1918); *Breakers and Granite* (1918). It hardly represents
the rich and various intelligence that is revealed in Fletcher's
remarkable, but poorly titled, autobiography, *Life Is My Song,*
published in 1937. But I suppose the truth is that even at
the age of fifty, when he had resettled in the United States,
Fletcher was still paying the price of having chosen exile
for the sake of art at a time when he could not have foreseen
the consequences of his choice.

In the peculiar history of John Gould Fletcher as exile, the
time element itself is important. Born January 3, 1886, at Little Rock, Arkansas, he grew up in a society—the society of
the middle and western South—that had in its cultural habits
as much of frontier as of establishment. His father, who came
of a family of hill-farmers, fought through the Civil War in
the Confederate army, became a cotton buyer after the war,
finally prospered, and was very prominent in post-Reconstruc-

tion politics, retiring when, in his old age, he failed in his campaign for the governorship of Arkansas against the once famous "one-gallus" politician, Jeff Davis. From his father, apparently, Fletcher inherited the combination of aristocratic and backwoodsy tendencies that social historians still find it difficult to understand in persons of Southern antecedents. From his mother, a sensitive woman of German ancestry, he derived a strong aesthetic bias which she spared no pains in cultivating. In the old Pike mansion the boy led at first a very sheltered life. His mother's influence predisposed him toward books and art. Frail of body, inept at games, he took refuge in a deeper bookishness when he entered the more active world of school. Graduated from high school at the age of sixteen, he was confronted with his parents' determination to send him off to Harvard. This was his mother's decision, Fletcher thought; the father, though consenting, planned that young Fletcher should eventually become a lawyer.

Doubtless life at Harvard, for a Southern boy in those times, was in itself a sort of exile. At any rate it brought to young Fletcher as complete a dissociation from his inherited background as any that is on record for a poet. From his college studies he got little that counted. By his third year he had become an ardent Nietzschean and had written much poetry, including a long composition entitled "Impressionistic Symphony." But he had already decided that the materialistic United States was no country for poets. At Harvard he had found only one other student who, like himself, dared to indulge seriously in the art. By this time his discontent was reaching a critical stage. After a futile excursion into archaeology, which led him into the Mesa Verde region of the Southwest and to other travel in the West, Fletcher deliberately absented himself from his college examinations. In 1909, after the settlement of his father's estate, Fletcher overrode the objections of his family, abandoned Harvard without his degree, and determined to use his income to finance his life as poet—in Europe.

In view of the brilliant achievement that soon followed this expatriation we are not entitled to say that young Fletcher's decision was wholly wrong. That it was in an ironic way untimely, we can now see. In 1909 the Europe to which he hopefully fled was only five years away from the debacle of total war. And in the United States, on which he turned his back, the greatest upsurge of the arts in American history was on the point of appearing. Fletcher came to Europe too late; he left America too soon. His tragedy, if it was tragedy, was in the timing of his exile. When Fletcher realized that the center of artistic vitality had shifted from Europe to America, he was already too deeply involved in Europe to convert his exile into a mere visit abroad. His virtuosity had established him as a leading experimentalist in poetry, and in a way his reputation rested on his being a notable expatriate. Furthermore, in his first marriage—to Daisy Arbuthnot, an Englishwoman—he had made the most responsible of all commitments.

And so for many years Fletcher experienced the agonized incertitude that only the exile knows. Abroad he had achieved, at least to outward view, what he had come for. But at home in the United States, not abroad, was the real audience for his poetry: the magazines like *Poetry, The Little Review, The Fugitive,* and many more; the friendly editors and thriving publishing houses; the congenial groups of intellectual and literary spirits. And Europe, to which he had trusted for salvation, was falling before his eyes into social disorder and ruin. The struggle of his life was now, while maintaining his integrity as man and artist, to face the painful contradictions, the enormous practical difficulties that this unanticipated state of affairs forced upon him.

Lonely, unguided, Fletcher had discovered for himself in France, and had striven to master, the French symbolist poets that, as Harvard undergraduate, he could sample only in the meager translations that he had found in the Boston Public Library. Still solitary, still unadvised, he had tried to write a new poetry that fused the effects of poetry, painting, and music—"the triple influence" (he afterwards said) of Mallarmé, Gauguin, and Debussy—and so was practicing his own version of symbolism before it had taken hold in English or American poetry. For a while unsuccessful in getting publication, he welcomed in Ezra Pound his first literary friend; but he resisted Pound's attempts to make over his poetry in the Pound model. Defending his methods to Pound, Fletcher cited the French symbolists, whom Pound, by Fletcher's account, had not yet actually read, but whom Pound then proceeded to read, in books borrowed from Fletcher, and to introduce to the English public in a series of articles. Though he declined to become Pound's disciple, Fletcher, with the generosity characteristic of him throughout his life, contributed from his own funds toward the financing of *The Egoist*.

Similarly, though he was aware of the poetic limitations of Imagist procedure, he was secretly shocked and disturbed by Amy Lowell's quick exploitation for her own use of techniques that Fletcher felt he had originated, and he writhed inwardly at many aspects of her championship of the new poetry. Fletcher conceded that the role Amy Lowell assumed was one she was peculiarly well fitted to play, as he was not, and he gave the Imagist movement his hearty support and Amy Lowell his sympathetic and grateful friendship. "My business," he afterwards wrote, "was to write poetry. . . . Whether or not she got the credit for her championship of the new poetry was to me a matter of complete indifference."

Again and again Fletcher opened fresh fields of endeavor, only to see others reap the fruit. His *Paul Gauguin,* written in 1918 but not published until 1921, anticipated a trend that others popularized. Years before the vogue of "world literature," Fletcher tried to interest American publishers in bringing out a series of translations, which he proposed to edit, of Unamuno, Spitteler, Berdyaev, Ramuz, Claudel; but with one voice the publishers declined to support his projected "Modern European Library." His prophetic study of Russia and America, *The Two Frontiers,* was rejected by his British publisher and appeared in America in 1930 only to be unheard in the din of the great depression.

Yet such defeats never left him long discouraged. In his devotion to his art there was a certain fierceness that, while it isolated him, also must have sustained him. Although from first to last Fletcher knew most of the writers of his generation, both the great and the less great, and will stand in our poetic history in association with Frost, Robinson, Pound, "H. D.", Masters, Sandburg, Lindsay, and Amy Lowell, and although he shared in many group enterprises, he was never truly of any group or coterie, never had the support of any claque or organization, cultural, commercial, or political, never was the darling of any publisher, never enjoyed a real popular success. He is an extraordinary, almost unique example of the isolated artist. Independent to the last degree, outspoken and frank, uncompromising where his principles were involved, yet wholly without guile, he won all that he won by the test of merit alone. Unflinching in his individualism, John Gould Fletcher was no man to bow his neck before Caesar. This is the stern and lonely poet who wrote in "The Black Rock" these self-descriptive lines—

> *Keel of the world, apart,*
> *I have lived like you.*
>
> *Some men are soil of the earth;*
> *Their lives are like harvest fields,*
> *Green in the spring, and gold in their season,*
> *Then barren and mown;*
>
> *But those whom my soul has loved*
> *Are as barren rock standing off headlands,*
> *Cherishing perhaps a few bitter wild flowers*
> *That bloom in the granite year after year.*

But Fletcher was also generous. With a gallantry so rare that it must seem archaic and quixotic to the present generation, he was always ready to risk everything for a friend or a good cause. Like the Sartorises of William Faulkner's novels, he was born into a world that no longer offered a good field for the exercise of gallantry; but he did not, like the Sartorises, waste his strength in jousting in lists where victory would be a worse calamity than defeat. He gave his strength to the cause of art and to those who were enlisted in that cause. To Fletcher, this was a chivalric pursuit, the only chivalric pursuit left to modern man to cherish. For this, and for much more, he will be remembered and honored, and I cannot think there will ever be a true follower of poetry who will fail to know what John Gould Fletcher meant when in his youth he wrote—

> *The morning is clean and blue and the wind blows up*
>   *the clouds.*
> *Now my thoughts gathered from afar*
> *Once again in the patched armour, with rusty plumes*
>   *and blunted swords,*
> *Move out to war.*

> *Smoking our morning pipes we shall ride two and two*
> *Through the woods.*
> *For our old cause keeps us together,*
> *And our hatred is so precious not death or defeat*
>   *can break it.*

> *God willing, we shall this day meet that old enemy*
> *Who has given us so many a good beating.*
> *Thank God we have a cause worth fighting for,*
> *And a cause worth losing and a good song to sing.*

Part II

TRADITION VERSUS ANTITRADITION
IN PROSE FICTION

THE TRADITIONAL BASIS

OF THOMAS HARDY'S FICTION

IN THE EIGHTY-EIGHT years of his life Thomas Hardy got used to a great many of the oddities of terrestrial experience, and was resigned to most of them, even to the seeming unapproachableness or indifference of the Deity. One thing, however, he never got used to, and was apparently not resigned to. I find a peculiar pertinence in the fact that the second Mrs. Hardy, in *The Later Years,* has inserted a rather lengthy reminiscence of Hardy's visit to Oxford in 1920, written by Charles Morgan, who was then an undergraduate at the university and one of the leaders in arranging for the performance of *The Dynasts* at Oxford on this particular occasion. After an account of Hardy's visit, Morgan goes on to record a later conversation with Hardy at Max Gate, on the subject of literary criticism. Hardy spoke out against the critics with an animus that startled the younger man. Dramatic criticism, Hardy thought, had some merit because the dramatic critics had less time "to rehearse their prejudices." But Hardy was bitter about literary criticism.

> The origin of this bitterness [writes Morgan] was in the past where, I believe, there was good reason for it, but it was directed now against contemporary critics of his own work, and I could not understand what general reason he had to complain of them. He used no names; he spoke with studied reserve, sadly rather than querulously; but he was persuaded—and there is evidence of his persuasion in the preface to the posthumous volume of his verse—that critics approached his work with an ignorant prejudice against his

"pessimism" which they allowed to stand in the way of fair reading and fair judgment.

This was a distortion of the facts as I knew them. It was hard to believe that Hardy honestly thought that his genius was not recognized; harder to believe that he thought his work was not read. Such a belief indicated the only failure of balance, the only refusal to seek the truth, which I perceived in Hardy. . . .

But Morgan was wrong, and Hardy was right, and the "bitterness" of the aged poet toward literary criticism, as thus recorded, is something to give pause to the presumptuous critical interpreter. Hardy could not explain himself clearly to the younger man, and perhaps the reference to pessimism comes in only for want of a better verbal statement of the strange misunderstanding Hardy felt he had encountered. There was a real intellectual distance between Hardy and the critics—indeed, between Hardy and almost three generations of critics. The critics had not so much underrated—or overrated—Hardy as missed him, in somewhat the same way as, in our opinion, Dr. Johnson missed John Donne. When we look over the impressive list of those who have made literary pronouncements in Hardy's time and ours, they do not seem to be the kind of people who would have affinity with Hardy. From George Meredith, his first literary adviser, up to T. S. Eliot, one can hardly think of a critic whose view of Hardy's work, however well-intentioned, would not be so external as to set up a gross incongruity like what we find in Marxian criticisms of Shakespeare.

Possibly the critics have been most in error in not realizing the comparative isolation of Hardy in modern literary history. Misled by the superficial resemblance between his work and the product current in their day, they have invariably attempted to treat him as a current author—or at least as a queer blend of tendencies receding and tendencies coming on. They have been further misled by Hardy's own attempt (not always happy) to shape his work into a marketable form or to bring it up to what he conceived to be a good current literary standard. For Hardy seems to have had little idea of being an innovator or an iconoclast. He sought to please and entertain, and perhaps to instruct, and he must have been amazed to find himself now acclaimed, now condemned, as heretic.

The appearance of Thomas Hardy among the temporal phenomena of the England of 1870 to 1928—that is the amazing, the confusing thing. I believe we ought to begin consideration by admitting that though Hardy was *in* that time, and was affected by its thought and art, he was not really *of* that time whenever he was his essential self. It is not enough to say that Hardy is "old-fashioned" or "quaint." Certainly he did not try consciously to be old-fashioned. Although there are archaisms of language in his poetry and prose, and much general display of the antique in subject matter, there is nowhere in Hardy the affectation of archaism (found in such an ironic romanticist as Cabell) or the deliberate exploitation of archaism (found in a great many of the literary specialties offered in America). The old-fashioned quality in Hardy is not in the obvious places, but lies deeper. It is in the habit of Hardy's mind rather than in "folklore" or the phenomena of language and style.

Hardy wrote, or tried to write, more or less as a modern— modern, for him, being late nineteenth century. But he thought, or artistically conceived, like a man of another century—indeed, of a century that we should be hard put to name. It might be better to say that he wrote like a creator of tales and poems who is a little embarrassed at having to adapt the creation of tales and poems to the conditions of a written, or printed, literature, and yet tries to do his faithful best under the regrettable circumstances. He is not in any sense a "folk author," and yet he does approach his taletelling and poem-making as if three centuries of Renaissance effort had worked only upon the outward form of tale and poem without changing its essential character. He wrote as a ballad maker would write if a ballad maker were to have to write novels; or as a bardic or epic poet would write if faced with the necessity of performing in the quasi-lyrical but nonsingable strains of the nineteenth century and later.

Hardy is the only specimen of his genus in modern English literature, and I do not know how to account for him. He has no immediate predecessors; and though he has some imitators, no real followers as yet. For his habit of mind has seemingly disappeared in England, and threatens to disappear in America; and without the habit of mind to begin with no real following can be done. I am almost ready to characterize Hardy (if he must be "placed") as an American whose ancestors failed to migrate at the proper time and who accordingly found himself stranded, a couple of centuries later, in the wrong literary climate. In this connection it is amusing to remember that Hardy has been charged with borrowing a description from Augustus Baldwin Longstreet's *Georgia Scenes* for use in *The Trumpet Major*. The truth is that his general affiliation with the frontier humorists of the Old Southwest is a good deal more discernible than his affiliation with Victorian romantic-realists or with French Naturalists. It is an organic affiliation, not a literary attachment, because the Southwestern humorists drew their art, such as it was, from the same kind of source that Hardy used, and wrote (when they had to write) under the same embarrassment. If Hardy's distant seventeenth-century progenitor had migrated to America at the time of the Monmouth Rebellion —as some of his progenitor's relatives and many of his neighbors did, in all haste, migrate—then Thomas Hardy might easily have been a frontier humorist of the Longstreet school. And then he would never have been accused of pessimism, though he might, to be sure, have caused eyebrows to lift in Boston.

In the two volumes which are the second Mrs. Hardy's memoir of her husband (*The Early Life of Thomas Hardy* and *The Later Years of Thomas Hardy*) there is a good deal of scattering and fragmentary evidence to indicate the bent of Hardy's mind. It is enough to aid a speculation, though not enough, probably, to prove the case for a professional researchist. I refer to the recorded experiences of Hardy's childhood and youth which seem to suggest his inward preoccupation better than the interests generally emphasized by critics, such as his study of Greek, his knowledge of architecture, or his tussle with Darwinian theory and modern social problems. Another age than ours would have made something out of the fact that when Hardy was born he was at first cast aside for a stillbirth and was saved only by the shrewd perception of a nurse; or that when the infant Hardy was reposing in his cradle a snake crawled upon his breast and went to sleep there. These are omens that I profess no ability to read. But the many little items that seem to make Hardy a "crusted character," like so many of the personages of his fiction, are not of minor or dubious importance.

Hardy was born early enough—and far enough away from looming Arnoldian or Marxian influences—to receive a conception of art as something homely, natural, functional, and, in short, traditional. He grew up in a Dorset where fiction was a tale told or sung; and where the art of music, always important to him, was primarily for worship or merriment. The Hardys, up through the time of Thomas Hardy's father, were "church-players" of the type of the Mellstock Choir—performers on the violin, cello, and bass who adhered to a traditional psalmody and instrumental performance (of which echoes are preserved here today in the music of the "shape note" singers of the South). Thomas Hardy, as a child, was "extraordinarily sensitive to music." He danced to "the endless jigs, hornpipes, reels, waltzes, and country-dances" that his own father played and, without knowing why, was contradictorily moved to tears by some of the tunes. Later he himself could "twiddle from notation some hundreds of jigs and country-dances that he found in his father's and grandfather's old books"—he was an "oldtime fiddler." Young Thomas played the fiddle at weddings and in farmer's parlors. On one occasion he bowed away for a solid three-quarters of an hour while twelve tireless couples danced to a single favorite tune. At one notable harvest home he heard the maids sing ballads. Among these Hardy remembered particularly "The Outland-ish Knight"—a Dorset version of the ballad recorded by Child as "Lady Isabel and the Elf Knight."

And of course he must have heard, in time, many another ballad, if we may make a justifiable inference from the snatches of balladry in the novels and tales, and if Dorset was the kind of countryside we are led to think it to be. Mrs. Hardy would have us believe that upon the extension of the railway to Dorset in the middle nineteenth century "the orally transmitted ballads were slain at a stroke by the London comic songs," but she underestimates the vitality of folk art. As late as 1922, one R. Thurston Hopkins published a book entitled *Thomas Hardy's Dorset,* in which he tells how he found a singing blacksmith at Lyme Regis, in Devon. Hopkins gives the blacksmith's song, but evidently does not know enough of balladry to recognize it. It is a perfectly good version of the ballad known as "Mollie Vaughn" or "Mollie Bond."

For what it may be worth I note that Hardy first conceived *The Dynasts* as a ballad, or group of ballads. In May, 1875, he wrote in his journal:

> Mem: A Ballad of the Hundred Days. Then another of Moscow. Others of earlier campaigns—forming altogether an Iliad of Europe from 1789 to 1815.

This, Mrs. Hardy says, is the first mention in Hardy's mem-oranda of the conception later to take shape in the epic drama. Again, on March 27, 1881, Hardy referred to his scheme: "A Homeric Ballad, in which Napoleon is a sort of Achilles, to be written."

To evidence of this kind I should naturally add the follow-ing facts: that Hardy wrote a number of ballads, like "The Bride-Night Fire," and balladlike poems; that his poems like his novels are full of references to old singers, tunes, and dances, and that many of the poems proceed from the same sources as his novels; that he is fond of inserting in his journals, among philosophizings and other memoranda, summaries of anecdotes or stories he has heard. Of the latter sort is the following entry:

> Conjurer Mynterne when consulted by Patt P. (a strapping handsome young woman), told her that her husband would die on a certain day, and showed her the funeral in a glass of water. . . . She used to impress all this on her inoffensive husband, and assure him that he would go to hell if he made the conjurer a liar. He didn't, but died on the day foretold.

Such notations should not be unduly emphasized. Yet they appear in his journal with such frequency that we are justified in assuming Hardy's special interest in such material. On the other hand, in the record of Hardy's life thus far available to us, there is little evidence to indicate that, in devising the greater stories, he had some specific literary model before him, or was trying out some theory of fiction, or had, at the beginning of his conception, a particular philosophical or social thesis. Critics may show that such and such a literary influence reached him, or that a theory or philosophy ultimately engaged his mind; but I cannot believe that such elements controlled the original conception or determined the essential character of the greater novels and stories. The poetry offers a somewhat different field of critical speculation, which I do not propose to enter, but it seems worth while to argue that his characteristic habit of mind, early established and naturally developed, has much to do with certain peculiarities of his fiction.

My thesis is that the characteristic Hardy novel is conceived as a *told* (or *sung*) story, or at least not as a literary story; that it is an extension, in the form of a modern prose fiction, of a traditional ballad or an oral tale—a tale of the kind which Hardy reproduces with great skill in *A Few Crusted Char-*

acters and less successfully in *A Group of Noble Dames;* but, furthermore, that his habit of mind is a rather unconscious element in Hardy's art. The conscious side of his art manifests itself in two ways: first, he "works up" his core of traditional, or nonliterary narrative into a literary form; but, second, at the same time he labors to establish, in his "Wessex," the kind of artistic climate and environment which will enable him to handle his traditional story with conviction—a world in which typical ballad heroes and heroines can flourish with a thoroughly rationalized "mythology" to sustain them. The novels that support this thesis are the great Hardy novels: *Under the Greenwood Tree, Far from the Madding Crowd, The Mayor of Casterbridge, The Return of the Native, The Woodlanders,* and *Tess of the D'Urbervilles*—in other words, the Wessex novels proper. *Jude the Obscure* and *The Trumpet Major* can be included, with some reservations, in the same list. The novels that do not support this thesis are commonly held to be, by comparison with those named above, of inferior quality: *The Hand of Ethelberta* and *A Laodicean,* for example. These are Hardy's attempt to be a fully modern—and literary—novelist.

The fictions that result from Hardy's habit of mind resemble traditional, or nonliterary, types of narrative in many ways. They are always conceived of as stories primarily, with the narrative always of foremost interest. They have the rounded, often intricate plot and the balance and antithesis of characters associated with traditional fiction from ancient times. It is natural, of course, that they should in such respects resemble classic drama. But that does not mean that Hardy thought in terms of dramatic composition. His studies in Greek (like his experience in architecture) simply reinforced an original tendency. The interspersed descriptive elements —always important, but not overwhelmingly important, in a Hardy novel—do not encumber the narrative, as they invariably do in the works of novelists who conceive their task in wholly literary terms; but they blend rather quickly into the narrative. Action, not description, is always foremost; the event dominates, rather than motive, or psychology, or comment. There is no loose episodic structure. Hardy does not write the chronicle novel or the biographical novel. Nor does he build up circumstantial detail like a Zola or a Flaubert.

Hardy has an evident fondness for what we might call the "country story"—the kind of story *told* by the passengers in the van in *A Few Crusted Characters;* or *sung* in ballads of the type attributed by scholars to the seventeenth and eighteenth century and sometimes called "vulgar" ballads to distinguish them from the supposedly more genuine "popular" ballads of an earlier day. In *Under the Greenwood Tree,* the coquettish behavior of Fancy Day is a delicate feminine parallel to the difficulties of Tony Kytes, the Arch-deceiver, related in *A Few Crusted Characters.* The coy maiden, after involvement with the solid farmer Shiner and the excellent Vicar, rejects them both at last for the brisk young country lad, Dick Dewy. Gabriel Oak, in *Far from the Madding Crowd,* is the "faithful lover" of many a ballad, who has many of the elements of a masculine "patient Griselda"; he endures a kind of "testing" not irretrievably remote from the testings that ladies put upon their lovers in romances and ballads; and he is also obviously the excellent lover of "low degree" who aims his affections high and is finally rewarded. Fanny Robin, of the same novel, is a typical deserted maiden, lacking nothing but a turtledove on her tombstone; or perhaps she is the more luridly forsaken girl found in "Mary of the Wild Moor." Her lover, Sergeant Troy, is the soldier (or sailor) of any number of later ballads. And it is worth remarking, in this connection, that Hardy's fondness for soldiers has everywhere in it the echo of many ballads about the military composed in the half century or more preceding his birth and even in his own time. It flavors strongly, that is, of such pieces as "Polly Oliver," "Bold Dighton," "Brave Wolfe," "High Germany," and "Bloody Waterloo."

The Return of the Native gives us far more complexity, but many of its focal incidents are the stuff in which taletellers and ballad makers delight. Mrs. Yeobright is bitten by a snake; Eustacia and Wildeve are drowned in one pool, to make a simultaneous romantic death, and we almost expect to learn that they were buried in the old churchyard and presently sprouted—a rose from her breast, a briar from his. We should not forget that Eustacia disguises herself in man's clothing (as heroines of traditional stories have long done) for the mummer's play.

Henchard, in *The Mayor of Casterbridge,* undergoes the rise and fall traditional in English story from Chaucer to *The Mirror for Magistrates.* More clearly, as the man who sold his own wife, he is of ballad or folk tale quality. And the man to whom he sold her is none other than a sailor, of all persons, who returns from the salt, salt sea to claim his woman, as sailors will do.

The Woodlanders, of the Wessex novels, seems furthest from the type; but again, the love of Marty South for Giles Winterborne is ballad love; and the women of *The Woodlanders,* like most of Hardy's women, have the frantic impulsion toward love, or the cruel and unreasoning capacity to reject faithful love, which we find in balladry. Then, too, Grace Melbury is caught, after the setting of the sun, in a murderous mantrap placed in the path to catch a poacher. Happily she is released, and so escapes the fate of Mollie Vaughn of the ballad; Mollie was *shot* by her own lover, who went hunting after the setting of the sun.

Tess of the D'Urbervilles, whatever else she may be, is once more the deserted maiden who finally murders her seducer with a knife in the effective ballad way. And she, with the love-stricken trio—Marian, Retty, and Izz—is a milkmaid; and milkmaids, in balladry, folk song, and folk tale, are somehow peculiarly subject to seduction.

The high degree of coincidence in the typical Hardy narrative has been noted by all observers, often unfavorably. Mr.

Samuel Chew explains it as partly a result of the influence of the "sensation novelists," and partly as a deliberate emphasis on "the persistence of the unforeseen"—hence a grim, if exaggerated, evidence of the sardonic humor of the purblind Doomsters. Let us pay this view all respect, and still remember that such conscious and artful emphasis may be only a rationalization of unconscious habit. The logic of the traditional story is not the logic of modern literary fiction. The traditional story admits, and even cherishes, the improbable and unpredictable. The miraculous, or nearly miraculous, is what makes a story a story, in the old way. Unless a story has some strange and unusual features it will hardly be told and will not be remembered. Most of the anecdotes that Hardy records in his journal savor of the odd and unusual. And occasionally he speaks directly to the point, as in the following passages:

> The writer's problem is, how to strike the balance between the uncommon and the ordinary, so as on the one hand to give interest, on the other to give reality.
>
> In working out this problem, human nature must never be abnormal, which is introducing incredibility. The uncommonness must be in the events, not in the characters. . . . [July, 1881.]
>
> A story must be exceptional enough to justify its telling. We tale-tellers are all Ancient Mariners, and none of us is warranted in stopping Wedding Guests (in other words, the hurrying public) unless he has something more unusual to relate than the ordinary experience of every average man and woman.

Thus, coincidence in Hardy's narratives represents a conviction about the nature of story as such. Hardy's world is of course not the world of the most antique ballads and folk tales —where devils, demons, fairies, and mermaids intervene in human affairs, and ghosts, witches, and revenants are commonplace. It is a world like that of later balladry and folk tale, from which old beliefs have receded, leaving a residue of the merely strange. Improbability and accident have replaced the miraculous. The process is illustrated in the ballad "Mollie Vaughn" (sometimes Van, Bond, or Baun), in which the speaker, warning young men not to go shooting after sundown, tells how Mollie was shot by her lover. I quote from an American version recorded by Louise Pound:

> *Jim Random was out hunting, a-hunting in the dark;*
> *He shot at his true love and missed not his mark.*
> *With a white apron pinned around her he took her for*
> *   a swan,*
> *He shot her and killed her, and it was Mollie Bond.*

In many versions, even the American ones, Mollie's ghost appears in court and testifies, in her lover's behalf, that the shooting was indeed accidental. But the ballad very likely preserves echoes, misunderstood by a later generation, of an actual swan maiden and her lover. This particular ballad is certainly unusual in admitting the presence of a ghost in a court of law. But at least the apparition is a ghost, not a swan maiden, and so we get the event rationalized in terms of an unlikely but not impossible accident: he saw the apron and "took her for a swan."

Hardy's coincidences may be explained as a similar kind of substitution. He felt that the unlikely (or quasi-miraculous) element belonged in any proper story—expecially a Wessex story; but he would go only so far as the late ballads and country tales went, in substituting improbabilities for supernaturalisms. Never does he concoct a pseudo folk tale like Stephen V. Benét's "The Devil and Daniel Webster." Superstitions are used in the background of his narrative; coincidence, in the actual mechanics. Tess hears the legend of the D'Urberville phantom coach, but does not actually see it, though the moment is appropriate for its appearance. In *The Return of the Native* Susan Nonesuch pricks Eustacia Vye for a witch and later makes a waxen image of her, just before her drowning; but coincidence, not superstition, dominates the action. Henchard visits the conjurer just before his great speculation in grain, but only out of habit and in half belief; and it is coincidence that makes Farfrae a winner just at the moment when Henchard is a loser. The supernatural, in Hardy, is allowed in the narrative, but in a subordinate position; the quasi-miraculous takes its place in the main position.

If we use a similar approach to the problem of Hardy's pessimism, it is easy to see why he was irritated by insensitive and obtuse critics. Are the ballad stories of "Edward," "Little Musgrave," and "Johnnie Armstrong" pessimistic? Were their unknown authors convinced of the fatal indifference of the Universe toward human beings? Should we, reading such stories, take the next step in the context of modern critical realism and advocate psychoanalysis for Edward's mother and social security for Johnnie Armstrong? In formal doctrine Hardy professed himself to be an "evolutionary meliorist," or almost a conventional modern. But that had nothing to do with the stories that started up in his head. The charge of pessimism has about the same relevance as the charge of indelicacy which Hardy encountered when he first began to publish. An age of polite literature, which had lost touch with the oral arts—except so far as they might survive in chitchat, gossip, and risqué stories—could not believe that an author who embodied in his serious stories the typical seductions, rapes, murders, and lusty lovemakings of the old tradition intended anything but a breach of decorum. Even today, I suppose, a group gathered for tea might be a little astonished if a respectable old gentleman in spats suddenly began to warble the outrageous ballad of "Little Musgrave." But Hardy did not know he was being rough, and had no more notion than a ballad maker of turning out a story to be either pessimistic or optimistic.

To be sure, Hardy is a little to blame, since he does moralize at times. But the passage about the President of the Immortals in *Tess* and about the persistence of the unforeseen in *The Mayor of Casterbridge* probably came to him like such ballad tags as "Better they'd never been born" or "Young men, take warning from me." He had a mistaken idea, too, that he could argue and philosophize with impunity in verse, whereas he might have to go carefully, say, in an essay or speech. "Perhaps I can express more fully in verse," he wrote in 1896, "ideas and emotions which run counter to the inert crystallized opinion . . . which the vast body of men have vested interest in supporting. . . . If Galileo had said in verse that the world moved, the Inquisition might have let him alone." The good and innocent Hardy could somehow not easily learn that a bard was no longer a bard but a social critic.

The most striking feature of Hardy's habit of mind, as traditional narrator, is in his creation of characters. The country characters of the Wessex novels, with certain important exceptions, are fixed or "nondeveloping" characters. Their fortunes may change, but they do not change with their fortunes. Once fully established as characters, they move unchanged through the narrative and at the end are what they were at the beginning. They have the changelessness of the figures of traditional narrative from epic, saga, and romance to broadside balladry and its prose parallels. In this respect they differ fundamentally from the typical characters of modern literary fiction. Our story writers have learned how to exploit the possibilities of the changing, of changeful, or "developing" character. The theory of progress has seemed to influence them to apply an analogical generalization to the heroes of their stories: to wit, the only good hero in a serious novel is one that *changes* in some important respect during the course of the narrative; and the essence of the story is the change. This has become almost an aesthetic axiom. It is assumed that a story has no merit unless it is based on a changing character. If the modern author uses the changeless character, it is only in a minor role, or as a foil; or he may appear as a caricature.

But we have forgotten a truth that Hardy must have known from the time when, as a child, he heard at the harvest home the ballad of the outlandish knight. The changeless character has as much aesthetic richness as the changeful character.

Traditional narrative of every sort is built upon the changeless character. It is a defect in modern fiction that the value of the changeless character is apparently not even suspected. But since the human desire for the changeless character is after all insatiable, we do have our changeless characters—in the comic strips, the movies, the detective story. Perhaps all is not well with a literary art that leaves the role of Achilles to be filled by Popeye.

At any rate Hardy made extensive use of the changeless character. The habit of his mind probably forbade him to do otherwise; or at least he could not with complete success build his stories upon the changeful character. And so his novels of manners and genteel society are failures. At the same time, Hardy was no untutored child of the folk but a great author who learned by trial and error how to utilize self-consciously the rich material which by unself-conscious habit crowded his mind. He was thinking of his problem, I believe, when he wrote: "The uncommonness must be in the events, not in the characters." He did not make the mistake of exploiting his material for its mere picturesqueness—its *special* quality. He did not write dialect poems like William Barnes or romantic reconstructions like Blackmore's *Lorna Doone*.

What Hardy did is, in its astonishing completeness and verity, a rebuke to superficial quasi-regionalists and to all who attempt to exploit "folk material" with the shallow assumption that the "folkishness" of the material is alone enough to dignify it. Hardy rationalizes the changeless characters by creating in highest circumstantiality not only the local environment in which they move, but the entire social order— the tradition itself, and the basis of the tradition—which will accommodate them. The basis of the tradition is a natural environment—a nature not very much despoiled or exploited, a town life neither wholly antique nor wholly modern, and the whole removed a little in time from the strictly contemporary, but not so far removed as to seem like a historical reconstruction. The antiquities, the local color, the folk customs are not decorative or merely picturesque; they are organic with the total scheme. They are no less essential and no more decorative than the occupations, ambitions, and interrelationships of the changeless characters. He accepts the assumptions of the society that he depicts, and neither apologizes for it nor condescends to it. The stories are stories of human beings, not of peasants or moor-dwellers as such.

The scheme is somewhat more complex than it might appear to be. The changeless characters of the Wessex world are of both minor and major order; and they are generally set in juxtaposition with one or two characters of a more changeful or modern type. The interplay between the two kinds of characters is the focus of the struggle that makes the story. Hardy is almost the only modern novelist who makes serious use of this conflict and at the same time preserves full and equal respect for both sets of characters. His great art lies in not setting up too great or obvious a distance between his changeless and his changeful characters. The difference between Hardy and other novelists will be clear if I cite a typical example. Ellen Glasgow's *Barren Ground,* a novel which seems to copy Hardy at certain points, reduces all the thoroughly rustic characters to a condition either of amusing oddity or of gross ineptitude; and the excellent Dorinda, who makes such an obviously admirable change from rustic backwardness to rural progressivism, is at all times infinitely above all the rest.

Nature, itself unchangeable and inscrutable, is the norm, the basis of Wessex life. Those who accept nature as unchangeable and passively accommodate themselves to nature in the ordered ritual of their lives, not rebelling against it or attempting rash Promethean manipulations—these are the changeless characters.

Nearest to nature, and therefore most changeless, are the rustics (all crusted characters) who throng Hardy's pages. In the rural comedies, like *Under the Greenwood Tree* and *Far from the Madding Crowd,* they dominate the scene. Only the Vicar, in *Under the Greenwood Tree,* with his newfangled church organ, and perhaps in a slight way Sergeant Troy, in the other novel, foreshadow the kind of disturbance set up by the changeful character. But these novels are essentially comedy, joyful and almost idyllic. In Hardy, tragedy does not arrive until changeless and changeful are engaged in bitter conflict.

Such a conflict is found in *The Return of the Native*. Here the rustics are Timothy Fairway, Grandfer Cantle, Christian Cantle, Susan Nonesuch and her son Johnny, and the mummers. It would be wrong to regard these persons as curiosities, or as interesting literary fossils planted in the environment for the verisimilitude that they give. They not only take part in the series of festivals that provide a symbolic chronological pattern for the novel; but they also participate in the critical action itself, as agents of destiny. Timothy carries the letter which was so fatally not delivered at last. Johnny Nonesuch is liaison agent between Eustacia and Wildeve. Christian Cantle carries the guineas, and gambles them away. Susan Nonesuch and her son intervene actively in the lives of both Eustacia and Clym. Their part is organic, not decorative; they are much more than the "Greek chorus" that they have been called. They are, in fact, the basic pattern to which other characters conform or from which they differ. Diggory Venn and Thomasin, at a slightly higher level, conform more or less; they are changeless characters who venture near the danger line of changefulness but do not pass over it. Eustacia and Clym have passed over the line, though not beyond the possibility of retraction. They are changeful characters, strongly touched by Promethean influences—as Wildeve, in a vulgar way, is also touched. Modernism has worked on Eustacia to lure her away from Egdon Heath; but Clym, who has already lived in Paris, has reached a second stage of revulsion against modernism. Yet when this native returns he brings with him a characteristically modern program of education and evangelism. Eustacia and Clym, as changeful characters, do not diverge extravagantly from the changeless pattern, but their rebellion is great enough to render their life courses inconstant and tragic.

Hardy has taken some pains to mark the essential nature of Clym's character. The motto for the chapter that describes Clym is "My mind to me a kingdom is." Clym is a Renaissance, or nontraditional, man. His face, already marked with disillusionment, foreshadows "the typical countenance of the future." Jude, another changeful character, is like Clym in some ways. He too is a rebel against nature, whose rebellion is also idealistic; but it leads him away from Wessex. His story might have been entitled: "The Migration of the Native." In Jude's life the changeless and the changeful are further represented in Arabella and Sue; Arabella, the changeless but too gross; Sue Bridehead, the changeful but too refined. In *Tess* there are two changeful and ruin-wreaking characters. In Alex Stoke-D'Urberville the changeful character takes on a vulgar form. He is an imposter, who has appropriated an old country name and bought his way into Wessex; and the Stoke-D'Urberville establishment, with its preposterous chicken culture, is a fake rural establishment. Angel Clare, on the other hand, is a rarefied form of alien. He is willing, condescendingly, to accept Wessex, and dairy farming, and Tess, provided he can possess all this in an abstractly "pure," or respectable form. The tragedy arrives when he cannot adjust (the sociological term is necessary) his delicate sensibility to a gross, but, in the natural order, an understandable biological fact. It is the changeful modern character in Angel that cannot abide Tess's delinquency. The changeless characters might have found fault, but would not have been shocked, would not have sulked, would have not been too slow to pardon. A similar opposition appears in *The Woodlanders,* where changefulness appears in Fitzpiers and Mrs. Charmond; changelessness in Giles Winterborne and Marty South.

Perhaps these are dangerous simplifications. I do not offer them as definitive explanations of Hardy's fictions, but rather as possibilities not yet explored. Hardy's habit of mind, and his method of using his habit of mind in fiction, seem to me the least discussed of the aspects of his work. I have found no other approach that does not seem to impose a critical explanation from without, with an arbitrariness that often seems to do violence to the art work itself.

There is surely no other example in modern English fiction of an author who, while reaching the highest levels of sophisticated artistic performance, comes bringing his tradition with him, not only the mechanics of the tradition but the inner conception that is often lacking. The admonitions we hear so often nowadays about the relation of the artist and his tradition seem dry and academic when we look closely at Hardy's actual performance. He seems to illustrate what we might think the ideal way of realizing and activating a tradition, for he did, without admonition, what the admonishers are always claiming ought to be done; and yet for that particular achievement he got no thanks, or even a notice. The achievement is the more extraordinary when we consider that he worked (if I read his career rightly) against the dominant pattern of his day. He did what the modern critic (despite his concern about tradition) is always implying to be impossible. That is, Hardy accepted the assumptions of a society which in England was already being condemned to death, and he wrote in terms of those assumptions, almost as if Wessex, and perhaps Wessex only, would understand. From his work I get few of the meanings, pessimistic or otherwise, that are commonly ascribed to him. His purpose seems to have been to tell about human life in the terms that would present it as most recognizably, and validly, and completely human. That he succeeded best when he wrote of rural Wessex is significant. He probably had strong convictions on one point—convictions that had little to do with his official inquiries into Darwinism and the nature of Deity.

FUTURISM AND ARCHAISM

IN TOYNBEE AND HARDY

Yᴏᴜ CANNOT TURN the clock back!" is the commonest taunt of our day. It always emerges as the clinching argument that any modernist offers to any traditionalist when the question is: "What shall we do *now?*" But it is not really an argument. It is a taunt intended to discredit the traditionalist by stigmatizing him as a traitor to an idea of progress that is assumed as entirely valid and as generally accepted. The aim is, furthermore, to poison the traditionalist's own mind and disturb his self-confidence by the insinuation that he is a laggard in the world's great procession. His faith in an established good is made to seem nostalgic devotion to a mere phantom of the buried past. His opposition to the new—no matter how ill-advised, inartistic, destructive, or immoral that new may be—is defined as a quixotic defiance of the Inevitable. To use a term invented by Arnold J. Toynbee, he is an Archaist. By definition, he is therefore doomed.

For the past century and a half the answers of traditionalists to the taunt, "You cannot turn the clock back!" have been rather weak and compromising. Too often they have made needless concessions, have accepted battle on disadvantageous terms, and have lost. In the argument which I propose to develop in the field of literature I shall make only one concession—namely, that it is futile to argue with a Futurist who holds, as all Futurists do, that science and industrialism as they now exist are examples of the Inevitable.

It is inconceivable that Chaucer's *Canterbury Tales* could have originated in a chartered bus ride to the shrine of Thomas à Becket, or in a vehicle moving at a speed greater than the speed of sound. But no modern materialist would ever be convinced, for such reason, that the bus or airplane or even space-ship are to be abhorred—or are anything but inevitable. He can always produce the bus or airplane, and he thinks the space-ship is the next inevitable development because there is nothing else left to produce. Through such pragmatism the materialist has won many a seeming victory, and he continues to win, though with increasing hazard. Yet the victory is never quite the victory he predicted and always has more of seeming in it than substance. So the modern materialist is not after all a very happy man. The tales that he tells have none of the assurance and repose that we can still find in the tales told by Chaucer's pilgrims as they plod crudely along the highway, at a little more than a foot-pace, without even the comfort of stagecoach or buggy. Somewhere in the chain of modern argument a link must be missing. Otherwise we should not be wandering, as we clearly are, in a state of painful frustration and error.

One missing link is supplied by Toynbee in his use of the term Futurism as the counterpart of Archaism. It is always the Futurist, and no other, who offers the rhetorical taunt, "You cannot turn the clock back." The proper rhetorical answer to him evidently is, "Neither can you turn the clock forward, for Time is beyond human control." But the Futurist's use of the clock metaphor is in fact an unconscious revelation of his weakness. He wishes to imply that his design, and his only, is perfectly in step with some scientific master clock of cause and effect that determines the progress of human events. The implication has no basis in reality, since the Futurist actually means to break off all connection with the historical process of cause and effect and to substitute for it an imagined, ideal process of quasi-scientific future development which is nothing more than a sociological vulgarization of Darwinism. The solution of any contemporary problem, social or personal, is to be calculated according to the ticking of an entirely nonexistent Darwinian clock of the future which is held to exert causal force upon human affairs *now*. Thus, it is argued, the curve of social evolution, projected far enough, reveals a theoretical development from the small tribal community, through the nation, to the great world community. Accordingly we should now behave *as if* the still unknown future events lying along the dotted portion of the curve were controlling us now; we should govern, marry, educate, speechify, and poetize *as if* we were already citizens of the anticipated world community and not American taxpayers named Smith or Brown whose establishments and hopes are predicated upon very different assumptions.

In Toynbee's historical analysis, both Futurism and Archaism are classified as phenomena of a disintegrating civilization. Toynbee says: "Futurism and Archaism are, both alike, attempts to break with an irksome Present by taking a flying leap out of it into another reach of the stream of Time without abandoning the plane of mundane life on Earth." Both, too, are "forlorn hopes" and differ mainly in the direction of the leaps they take, one into the unknown Future, the other into the familiar Past. Futurism, Toynbee admits, "goes against the grain of human nature," since the Past, being familiar, offers some direct comfort, and even the disagreeable Present may seem preferable to the dark unknown. Yet Futurism has its hopeful points, since "it is sometimes rewarded for its greater transgression by being allowed to transcend itself through rising into Transfiguration." Through the process of Transfiguration the Futurists of the first century B.C.—involuntarily, it would seem—achieved Christianity. Christianity, in this Toynbeean interpretation, embodies the idea of "A Kingdom of God which is not in Time at all . . . and which differs from all temporal mundane states in the radical way of being in a different spiritual dimension, but which, just by virtue of this difference of dimension, is able to penetrate our mundane life and, in penetrating it, to transfigure it."

The emphasis given by Toynbee, in the sixth volume of his *Study,* to Transfiguration, and particularly to the Christian concept of the Kingdom of God as preferable to "mundane Futurism," seems to impart some quality of positive assurance to his otherwise disheartening analyses. Yet we become uneasily aware, if we read far enough and closely enough, that Toynbee's scheme fails to provide what we most desire and need— a valid means of determining our course of action in the insistent Now. All the societies of all time seem to have been hopelessly disintegrating; the Archaists are always defeated; the Futurists never succeed unless somehow mysteriously "transfigured"; and it is no great comfort to be told by Toynbee that the Christian "transfiguration" was something of a happy accident that owed much to the Greek mythical fumblings that preceded it.

Toynbee himself, when attempting a contemporary application of his scheme, is extraordinarily prejudiced and inept. Indeed he is suspect as something of a "mundane Futurist." For example, in a revealing footnote, Toynbee stigmatizes as archaistic "the well-known human weakness of recalling 'elder statesmen' to power in times of crisis. . . . A rational calculation would lead to the conclusion that these 'elder statesmen' are the last people to whom a community can safely commit its destinies in an emergency, since, *ex hypothesi,* these 'dugouts' are doubly incapacitated—in the first place by the lassitude of old age and secondly, and more seriously, by the obsoleteness of their outlook and habits."

An application of this Toynbeean judgment to American events would have led, presumably, to the rejection of Washington and Jefferson for the Presidency on the grounds of their Archaism, and no doubt—by the principle of "rational calculation" that Toynbee seems to recommend—to the election of Tom Paine Francophiles and Aaron Burrs. But if it was, in Toynbee's language, "a vein of Archaism that is instinctive and unreasoning" that led Americans of the early republic to choose as leaders such elder statesmen as Washington, John Adams, Madison, and possibly even Andrew Jackson, then historical experience would justify us in suspecting now that instinctive and unreasoning judgments of this kind have something in them to recommend them over "rational calculation"—that is, if "rational calculation" and the "instinctive and unreasoning" element are held to be mutually exclusive and opposite, as Toynbee would have us believe.

The weakness of Toynbee's analysis is evident. It is the weakness of any history that tries to interpret human events in the light of a hypothesis which the historian applies in order to test—and generally to demonstrate—the validity of a "theory" of history. The method used must be schematic; and, being schematic, it may misinterpret, or pass over as unimportant, or simply fail to notice, phenomena that are not revealed in their true light by the application of the hypothesis. Furthermore, since the schematic method, however useful and interesting within its limits, is an abstraction like other scientific and quasi-scientific operations, it cannot express, as works of art do, either the rich totality or the vital essence of human experience.

Thus Toynbee, like the Futurists and Archaists whom he criticizes, can never account for or even characterize adequately Tradition as an abiding continuum of man's social history—a continuum which may be influenced by Futurism and Archaism, but which is properly neither one nor the other. For example, in Toynbee's terms, Ireland must be viewed as a remnant of "an abortive Far Western Christian Civilization." In modern times, according to Toynbee, Ireland falls into the category of Archaism because of its attempt to restore Old Irish as a national language. But when Toynbee thus indexes modern Ireland, he leaves us with no notion whatever of the role that living tradition has played in making Ireland an independent state and a going concern. He is similarly Procrustean and inept in gauging the quality and force of the "disintegration" that may afflict a failing society. His scheme affords him no adequate means of distinguishing the peculiarly destructive disintegration generated by modern industrial society from the seemingly parallel but possibly quite different types of disintegration that he can trace in previous societies. He seems incapable of realizing that the Futurism of our industrial age is the most dangerous of all types of Futurism and that, in its assault upon Tradition, it offers the most destructive threat to the continuity of human life that any civilization has ever had to face.

These are indeed the common inadequacies of history, to which Sir Philip Sidney called attention long ago when, in his *Defense of Poesy,* he set poetry above both history and philosophy. But in Toynbee's case the common inadequacies are obscured and may pass unnoticed because of the bold sweep and seeming definitiveness of his *Study,* as well as the authority that in our day attaches to works that seem to rest upon a skilful application of a scholarly and scientific method. In preferring "poetry," or in the present instance, Thomas Hardy's prose fiction to Toynbee's "history," I do not mean to reject either Toynbee or history as empty of merit. But an excursion into Toynbee, who in so many ways reflects the crotchets and blind assumptions of our modern age, has its value as a preliminary to an examination of Thomas Hardy. In a Hardy novel—especially in *The Mayor of Casterbridge,* which has been something of a puzzle to critics—we face the same phenomena, the same issues that Toynbee attempts to reduce to a historical scheme. But we are free from the rule of categories and can apprehend both the totality and the essence of the experience presented. We are put face to face, dramatically, with the struggle between tradition and antitradition that the historians and many of the critics seem strangely unable to define.

An insistent follower of Toynbee could plausibly argue that the conflict in almost any one of the greater Hardy novels may be reduced to a conflict between Futurism and Archaism. Wessex in general looks like an Archaist country which, if it has not leaped backward upon the stream of Time, has remained by stubborn preference in the backwaters. Tragedy occurs, then, when a convinced Futurist like Clym Yeobright in *The Return of the Native* intrudes his intellectual progressivism upon the Archaistic scene.

But a Hardy novel, like life itself, is not that simple. The "Promethean" or changeful characters—Clym Yeobright, Angel Clare, Sue Bridehead—are indeed self-conscious Futurists; but the unchangeful characters that the modern critic may deem "Archaist"—Gabriel Oak, Tess, Marty South, Michael Henchard, as well as numerous "crusted characters" among the country folk—are not at all self-conscious Archaists attempting a *revival* of outmoded ways and beliefs. The deliberate Archaist, in fact, makes no appearance in any Hardy novel or story that I can recall.

What we have instead is a consistent pattern of opposition between the Traditional and the Antitraditional. Tragedy, when it occurs, is of two sorts: (1) an Antitraditionalist (who may well be called a Futurist) brings down calamity upon himself and others by his Promethean disregard of Tradition or by his overt attempt to dislocate the firm continuum of nature and human experience; or (2) a Traditionalist is caught in the web of Futurism—as in *The Mayor of Casterbridge*— and tragically fails to disentangle himself.

Modern critics do not, of course, state the issues in these terms. They are conscious or unconscious Futurists, and their vision is limited by their Futurist bias, no matter whether they are looking at Dostoevski's novels, Mozart's *Figaro*, Yeats's poetry, or some trivial tendentious thing like *South Pacific*. If they are looking at history, they will, like Arthur Schlesinger, Jr., see Andrew Jackson as an American Marxist anticipating class warfare and the New Deal by one hundred years.

To a critic like Albert Guérard, for example, any sort of Prometheanism is a normal, sensible, or perhaps heroic way of life, and Tradition at best is only an obstructive kind of quaintness. The Futurist critic is as blind to his own Futurism as George F. Babbitt was blind to his own Babbittry. In a Hardy novel he discounts or misses altogether the destructive aspects of Prometheanism and concentrates with much fervor upon any evidences of naturalism or realism that he professes to discover. He looks for signs of hidden conflict in the psyches of the leading characters and emerges with a Freudian diagnosis and a lecture on somebody's "sense of guilt."

This is not surprising. The tendency goes far back in Hardy criticism and in all modern criticism of the novel. We are led to suspect that the tenets of naturalism and realism have won far more converts among the critics than among the novelists themselves. For the actual practice of the novelists does not at all consistently support the preaching of critics and literary historians. Hardy, in particular, is out of line with that preaching and suffers when the Futurist critic comes probing him with a questionnaire. To the majestic tragedies of the Wessex people, assailed among their heaths, forests, and earthworks by external and internal foes, the Futurist questionnaire applies the ridiculous illumination of a pocket flashlight. A few minor objects are dubiously revealed, but the rich and massive context is utterly lost.

Thus Henchard, in *The Mayor of Casterbridge,* may seem to a Futurist critic a perfect example of an Archaist caught in hopeless and quixotic contention with processes of change which, to such a critic, seem normal and salutary. The easy solution of the critic's problem, then, is to say that *The Mayor of Casterbridge* is a "life novel" of a familiar modern type, with realism as its dominant technique. The strong man of the older generation (Henchard) cannot "adjust" to a new social-economic situation. Accordingly, by a deterministic operation of cause and effect, he is knocked out, or knocks himself out, and is replaced by his progressive counterpart (Farfrae). Then the novel ought to be, not a tragedy, but a realistic chronicle of which Farfrae should emerge as hero. But that is not at all the impression the novel leaves upon the awed reader. Obviously Hardy intended no such thing. This oversimplified interpretation, furthermore, does not account for the peculiar organization that Hardy gives the novel, which is certainly not the organization that Balzac, Flaubert, Zola, or Bennett would have given it. The detached prelude, for example—in which the moody and drunken Henchard auctions off his wife and daughter to a passing sailor who fortuituously appears in the furmity woman's tent—moves, like the opening scenes of *King Lear,* at the level of ballad and folk tale. It is sufficiently "realistic," but the realism is not modern. And this wife-selling episode, though linked in the plot with critical events of Henchard's later career, does not operate as a prime determinant upon those events, as does, by way of comparison, the only slightly detached treatment of the heredity and environment of Emma and Charles with which Flaubert begins *Madame Bovary.*

There is evidently a dramatic logic impelling Hardy's use of "realism," but it is not the logic of nineteenth-century naturalism or twentieth-century realism. Mr. Guérard recognizes this in his declaration that Hardy consistently fuses realism and antirealism. The two techniques appear in combination, Mr. Guérard notes, in the scene in which Henchard stands on the bridge, meditating suicide, but recoils when he sees the image of himself floating in Ten Hatches Hole. Here (to follow Guérard) we find "straight realism," since the effigy used in the skimmity-ride is *actually* floating in the pool, and "sublimated realism," since the stress of the moment produces in Henchard a momentary "neurosis" and a hallucination that he mistakes for supernatural revelation. But this is condescension on Mr. Guérard's part. Hardy does not thus condescend. A page further on, Henchard declines to be persuaded when matter-of-fact Elizabeth-Jane descends to the bank and shows him the effigy. "It seems that even I be in Somebody's hand," Henchard insists.

The ethical problem of the novel cannot be solved, or even stated, in terms of "realism" and "antirealism," viewed as technical devices for revealing a psychic state. Hardy makes it clear that Henchard's acceptance of the miraculous must be taken into serious account. Nor will it suffice to interpret the novel as a tragedy of character, even though Hardy seems to invite such interpretation by his subtitle, "A Story of a Man of Character." The tragic flaw in Henchard as a "man of character" would then have to be his impulsiveness, or his inability to balance passion with reason. But though Henchard can be viewed as a "man of passion," and though his errors are errors of passion, not of calculation, still excess of passion is not enough to account for Henchard's ruin. The flow of feeling that leads him into his mistakes also develops in him the remorse, generosity, and sense of fair play that put him on the road to recovery. His drunken casting off of Susan is redeemed by his great penitential oath, his search for the lost wife and child, and his reparation when the lost ones reappear.

Mr. Guérard gets around this difficulty by arguing that Henchard is "a man of character obsessed by guilt and so committed to his own destruction," and puts him with such heroes of modern tragedy as Conrad's Lord Jim and Rasumov, Melville's Captain Ahab, and similarly introspective character-inventions. This view requires us to believe that the whole narrative structure rests upon the sense of guilt felt by Henchard for "the crime of selling his wife," a fantasy which Mr. Guérard attempts to bolster up by citing the Freudian theory of the psychology of errors: Henchard, he argues, is under a psychological compulsion to destroy himself.

But it is absurd to reduce the area of conflict in this complex novel to some mere subjective struggle in Henchard's psyche. He is one of the least subjective characters in modern fiction and anything but a psychotic individual. The "sense of guilt," so far as it operates in Henchard as an entirely normal man, is only one of the motives determining his conduct. His sense of outrage, when once caught in the net of events, is infinitely stronger than his sense of guilt. The great frustrating element that brings bafflement and finally despair and defeat is external, not internal. It is incomprehensible to Henchard, as something foreign to his experience and outside the range of his convictions. To identify this external frustrating element is to define the opposing force that causes the tragic conflict. And the opposing force is dramatically represented by Farfrae, whom the Futurist critic somehow is never quite able to "see."

Donald Farfrae, is the "villain" of *The Mayor of Caster-bridge,* if so inadequate a catchword can be used to designate the agent of the Promethean forces that wreck the life of Michael Henchard. Farfrae is a man of calculation who has the typically modern faculty of being able at will to divorce "rational calculation" from whatever he possesses of the "instinctive and unreasoning" qualities that would ally him with erring, pulsating humanity. Lucetta, the adventuress who belongs, more vaguely, to the same Promethean strain, instantly perceives the duality of Farfrae's nature when he visits her at High-Place Hall.

" 'You are animated . . . [she says to him] Then you are thinking of getting on. You are sad the next moment—then you are thinking of Scotland and friends.' "

Presently Hardy adds, with the forthrightness of a novelist who is troubled by no timid modernist scruples about the aesthetic necessities of "the limited point of view":

> Whether its origin were national or personal, it was quite true what Lucetta had said, that the curious double strands in Farfrae's thread of life—the commercial and the romantic— were very distinct at times. Like the colours in a variegated cord those contrasts could be seen intertwisted, yet not mingling.

Farfrae prefigures, as no other Hardean character so effectively does, the ominous arrival in traditional Wessex of business and applied science, capable through "rational calculation" of delivering material benefits which nevertheless carry with them incalculable elements of destruction. Farfrae foreshadows the modern industrial plutocrat—*vide* Henry Ford and many others—whose enterprises can dislocate the social and even the political structure of an entire nation; but who, using a different part of his mind, can nostalgically picture himself as an American of the old tradition and, at leisure in some Georgia Sea Island estate or some bought-up Virginia mansion, can surround himself with the appurtenances of a country squire. It is Farfrae's exactly similar capacity for separating the "commercial" and "romantic" that makes him completely dangerous. To Henchard and other traditionalists of Casterbridge, who do not thus separate "thought" and "feeling," Farfrae is unfathomable.

That Hardy intends dramatic opposition between Henchard and Farfrae, and not mere dramatic contrast, is evident from the structure of the narrative and from the comments of the persons of the tale, minor and major. From the moment of Farfrae's entrance to the end of the reversal of Henchard's fortunes which Farfrae brings about, this opposition is so clear that one can only marvel how critics have made so little of it. He is not only the efficient cause of Henchard's ruin but also a herald of the general disintegration that will seize "Wessex" and other traditional societies.

Farfrae the destroyer enters the drama in the guise of ingenious benefactor—very much as the industrial revolution entered European society during the period depicted in Hardy's novel. He has a scheme for converting inferior "grown" wheat into usable—though still admittedly inferior —grain. His intervention in the Mayor's affairs comes at a time when Henchard, through a combination of accident and indiscretion, is exposed to Promethean seductions. Bad weather has injured the quality of the wheat that Henchard, as corn-factor, has to sell, and there is public complaint—however unjustified—against him. At the same moment he is forced to meet two personal crises, in the return of the lost wife and daughter and the sudden necessity for settling, somehow, his illicit affair with Lucetta.

To a modern sociologist it would be entirely "rational" and proper that Henchard, the self-acknowledged "rule o' thumb

sort of man" who is "bad at science," should insist on hiring
Farfrae as his manager. It is a "progressive" act for an agricultural entrepreneur to enlist science as his guide. But in this
judgment the sociologist would entirely miss the point of the
dramatic irony, Sophoclean in its meaning and its economy,
that Hardy uses here and elsewhere. He might also overlook
the subtle touch that Hardy uses to suggest that Henchard is
drawn to Farfrae by intangible elements which, however
wrongly, he thinks he perceives. In good country tradition
he tries hopefully to find some basis of kinship: "Your fore-
head, Farfrae, is something like my poor brother's—now dead
and gone; and the nose, too, isn't unlike his."

But Farfrae is an alien intruder, not a kinsman. A flair
for public entertainment and skill in calculation—or, in other
words, a "romantic" and, to Casterbridge folk, an exotic display of emotionalism, plus cold efficiency and success in business—these are the sources of Farfrae's popularity and his
quick rise to power. It is a formula not far off from the bread
and circuses of the Caesars and the television–plus–social
security program of the modern Leviathan state. At the Three
Mariners Inn, Farfrae charms the rustic company with his
nostalgic Scottish song, "Hame to my ain countree." For interpretation of this and similar performances by Farfrae, all
the clue we need is Christopher Coney's doubting comment:
"What did ye come away from yer own country for, young
maister, if ye be so wownded about it?" Farfrae is an op-
portunist and a *déraciné,* bound for America to seek his fortune, but ready enough to stop at Casterbridge. His nostalgia
is meaningless, or has only momentary genuineness. It is not
an expression of the whole man, but only a superficial adorn-
ment of the dominant principle of calculation. The efficiency
of Farfrae as calculator requires that his singing and dancing
be kept distinct from his calculation; they can never really
be "meant." But neither Elizabeth-Jane nor Lucetta nor the
Casterbridge public can see any harm in the man, and so the
special public entertainment arranged by Farfrae in his im-

provised tent (to which entertainment, significantly, he charges admission) draws off the crowd, while Henchard's outdoor fair of the old traditional kind, which is free to the public—and has no star performer—is deserted when rain sets in. The alliance of Henchard and Farfrae, which to the older man represents warm friendship fused with commercial interest, quickly collapses and is followed by open trade rivalry. In this rivalry Henchard cannot win. The traditionalist who "means" everything he does is helpless against the cool, strictly business methods of Farfrae—who is not only strictly business but machine-minded. Farfrae can hum the love ballad, "The Lass of Gowrie," while inspecting the interior of the new-fangled mechanical corn-drill.

But for Farfrae's intervention, Henchard's difficulties with Susan and Lucetta could have been solved—as Dickens might have solved them, or Thackeray, or Jane Austen, or Charlotte Brontë—and we should then have had a comedy. It is the role of Farfrae, in subtle opposition to Henchard, that makes *The Mayor of Casterbridge* definitely and uniquely a Hardy novel, which dramatizes the dilemma of modern civilization more sharply and impressively than all of Toynbee's volumes can expound it.

For Farfrae as Promethean, everything becomes a means to power. He is able to reverse relationships—to become master and owner of the business, with Henchard his employee, a mere humble worker at that. He becomes mayor, and he is the successful suitor, first, for the hand of Henchard's former mistress, Lucetta, and, after her death, of Henchard's "daughter," Elizabeth-Jane. In all this there is no self-conscious, intended malignancy of purpose. At every turn Farfrae is "doing right" by modern standards—that is, acting reasonably and providently, without respect for the "imponderables," whereas Henchard, by those same standards, is improvident, unreasonable, and therefore "in the wrong." At the official reception of the Illustrious Personage, Henchard seems grotesque in the eyes of the public and by common consent is held to be nothing less than a nuisance. Yet all the while, in this remarkable narrative, our sympathy is with the heroic nuisance. Thus it is that Hardy means for us to understand, as J. F. A. Pyre has pointed out, that Farfrae's triumph is "a defeat of the superior by the inferior nature."

This is a hard pill for the modern reader and for many a high critic to swallow. It is tantamount to saying that the defeat of a small-town wagon manufacturer by Ford or General Motors is a defeat of a superior by an inferior nature. And by modern standards, that is nonsense.

But it is modern standards that are warped, not Hardy's scale of dramatic and ethical values. The meaning of *The Mayor of Casterbridge* is that what Henchard is as a valorous human being, with all his human imperfections, is superior to what Farfrae is, as the finally repugnant representative of a logic which in the last analysis is not only antitraditional but antihuman.

In this antithesis of forces Elizabeth-Jane is almost completely passive and neutral. To Elizabeth-Jane, who with Farfrae survives the wreck that engulfs Susan, then Lucetta and her unborn child, then Henchard, Hardy attributes certain meditations that are sometimes taken as providing the "key" to the novel. When Elizabeth-Jane perceives that both Farfrae (with whom she is secretly in love) and Henchard, her pseudo-father, are courting Lucetta, we are told by Hardy that her thoughts were as follows:

> She had learnt the lesson of renunciation, and was as familiar with the wreck of each day's wishes as with the diurnal setting of the sun. . . . Yet her experience had consisted less in a series of pure disappointments than in a series of substitutions. Continually it had happened that what she had desired had not been granted her, and that what had been granted her she had not desired. So she viewed with equanimity the now cancelled days when Donald had been her undeclared lover, and wondered what un-wished for thing Heaven might send her in place of him.

At the end, when she is at last married to Donald, and Henchard has met his lonely death, she is represented as being thankful for her good fortune—but not effusively thankful:

> . . . her strong sense that neither she nor any other human being deserved less than was given, did not blind her to the fact that there were others receiving less who had deserved much more. And in being forced to class herself among the fortunate she did not cease to wonder at the persistence of the unforeseen, when the one to whom such unbroken tranquillity had been accorded in the adult stage was she whose youth had seemed to teach that happiness was but the occasional episode in a drama of pain.

We should resist the temptation to view Elizabeth-Jane, in her detached, seemingly philosophical role, as Hardy's spokesman. The sentiments that Hardy puts into her mind—but not into her mouth—do not really clarify the pattern of events in the novel as a whole, but rather signify that Elizabeth-Jane, from her personal angle of vision, can make no sense out of them. What she has learned is how to come to terms with catastrophe. Throughout the narrative Elizabeth-Jane yields to events. A thoroughgoing passivist, she never fights back, and she never plans ahead. Only once does she display outspoken anger. That is when, at her wedding festivities, she reproaches Henchard for deceiving her as to the identity of her father—and therefore as to her own identity.

This is the moment, we should remember, when she is at last certain that she is Elizabeth-Jane Newson, not Elizabeth-Jane Henchard, and is also Mrs. Farfrae, wife of the new mayor. Her detachment is not so much a philosophical attainment as a pragmatic facing of conditions. Her resignation, renunciation, and neutralism, as well as her awareness of "the persistence of the unforeseen," are the product of a kind of orphanage and dissociation. Necessity has shaped her into a canny female counterpart of Conrad's Axel Heyst; she does not act, but awaits action. Like a character in a Robert Penn Warren novel, she must perpetually be asking, "Who am I?"

It is dramatically appropriate that her Neutralism should wed Farfrae's Prometheanism at the moment when Henchard falls. It is a very modern situation—and a very modern wedding. Neutralism permits survival—if it is lucky enough to make terms with the victor.

Should we then conclude that if Michael Henchard had been shrewd enough to develop Elizabeth-Jane's philosophy of life, he too could have survived? He would have had to practice renunciation; expect more defeats than victories; accept substitutes for the objects of his most passionate desires; be content with less than he hoped for; and, though conscious of his own "deserts," not expect others necessarily to recognize those deserts; but hope for the persistence of the unforeseen, which might just possibly bring some period of happiness if he could cultivate "equanimity" and hold out long enough.

Such conduct is not possible to Henchard. Elizabeth-Jane's pattern—which closely resembles the diplomatic pattern known in our day as "appeasement"—does not suit the strong man who acts on intuition and conviction and makes his commitment, no matter what the cost.

Henchard is neither Neutralist nor Promethean, nor is he an Archaist. He is the kind of man that the modern Promethean regime can neither define nor use—nor even see. For the eyes of this regime are adjusted to historical discontinuity, and, like Toynbee, simply fail to notice or to take into account that vital continuum of human existence to which we give the somewhat inadequate name, Tradition. It is Henchard's misfortune—as it is now the misfortune of a great part of the world's traditional societies—that he, for his part, cannot identify Prometheanism and Neutralism for what they really are, but interprets them, with disastrous results, in terms of his unself-conscious traditionalism, which has been weakened in one or two important respects.

To begin at the folk level—as Hardy himself does—Henchard is in many ways the traditional "bold" Englishman of song and story—as Robin Hood was "bold" in the ballads, and Wolfe and Nelson were "bold" in later times. He is great of frame—and great of heart; reckless, but generous; quick to make friends and ready to fight his enemies openly; quick to wrath, but also warm in affection—"emotional" in his judgments, the modern sociologist would say. But with this emotional capacity goes an intuitive ability to sense the feelings of others—a trait lacking in his rather dense opponent. A "rule of thumb man," as he admits, Henchard is crude and inept in calculation. But he knows how to command men, as Farfrae does not. His harshness toward Abel Whittle is not "bad employer-employee relationships" but comes from his knowledge of men, and it binds the lad to him in the end. His masterful discipline is preferable to Farfrae's spinsterish, bureaucratic concern over mere appearances. Henchard's "March on; never mind your breeches!" is the right thing to say to sleepy-headed Abel, when the wagons are waiting; not Farfrae's "Go and dress yourself instantly, Whittle." The men know, as Farfrae does not, that Henchard had kept Abel's old mother in coals and snuff during the winter. For Henchard, human relationships do not rest on a wage scale. Loyal himself, he expects loyalty of others. He is over-trustful, as is the way of chivalrous souls. He is subject to rages and black moods, but he responds to frankness and affection.

Henchard is, in short, a positive, very masculine man—by far the most masculine and positive of all Hardy's heroes. True masculinity of this strong and open kind is so rare in modern fiction that the seekers after symbolism and the Oedipus-complex doubtless have some difficulty in knowing how to take Henchard. A man in a Hemingway novel, by comparison, is little more than a whining forked radish dressed up in a sports coat.

The tragedy of Henchard is the tragedy of a truly masculine man in collision with forces that turn the traditional masculine virtues into liabilities. Henchard is a pre-Renaissance individual, born into a time (identified by Hardy as the period immediately preceding the repeal of the Corn Laws) that was already beginning to sacrifice religion for humanism and that, in so doing, had already released the calculating principle to work unchecked upon society. In Edmund Burke's terms, Henchard is a member, though not an aristocratic member, of "the age of chivalry"; and Farfrae (as also Lucetta in her rather vaguely depicted, somewhat urban character of woman in the abstract) belongs to the new age of "sophisters, calculators, and economists." Henchard, strong though he is with the strength of his masculinity and his tradition, does not yet know that the leaders of his society, who have become the masters of his destiny, have sold him out in the name of progress and scientific improvement. And his society—still traditional, but somewhat shaken, as Henchard himself is—does not know what has happened. Casterbridge and Henchard are open to invasion.

What are the masculine virtues? They are bodily strength, hardihood, valor, fidelity, piety, and chivalrousness. In the regime foreshadowed by Farfrae these virtues lose meaning and importance. The regime has no place for them to be exercised. Henchard of Casterbridge can still save Lucetta and Elizabeth-Jane from the onrush of a savage bull, as Farfrae cannot. But modern society allows few occasions for rescuing ladies in distress. The business executive does not need muscle; neither does the operator of a bulldozer. Strength is for professional athletes. Valor, fidelity, piety, chivalrousness do not prepare either man or woman to take financial advantage, as Farfrae and his successors do, of a purely economic situation.

The more Henchard struggles, the more he is entangled. His struggle is the more pitiful because he lacks any firm religious guidance. Religion in Casterbridge society (as in Hardy's Wessex in general) has been weakened. The Church, visibly present in *Tess of the D'Urbervilles*—though in diluted form—is significantly absent from *The Mayor of Caster-*

bridge. Yet the religious impulse survives in Henchard, as in his lone vow at the church altar and, more significantly, in his invocation of a curse on Farfrae, during the great scene in which he forces the villagers to sing the comminatory One Hundred and Ninth Psalm. So far as Henchard is concerned, the song in this case is completely *meant.* It is no romantic flourish, like Farfrae's entertaining ditties. Indeed, all that Henchard does, he does with his whole being. Toward the end, he truly believes that the image of himself in the pool is nothing less than a miracle. Whatever vestiges of religion remain to him are from the religion of tradition and true belief, not of the religion supported by modern humanists. Henchard's supernaturalism is not supported by Elizabeth-Jane. She seeks at once to "explain" the miracle.

In the final scenes, the apparently tawdry and jangling actions of Henchard, like the "reason in madness" of King Lear, are a dramatized ironic commentary on the false majesty of the Farfrae regime. When Henchard unrolls his "private flag," steps to the side of the Royal carriage and blandly extends his right hand to the Illustrious Personage, thus bringing consternation upon Mayor Farfrae and the committee of welcome, it is no mere display of a wounded ego. It is a proclamation that the proceedings are empty of meaning. Henchard, speaking *in vino veritas,* might well say the words that Shakespeare puts into Lear's mouth:

> *There thou might'st behold the great image*
> *Of authority: a dog obeyed in office.*

Finally there is Henchard's will, which is found pinned on the headboard of his deathbed:

"That Elizabeth-Jane Farfrae be not told of my death, or made to grieve on account of me.
"& that I be not bury'd in consccrated ground.
"& that no sexton be asked to toll the bell.
"& that nobody is wished to see my dead body.

"& that no murners walk behind me at my funeral.

"& that no flours be planted on my grave.

"& that no man remember me.

"To this I put my name.

MICHAEL HENCHARD."

Here Hardy uses the traditional device of the satirical will—employed by the "Archpoet" of the Latin Goliardic poems, by Villon, by John Donne in "The Legacy," and by the unknown authors of the ballads—to declare, as plainly as words can say, what is the conclusion of the whole matter. Under the Farfrae regime that conclusion can no longer be, as of old, to fear God and keep His commandments. In the Promethean world of science and Futurism, nothing is any longer sacred. Therefore the rites of Christian burial, if instigated and performed by Neutralist Elizabeth-Jane and Futurist Farfrae, would not only be—in the language their descendants might learn to use—an example of naïve Archaism, but also a gross insult to the man Henchard. Like Swift in "A Modest Proposal," Hardy reveals the false pretensions of modernism by dramatizing its logical extreme. Henchard's will is the parallel, in prose fiction, of the heap of broken images in T. S. Eliot's *The Wasteland*. It is also a realistic anticipation of the modern funeral, which in its progressive and "enlightened" form forbids exhibitions of grief and mourning; ignores consecrated ground in favor of a commercialized cemetery with a fancy name; asks that flowers be omitted; considers it bad taste to toll the bell or view the body; and, since processions obstruct traffic, whisks the deceased away from the funeral home and into oblivion with the least pretense of a funeral procession.

In a novel like *The Mayor of Casterbridge* there can be no Sophoclean chorus to admonish us to seek wisdom and reverence God. If a final chorus were to be added it would have to declare that the regime prefigured in Hardy's story of Casterbridge and its Mayor has despoiled us and continues to despoil us of what the long generations of the past understood to be the true quality of human life. To be reduced to mere func-

tions is to lose all manliness, all womanliness; and it is to invite
the curse that Michael Henchard invoked on those who despoiled him. Who is so bold as to say that that curse has not
already come true, for the descendants of Elizabeth-Jane and
Farfrae, in just the terms Henchard meant when he commanded the loitering choir to sing "Psalm the Hundred and
Ninth, to the tune of Wiltshire"—

> *His ill-got riches shall be made*
> *To usurers a prey;*
> *The fruit of all his toil shall be*
> *By strangers borne away. . . .*
>
> *A swift destruction soon shall seize*
> *On his unhappy race;*
> *And the next age his hated name*
> *Shall utterly deface.*

THEME AND METHOD IN

SO RED THE ROSE

DURING THE nineteen-twenties, when H. L. Mencken, Sinclair Lewis, and Theodore Dreiser were still the flourishing idols of the new American literature, realism was consistently recommended as a sovereign cure for the sentimentalism with which the South was said to be afflicted. Sentimentalism, it was argued, had produced the so-called magnolias-and-moonlight type of Southern literature. But realism in heavy doses would purge the South of the infection, much in the way that the medical doctors were conquering hookworm and pellagra. T. S. Stribling, Laurence Stallings, Howard Odum, Gerald Johnson, Paul Green, and even DuBose Heyward and Julia Peterkin (at that time the darlings of the liberal *avant-garde*) were held to be administering the cure with much success in what seemed to be regarded as a series of clinical demonstrations.

Preposterous though this school of thought may now seem, its influence has lingered on. A good deal of its sustained momentum has come, doubtless, from the great prestige of Vernon L. Parrington and such professors of American literature as have followed his social type of diagnosis. And this lingering tendency, I suppose, would explain why a critic, as late as the mid-nineteen-thirties, could say that Stark Young's *So Red the Rose* was "heavy with the scent of camellias." He did not know that camellias have no scent; but since magnolias do not flower prominently in Young's novel, while camellias do occasionally appear, he wished to damn the book by connecting it with what he considered a deplorable nonrealistic tendency.

The times have changed, and critics who think that camellias have an exotic odor are fewer—and more careful. They can no longer afford the luxury of an ignorance that would make a Florida tourist laugh. Under the new critical regime William Faulkner and other once neglected authors have received extended consideration, but the writings of Stark Young, particularly his prose fiction, have been given no such attention. They have remained an unexplored realm, to which hardly even a reportorial Marco Polo has journeyed.

This neglect seems the more remarkable when one recalls Stark Young's astonishing versatility and productivity. Since the beginning of his literary career, early in the nineteen-twenties, he has been, first of all, one of the few really distinguished dramatic critics writing in English. His dramatic criticism, furthermore, has been translated into foreign languages as distant as the Chinese and Japanese. His fine articles and essays on nondramatic subjects have had wide circulation, and some have been gathered up, selectively, with his stories, in such books as *The Street of the Islands* (1930) and *Feliciana* (1935). Then, most important of all for the present discussion, there are his four novels: *Heaven Trees* (1926), *The Torches Flare* (1928), *River House* (1929), and *So Red the Rose* (1934). The six books named are closely related. Taken all together, they form a definite organic unity—a kind of "war and peace" of the American scene, with the focus chiefly but not exclusively on the South; and they apply in the medium of prose fiction the artistic principles and moral philosophy that animate the dramatic criticism and that Stark Young has more recently expressed in his book of reminiscences, *The Pavilion* (1951).

Although all these books have claims upon a critic's sober attention—and *Heaven Trees,* among them, has a peculiar and charming perfection of its own—*So Red the Rose* is clearly the greatest. In this instance the judgment of readers has run ahead of the judgment of critics. From the time of its first publication, *So Red the Rose* has commanded a large audience of devoted readers. For twenty years it has remained in print without benefit of criticism new or old. Since it is a complex and difficult novel—not at all the simple romance that a camellia-minded critic might guess it to be—the phenomenon of its popularity is not easy to explain. Some would explain it, I suppose, by calling the book a "Civil War novel."

But though it deals with events of the eighteen-sixties, *So Red the Rose* is no more to be catalogued as a mere "Civil War novel" than the *Antigone* of Sophocles is to be catalogued as a drama of the Theban civil war. The dramatic conflict of *So Red the Rose* is not some special sort of conflict that pertains only to the people of the South or of a limited region of Mississippi. It is a conflict of the same order and nature as we find in the works of Dostoevski, Hardy, Yeats, Eliot, or Faulkner. The novel draws into focus the battle between tradition and anti-tradition that has been waged with increasing vehemence since the Renaissance. In it Stark Young deals with what is, for the serious artist, the great inescapable subject, and he dramatizes that subject in its own terms, without imposing special views upon it. By his method he "realizes" that subject in a full-bodied fiction that implies in every part the whole of which it is a symbolic rather than a merely pictorial or argued representation. There is no other "Civil War novel" that can compare with it because no other such novel has so convincingly brought the special historical subject matter into the realm of the high art that alone can give a local fiction general application and lasting relevance.

So Red the Rose is a large-scale narrative in which events of national importance exert catastrophic force upon the life of the Bedfords, the McGehees, and their kin, friends, visitors, slaves—the whole complex of plantation life and, by implication, of Southern life in general. Beginning with the birthday party for Hugh McGehee, in November, 1860, the narrative covers the period of the election of Lincoln, Southern secession, formation of the Confederacy, and the Civil War. It ends in November, 1865. More than fifty characters appear in the novel, and at least a score of these are of major importance.

Yet despite its large scope, numerousness of characters, and wealth of detail, *So Red the Rose* is singularly compact and at every point sharply dramatic in its method of rendering characters and events. This dramatic quality and compactness are the more remarkable if one recalls, by comparison, the diffuse or laborious treatment generally found in novels dealing with the same period. It would seem that a writer who chooses the Civil War period can hardly achieve dramatic concentration unless, like Stephen Crane in *The Red Badge of Courage*, he takes the safe course of centering his narrative on a single person to whose point of view everything is related. This limitation of course assists the dramatic concentration, but at the cost of impoverishing the context of great events and great persons in which the chosen mentality must perform. On the other hand, writers who, wishing to offset this limitation, attempt to supply richness of context by romantic, panoramic, or documentary devices inevitably lose dramatic concentration and produce mere "historical" novels.

In *So Red the Rose* there is no single character on whom the narrative is focused throughout; nor is there any narrator or disinterested participant whose angle of vision affords a consistent point of reference. A single point of view may be maintained for a while during a single episode. We may enter the brooding mind of Lucy McGehee when, after the battle of Shiloh, she has her vision of dead Charles Taliaferro riding through the gate, putting his hand to his side, and saying, "That night at Shiloh, lying in my blood, I remembered how you sang." But after such moments the focus soon shifts or, rather, merges into the impersonal current of the general narrative.

Evidently Stark Young wished to retain the breadth of perspective and richness of context afforded by the "omniscient point of view"—that is, the method of classical narrative. But he also wished each scene or narrative bit to carry the sharp particularity, the firm dramatic immediacy, afforded by the modern method of dramatization in prose narrative. This method bars intruded explanation. It noncommittally subjects the reader to the flow of inferences and sensations and ideas that the performing characters encounter at any given moment.

It is this combination of methods, applied with consummate skill, that gives *So Red the Rose* its wonderful compactness and dramatic force, together with its richness of narrative meaning. But though the classical method allows the author to shift the focus continually and also, by way of "exposition," to orient the reader as to the course of events in general—the war, for example—the dramatic method requires that the author never "intrude" the meaning of the dramatization itself; it must be implicit in the action. Therefore, in combining the two methods, Stark Young had to take, first, the risk of some confusion or uncertainty of orientation, especially during the opening chapters of the novel; and, second, the far greater risk that the total and true meaning of his narrative would be missed or only dimly apprehended. For the conscientious Southern writer in our time, the latter risk is peculiarly painful. Anything that looks like a declaration on his part will be viewed as partisanship. Yet if his real meaning does not somehow emerge, it will not be grasped at all or else will be confused with some conventional interpretation of Southern life.

It might be argued that confusion of orientation is, in a way, a part of the dramatic effect. Stark Young has said, in *The Pavilion:* "It does not matter at all if some reader of these pages should find he cannot keep straight various characters or stories that appear in them. . . . The point is the quality represented here and there in one name or one story and another and the memory that remains of them." This would apply to *So Red the Rose,* to some extent.

When we encounter Malcolm Bedford, in Chapter I, writing his humorous obituaries of relatives and friends—a remarkable scene—we may suppose, accustomed as we are to the limited point of view, that we will continue with Malcolm's point of view for at least one complete episode. But no, presently we are in the carriage with the Bedfords and Mary Cherry, proceeding to Hugh McGehee's birthday party, without knowing very precisely who the Bedfords and McGehees are. Momentarily, as we look back at Portobello from the avenue, we slip into Mrs. Bedford's mind. But on the next page we reach Montrose and are in the midst of a very large group of interesting people who know one another but do not stop to lecture us on their identities and backgrounds. The author is not going to lecture us either. And we may proceed for fifty pages, even a hundred, before the identity of the characters and their relation to historic events begins to form a narrative pattern that can be completely and definitely grasped. This confusion, as Stark Young says, "does not matter"— meaning that perfect clarity, if striven for by rigid outlining and explanation, would destroy the sense of vitality and spontaneity that are needed at the outset.

Still, in *So Red the Rose*, it is not a question of a few names and relationships but of a convergence of many names and multiple relationships. And the narrative is complicated by the fact that the author presents two complete households, where most novelists might have been content with one. At Portobello, the Bedford plantation, there are Malcolm Bedford; Sallie, his wife (née Tate); Duncan, their son; Valette Somerville, their adopted daughter. At Montrose, the seat of the McGehees, there are Hugh McGehee; his wife Agnes (sister of Malcolm Bedford); their son Edward; and their daughter Lucy. Adding to these two groups Mary Cherry and General Sherman, we have ten major characters to deal with, as persons of critical importance. There are also forty or more "minor" characters—none of whom, however, can be dismissed as unimportant. It would seem that we cannot really "know" the characters of the novel and establish them in the pattern of the narrative until the two families are understood, as families. It is clear that the minor characters of the book either belong to the Bedford or McGehee households by blood or principle; or else are pathetically unattached; or represent, like Sherman, a hostile principle. And the two families, united by ties of marriage and blood, are in a sense one family as the South in a still larger sense is one family. The Bedfords and McGehees, in their histories, dwellings, and personal peculiarities, represent different and complementary aspects of Southern life.

The Bedfords seem to represent a strain more definitely English, in certain ways, than the McGehees. This is the strain deriving from Virginia antecedents that became dominant in Tennessee and Kentucky and blended with other strains in settling the western parts of the Deep South. The name Bedford is English. The Bedfords' house repeats the name of an ancestral house in Virginia, Portobello, which, like its contemporary, Mount Vernon, echoed the English affiliations of the pre-Revolutionary Washingtons and their friends. At the outbreak of the war Duncan Bedford, son of Malcolm, is attending the University of Virginia. His war service is with the Army of Northern Virginia, under Lee and Stuart.

These small particulars, perhaps only mildly symbolic, belong to the frame of reference by which the Bedfords are to be differentiated from the McGehees. The Bedfords are rather extrovert, practical, and realistic; inarticulate in the expression of strong feeling; reliant on good sense rather than intuition—while the McGehees tend the other way. The Bedford household has grown by generosity as well as by biological increase, for it includes their adopted daughter Valette, the child of friends who perished in a yellow-fever epidemic, and little Middleton, the child of Malcolm's dead sister, as well as Rosa Tate ("Aunt Piggie"), Mrs. Bedford's sister, and Rosa's senile brother Henry, in addition to the Bedford children themselves. The good-humored tolerance of the Bedfords is further suggested by the near presence of that curious savage, Uncle Billy McChidrick, and his famous parrot which can make noises like a seasick person. Dock, the Choctaw Indian, retained in an anomalous relationship as hunter and hanger-on, links the family and the plantation with frontier days that are, after all, in the very recent past.

Since realism and good sense are not in the end a sufficient defense against all the irregularities of life, Malcolm is likely to confront serious issues with his sense of humor rather than with a system of philosophy. That humor, especially when aided by large potations, turns prankishly toward thoughts of the grave. Like John Donne, Malcolm makes quips about the shroud when he is faced with a conflict between idea and reality. The humorous obituaries are products of this mood. And in general Malcolm (like Dr. Clay in *Heaven Trees*) is an inveterate practical joker and tease, not far distant from the Sut Lovingood tradition. Off at the war, he writes his wife to send him some shirts with his name marked on the tails, together with his copies of Sterne and Lucretius. But for all his addiction to the classics, his talk is homely. "I could stand my children being taught transcendentalism, witch-burning, even abolition," he says, "but I'm damned if I'll have them taught that all things work together to make life sugar-coated." Sallie, his wife, is cut from the same cloth. "She was a woman who naturally, in whatever ways a man seemed to her to be like a man, let him alone."

If the Bedfords seem somewhat more definitely to stand out as a family established in Mississippi but otherwise not shown to be widely connected, the McGehees are a clan of which the McGehees of Montrose are only the part that appears in the foreground for the purposes of this particular novel. They are Celtic rebels, descendants of the outlawed McGregors of seventeenth-century Scotland. Hugh McGehee's choice of "Montrose" as the name of his home suggests this rebellious past. The McGehees incline to be mystical and intuitive. In the old Scottish sense they are "fey." Montrose, like the house of Airlie, is doomed to be burned by a foeman as cruel as "the great Argyle," though more self-assured logically. Edward is doomed to die in battle. His mother Agnes (though a Bedford by blood) "knows" beyond all reasonable persuasion to the contrary, when news comes of a battle at Shiloh, that her son is dead. Like the mother in some ballad, she must straightway go to seek him among the slain and to fetch his body home. In this same moment of tragic tension Lucy McGehee has her balladlike vision of the boy for whom she had cherished an unavowed love. While the Bedfords send their son far away to the University of Virginia, the McGehees, more locally attached and "clannish," send their Edward to Louisiana Military Academy, where in 1860 W. T. Sherman is commandant.

But though the McGehees, in comparison with the Bedfords, are more clearly exemplars of the frontier wanderings that peopled the western South, this frontier restlessness, as the historians like to call it, has nevertheless seated a part of the McGehees firmly in Mississippi. Hugh McGehee, elegant, philosophical, and well-provided, has put the frontier behind him and thinks in terms of an established society.

In Hugh McGehee, the wild Celtic strain has been tempered. The combination of fierce passion and cool reason that gave the South such a political leader as Calhoun and such a military leader as Stonewall Jackson is, in Hugh McGehee, a fusion of tenderness and wisdom. Completely articulate, he is able to detach his mind from the melee of raw events and to judge them under the laws of reason, but never with a logic that is merely logical. No doubt we are to assume—although Stark Young as author does not say so—that in Hugh McGehee Southern society has produced an example of the unified personality, in tune with its environment while also commanding it; and that Southern society at the outbreak of the war was tending toward such an ideal. When war comes, the Celtic intuition seems in Hugh McGehee to become prophetic insight, so that, while intensely loyal to the Southern cause, he can also stand apart from it in his thought about events and judge what the fruits of war will be both in North and in South.

To follow the code of the Bedfords and McGehees requires

an establishment like theirs in principle but not necessarily
of the same scale. It means ownership of land, respect for God
and nature, devotion to agriculture and its allied pursuits,
and, with these, a healthy mistrust of what towns and trade, or
in the later phrase, "industrialism," may seductively offer. In
So Red the Rose this is everywhere the underlying implication. In his contribution to *I'll Take My Stand,* four years
prior to the publication of the novel, Stark Young is explicit.
It was, he says, the landed class that gave Southern society "its
peculiar stamp." He is willing to concede that other classes
"reflected certain traits from the planter class," but in his
opinion "the manners and customs of the South do not wholly
arise from the bottom mass; they have come from the top
downward." At the same time he speaks sharply against those
who would defer to the mass in order to exploit it and warns
against false notions of "aristocracy," which, if it means anything at all, is nothing boastfully pretentious, but rather "a
settled connection with the land . . . the fact that your family had maintained a certain quality of manners throughout
a certain period of time, and had a certain relation to the
society of the country."

With such cues to interpretation, it is possible to understand the role of Mary Cherry and of certain minor figures
who appear in the narrative. Mary Cherry has neither husband
nor lover. Worse still, she has no kin. She owns no property
except the famous trunk and a few meager personal belong-
ings, and she will never inherit or acquire any. She has no occupation. She spends her time in long visits at household after
household. Under the inviolable code of hospitality, it would
be a breach of manners not to receive her and allow her the
privileges of a lady and, as it were, of a member of the family,
even though, away from her presence, the family groan under
her loud assertiveness and domineering exactions.

In *Heaven Trees* Mary Cherry is treated at greater length,
and it is in that novel that she avows her personal credo: "The
world owes me a living." This she interprets as meaning that

she can walk into a merchant's establishment and demand shoes or a coat, with no questions raised either as to cash or credit. In *So Red the Rose,* although she remains "an Amazonian in buckram," her rougher traits are toned down somewhat, except as, during the fearful abstraction of war, they can be turned to account against the enemy. Nevertheless, if we take the Mary Cherry of *Heaven Trees* and of *So Red the Rose* as one and the same person, it is clear that she is, in contrast to the Bedfords and McGehees, the perfect semblance of the individual who, having neither kin nor property, has no place whatever in society. In the modern term, she is dissociated. The orphan Valette might have grown up into a Mary Cherry if she had not been adopted by the Bedfords. Mary Cherry, less fortunate, must remain unattached. The society of the Bedfords and McGehees, acknowledging the tragedy, takes the private responsibility of accepting her as a charge. This is charity, which, however, must never be publicly advertised as charity. The Bedfords and McGehees prefer the private obligation, however onerous, to any plausible schemes that might be devised for shifting Mary Cherry onto the shoulders of the general public.

In her behavior Mary Cherry necessarily represents a kind of a parody of the culture by which she benefits and in which she heartily believes—though without understanding. Her exaggerated independence, her loud voice, her dictatorial sending away, at table, of dishes that do not please her, her solitary singing of hymns, her fire-eating pronouncements—all such mannerisms, which are her crude exercise of what she conceives to be the prerogatives of a lady, naturally are grotesque and even when amusing are empty of real meaning because there is no substance back of them to give them meaning.

As long as the Bedfords, McGehees, and their ilk flourish, Mary Cherry can do little real harm. Her gaucheries are ignored because she is an isolated case; and a similar tolerance is extended to the northern governess, the seamstress from

Iowa, and the invalids from the North who are visiting Montrose for the climate; all of these are in something of a Mary Cherry condition. Later on when the society of the Bedfords and McGehees is weakened and partly destroyed by the war and its aftermath, the Mary Cherrys will multiply enormously and become a menace. In one form they will become that familiar nuisance, the "professional Southerner"; in other forms, the homeless, rootless, isolated individuals of the modern world, whether of the industrial proletariat or intellectual elite.

Opposed to the Bedfords and McGehees are, of course, the armies, political leaders, and people of the North. In a very general sense all these together may be thought of as the Antagonist, which, in the trite and empty modern phrase, could be called a Social Force. The term is invalid, however, with reference to *So Red the Rose,* which is nearer to Aeschylus and Sophocles than to Zola or Dreiser. Since to depict the Northern counterparts of the Bedfords and McGehees with any great circumstantiality would merely increase the size of the novel at the risk of blurring its focus and diluting its dramatic power, Stark Young uses General William Tecumseh Sherman to represent what is most hostile, in principle and in deed, to the Bedford-McGehee tradition. Sherman is the Enemy in military fact as well as in fully rationalized intent. In trying out his policy of "total war" in the Natchez-Vicksburg area—long before it was applied in Georgia and elsewhere—Sherman represents the logical and realistic side of the humanitarianism to which Lincoln at this time was giving a very persuasive but misleading rhetorical expression.

But while the historical facts of Sherman's military career bring his path directly and jarringly athwart the Bedford-McGehee orbit, and therefore make him highly eligible for the role of chief antagonist, it is even more important to note that, in person, he typifies the opposite of what the Bedfords and McGehees stand for. If they represent the culture of the whole personality, Sherman is a grand apotheosis and cataclysmic realization of the cult of the divided personality. Between Sherman the man and Sherman in his efficient function as general there is no connection. The man may be courteous, gentlemanly, artistic, kind, and "good," but the code that determines his behavior as man does not carry over into the behavior of the general, the political thinker. In Sherman, then, "thought" and "feeling" act in separate compartments. A code is allowable for matters of "feeling," but it must not go beyond ordinary drawing-room behavior—manners in the superficial sense. In practical matters, to which logic must be applied, "thought" rules absolute, and therefore no code operates. So, while the code of the Bedfords and McGehees, not thus split, but having a certain all-inclusiveness, can distinguish between soldier and civilian and confine destruction to the field of war proper, the rational philosophy of Sherman denies the validity of any such code, refuses to distinguish between soldier and civilian, and thus infinitely extends the sphere of destruction.

For Sherman the man we should also note that it creates the peculiarly modern kind of tragedy. For Sherman in his grief over the death of his son Willie, there is no consolation. The logical half of the man, divided from the hurt emotional half, has no comfort to offer. Sherman is incapable of grasping the assumption of Hugh and Agnes McGehee that his grief for Willie will naturally lead him to pity and regret for the slaughter that has brought low their Edward—symbolic of the Southern dead. Sherman's view of that is strictly rational: "If the Southern people don't like what they are getting, all they have to do is to declare their loyalty and come back into the Union." He is convinced of the expediency of his war plan, but nevertheless on the one hand he writhes under the ill impression the Southern people have of him, and on the other hand he uses that ill impression as an instrument to further his ends. Agnes McGehee, intuitively, sees Sherman as "tormented and wilful." "This conflict of policy had become a conflict in his own nature, and . . . the story that was build-

ing up of him as a ruthless monster did at the same time both
serve him and his purposes as a picture of war, and antagonize,
grieve, and enrage him as a picture of himself."

Once the leading characters and groups of characters are
thus differentiated, the profusion of persons, scenes, and particulars that marks *So Red the Rose* is no longer bewildering,
and the dramatic structure can be apprehended, not as elaborate and pretentious, but as simple to the point of austerity.
The action of the narrative divides naturally into successive
stages, of growing intensity, from the time when war is a mere
probability to the time when it becomes an actuality and yet
is still distant as a physical fact; and then on to the stage when
war, at last physically present, is known for what it truly is.
What it truly is, in terms of this particular conflict, is not
wholly apparent until Sherman enters the scene—until, in
fact, after making his courtesy call on the McGehees, as the
parents of one of his former cadets, Sherman has his private
conversation at the gate with Hugh McGehee and tells him
the planter class must be "replaced" after the victory of the
North.

Thus the focus of the general narrative, very wide at first,
is steadily narrowed until the point of greatest significance is
reached. That point comes, it would seem, when Hugh Mc-
Gehee says, after his conversation with Sherman, "Yes. He's
good. I can't understand it." At once, like a commentary on
Hugh's generous restraint, comes Lucy's violent emotional
reaction. She is outraged that Sherman has been received into
the house. "How could you all, how could you, when they
killed—?" Almost immediately, confirming Lucy's bitter personal judgment, comes the burning of Montrose by Negro
soldiers under the command of a white officer:

> She [Agnes] could hear them tramping in the parlors and
> the rattle of their sabres and spurs. She rushed in to her
> daughter. There they were. Lucy was in the bedroom and
> the negroes were tramping through the sitting-room, threaten-
> ing, cursing.

"Get out," Agnes ordered. "Get out of my house. Get out of my sight!"

A big black who seemed to be in command gave a guffaw, and the other negroes, watching him evidently, followed. One of them came up to her and with his open hand boxed her on the cheek. At once another negro put a pistol against her breast; she could smell his sweat. Then the big negro who had struck her said, "Don't shoot her, Mose, slap her. Slap the old slut." He broke into a stream of abuse.

The powerful scene in which the sack and burning of Montrose are depicted is rendered in straightforward prose, unornamented, matter-of-fact, without any officious coloring or pointing-up to connect its dramatic meaning explicitly with the episodes immediately preceding. It is as "objective" as, say, Hemingway's account, in *A Farewell to Arms,* of the Italian retreat from the Caporetto, but is far richer in its complex of meanings, since Stark Young's total narrative scheme ranges further and wider than does Hemingway's, and his use of a shifting focus allows a depth of perspective which Hemingway, committed to the limited perceptions of Lieutenant Frederick Henry, cannot possibly attain.

For the scene, brief though it is, reveals not only the gross violation which ultimately implies (as Hugh McGehee says later on) the collapse of civilized society, but also the plight of the Confederacy, symbolized in the futile skirmishing of the little Confederate detachment for which the McGehees have been cooking a hasty breakfast, as well as, in the details of the ravaging, the catastrophe that the McGehees and the South are experiencing and must continue to face. Nor is the narrative so ordered as to deprive the individual invaders of all humanity or the McGehees of all their natural charity. The Negro soldiers, raw recruits under a white man's orders, are both brutal and scared. In parody of their wantonness and fear we are shown, with almost a kind of tenderness, a brief picture of the little black boy who steals a handkerchief and starts to run. Bessie, one of the house-servants, catches him as he runs.

> "What you got in yo' han', boy? Show me what you got in yo' hand," the girl was saying, as she jerked his elbow and shook him. She snatched his arm from behind him and pried open the little black fingers, which were clutching a red silk handkerchief. Hugh McGehee, who liked anything that was alive, stood watching the little negro's eyes, from which the tears ran down to make a worse smudge of his sooty face. It eased Hugh to see the destruction and pillage reduced to this level, when a piece of red cloth gave the feeling of excitement and booty. He looked down at his daughter with her drawn features and shut eyes, and at the green grass around her pallet. "Let him have it, Bessie," he said.

Considered in narrative terms, the burning of Montrose is a dramatic continuation of the talk at the gate during which Sherman reveals to Hugh McGehee the pitilessly logical half of his schizoid personality. Such, too, is the nocturnal episode in which Sallie Bedford witnesses the hanging of Federal marauders by a small group of Confederate cavalry who are taking Sherman's abandonment of ethical principle to a vengeful extreme—correspondingly "logical" on their side.

These and other such scenes in the closing phase of the novel are "historically" true in that they could be documented from the *Official Records of the War of the Rebellion* or the reminiscences, diaries, and letters of numerous participants on both sides of the conflict. In 1864, after the initiation of Sherman's famous policy, the war in all parts of the western theater of operations took on precisely the character indicated in Stark Young's narrative. Much of his material comes from papers of his own family or from oral reminiscence. The source of his information about the burning of "Montrose," for example, was a manuscript of his Aunt Mary's—an account which she composed and finally published in a Mississippi newspaper. Bowling Green, the plantation at Woodville which belonged to Edward McGehee, Sr., was sacked and

burned by the Third United States Colored Cavalry, commanded by Colonel J. B. Cook. A similar "documentation"
could be supplied for other historical details and episodes.
Portobello, for example, is drawn from Rosedown, a house
still standing, two miles from St. Francisville, Louisiana. The
real Billy McChidrick belonged to Stark Young's own Uncle
Hugh McGehee of Panola, Mississippi. The selection from
the diary of Agnes McGehee—at the end of Chapter LIII—
originates in a note by Mrs. Edward McGehee—and so on.
Furthermore, the details of manners, dress, and speech have
been worked out with minute and subtle scrupulousness. And
while a large chapter could be written on the prose style in
general, it may here be said, with regard to speech in particular, that *So Red the Rose* stands without a rival in its skilful
representation of the nuances of tone, pronunciation, and
idiom of Southern speech. The Southerners of this book talk
like real Southerners, not like stage Southerners.

But *So Red the Rose* is literature, not documentation. The
question of the "authenticity" of historical material of course
arises in a work of fiction dealing with the Civil War. Any
novelist who deals with the past knows that his fiction in some
sense is in competition with documented history as Homer's
fiction was not. But such authenticity, however necessary, is a
subordinate, not a major element in a work of art. *So Red the
Rose* is literature, not because of mere documentary authenticity but because it strives to evoke reality at the highest plane
of which the art of prose fiction is capable, and because it
succeeds in this evocation. It is literature in the full sense,
not with the partial meaning we use when we apply such
terms as realistic, romantic, propagandist, or the like.

The tragic scenes of *So Red the Rose* rise above any specific
feelings of resentment or horror such as might be aroused by
a more partisan account in a reader whose particular sympa-
thies might naturally be engaged on the Southern or the
Northern side of the actual historical conflict. Sherman, the
historical general, can be investigated and argued about in

matter-of-fact terms; and the Bedfords and McGehees, or their numerous parallels, can be studied in the various aspects of the social and economic situation. But Sherman the fictional character and his fictional opponents and victims appear here not for argument but for the kind of contemplation we would give to *Richard III* or *Macbeth* or *Antigone.* The characters of *So Red the Rose* move upward toward the large conceptions of "myth," in the high sense, not downward toward the always arguable and provocative issues of "realism." They submit to the Aristotelian principle and can be viewed as universals. What we see, if we look closely enough, is not only the specific personal tragedy of the Bedfords and McGehees confronted by a clearly identifiable and historic soldier-leader, but the two parties of a great conflict recurrent in one form or another throughout human history, though brought to an intense pitch in modern times. One party integrates, in terms of a harmonious life that blends substance and spirit, subject to God's inscrutable will and the contingencies of nature; the other disintegrates and, using disintegration itself as a tool of power, presumes to mount beyond good and evil and to make human intelligence a quasi-God. Since the Bedfords and McGehees of the South are by no means the only possible representatives of such integration, past or present, or Sherman the only possible representative of disintegration, the modern reader of *So Red the Rose* should be able to say, "There, but for the grace of God, go I," and find in this remarkable novel a mirror reflecting a state and a prospect to which we are more than ever disastrously and tragically liable.

Part III

THE ORAL TRADITION:

BALLAD, FOLKSONG, AND MYTH

THE TRADITION OF IRREVERENCE

IRREVERENCE IS ONE of the strongest traits of the in-digenous American character. As a matter of course, Americans are prone to be irreverent toward all kinds of persons, particularly those of high pretensions, and on all kinds of occasions, including, too often, the very occasions that seem to call for an opposite attitude. Irreverence, generally masked as humor, but amounting often enough to frivolity, is so much an accepted part of our common behavior that we practice it unconsciously, under an almost ritualistic compulsion, as a habit of our public and private life. We never think of it as symptomatic of social disease and cultural degeneration. On the contrary, it is likely to be rather proudly cited as evidence of democratic independence, and therefore of good social health. The tradition of irreverence is inherited, we are often told, from our "boisterous" frontier days when an American actually still could "look any man in the eye and tell him to go to Hell." This theory is particularly favored by the scholars and critics of American literature, who have only rather recently discovered Sut Lovingood, Davy Crockett, Artemus Ward, Bill Arp, and other representatives of American humor, and have the difficult task of explaining just how these irreverent characters could flourish in a civilization dominated (as their textbooks bear witness) by the solemn, portentous procession of the Worthies of New England.

Whatever influence frontier "boisterousness" may have had on American humor in the past, the theory of frontier origin will hardly account for certain manifestations of irreverence that appear in native American balladry and folk song. The nature of these manifestations is instantly apparent when we compare our native American ballads, however excellent, with the imported and inherited parts of our stock of ancient balladry, which we have preserved rather faithfully despite frontier influence and the supposed cultural disruption attributed to it—and despite, also, the cultural damage to oral art quite definitely attributable to universal compulsory education and urbanism in general.

All of the greatest traditional ballads of our inherited stock move at the heroic and tragic level and have much of the dignity and finality of high drama and epic. Taken together they constitute, in fact, for us as for our forebears, an approximate cultural equivalent of an epical literature. To us they are, or ought to be, something like what the Homeric poems were to the Greeks. At least they are this to the extent that they are, or can be, the common possession of all people, from the highest to the lowest, accepted, valued, and indeed loved by the greatest scholar or poet or the meanest farmer or mechanic. They have no rival in this respect in Anglo-American culture except the King James Version of the Bible and what is left to us of the traditional folk tale. The ballads are of unusual importance because, of the high and serious art of the remote past, they are the only portion that is still actively present in our folk-memory in a fully meaningful and authentic form.

Some of the ancient ballads are romantic, of course. A few are humorous or satirical—but in the canon of traditional ballads established by Child, only a few. Often enough, romantic elements may be mingled with the tragic and heroic. But the humorous element is rarely so mingled. It is kept rigidly separate. Tragic events are never told in a humorous manner. Sentimentalism occasionally appears, but it is generally considered a mark of late composition or of a degenerate text. By a tragic ballad I mean, naturally, such ballads as "Lord Randall," "Edward," "The Wife of Usher's Well," and the like; by a heroic ballad, I mean the best of the Robin

Hood ballads, "The Hunting of the Cheviot," "Johnnie Armstrong," and other such familiar examples.

On the American side, what have we to compare with this notable array? We have a large number of truly American ballads, ruggedly persistent in oral tradition and, for that and other reasons, authentic enough by the usual tests. That these should often be infused with a "lyrical" or "subjective" quality constitutes no necessary imputation against their genuineness as ballads. As Mr. Malcolm Laws has pointed out, it is high time to revise the definitions of "ballad," which, applicable though they may be to the pre-Renaissance genre, are far too rigid and exclusive if the whole range of balladry, European and American, is to be taken into consideration. It is not the "lyrical" or "subjective" element, as such, of "Fuller and Warren" that makes it inferior to "Lord Thomas and Fair Annet." And on the other hand, it is the presence of a "lyrical" and "subjective" quality that gives "Little Mohee," "The Cowboy's Lament," "The Trail to Mexico," "Old Paint," and other American ballads their peculiar attractiveness. It is doubtful whether these or similar American ballads would have been any better than they now are if their unknown authors had attempted to cast them in the approved "objective" mould of "Lord Lovel," or "Robin Hood's Death and Burial," or "Barbara Allen."

But they are not, for all their merit, really "tragic" ballads. And, as we survey the corpus of our folk accomplishment, we are entitled to doubt whether we have a single genuinely tragic or genuinely heroic native American ballad. We have pathetic ballads, infused often with romance, more often with elaborate sentimentalism or didactic moralizing. We have ballads of murders, executions, wrecks, and accidents. We also have ballads of undoubtedly heroic persons that somehow always manage to fall short of true heroic quality. Above all we have a great many humorous, bantering, satirical ballads, and in this group we have a certain number of ballads that treat tragic events in a vein of humor or straight burlesque. It is this last group that I wish to examine, for whatever light the examination may shed upon the cause of our American inability to compose in genuinely tragic terms. The examination may well begin with "Springfield Mountain," since the numerous texts of this ballad provide us with a more or less complete case history of the transformation of an initial "tragic" rendering into a "comic" ballad.

In 1937, the late Phillips Barry, summing up the results of his long investigation, wrote: "One fact, fully documented, has been established: Timothy Myrick of Wilbraham, formerly Springfield Mountain, died of snake bite in Farmington, Connecticut, August 7, 1761, the date recorded on his grave-monument in Wilbraham (Mass.)." Like other "fully documented" conjectures relating to balladry, Barry's categorical assertion is open to some question. For Springfield, Vermont, which has a Rattlesnake Hill, a convenient meadow, and an established local tradition, can also claim to be the scene of the tragedy, and evidence can be advanced to support the claim.

The scene, or for that matter, the date, does not concern us here, since in any case we can assume that a promising young man—who may have been either Lieutenant Myrick's or Lieutenant Curtis' "only son"—was bitten by a rattlesnake while mowing hay and died of the poison. If we accept the unofficial town record kept by Samuel Warner—so assiduously exact—he was "twenty-two years two months and three Days old and vary near the point of marridge." * In its essentials, then, the tragic situation contains the Orpheus-Eurydice motif with the roles reversed, but with little prospect, given the American environment, for a development of the ballad narrative beyond the plane of humble realism.

* Phillips Barry, *Bulletin of the Folksong Society of the Northeast,* No. 7, p. 5, quoting R. P. Stebbins' *Historical Address* of 1831, at Wilbraham, Mass.

If we accept the conjectures of W. W. Newell,† the eight-eenth-century contemporaries of the unfortunate Timothy Myrick nevertheless felt that he deserved to be memorialized in a dignified way, and accordingly, soon after Myrick's death or possibly for his funeral, someone composed an "ode" or "elegy" in typical ballad form. This elegy may have been printed in a local newspaper or in a broadside sheet, but if so, no copy has yet been found. It may not have been printed at all, but could have circulated in handwritten copies. The elegy may have been sung at the funeral by a group of Myrick's friends, perhaps to the tune of "Old Hundred," or so Newell declares. Newell reports that such a dirge was sung by six young women at the burial of one Isaac Orcutt, who was killed in a logging accident. The date of the Orcutt burial and dirge was about 1800. Newell's information came from Julia D. Whiting, whose grandmother was one of the six young women who rendered the Orcutt dirge at the graveside, and Newell holds that such funeral dirges were customary in western Massachusetts during the eighteenth century. This is only an argument by analogy and is not proof as to the specific origin of "Springfield Mountain." Yet it is true that even today a reader of country newspapers (and some city papers) may find a vestigial survival of the elegiac impulse in the ver-sified tributes to deceased relatives published in the Funeral Notices column.

At any rate, the fatal accident must have created more than a local impression in its day. Four years after the event, in 1765, Joseph Fisk took note of it in his versified *Ten Year Almanack.* Seemingly, Joseph Fisk was a lay preacher or ex-horter* who wandered from Vermont to the coast in various parts of New England. He believed in the near imminence of the Judgment Day, and therefore recorded in his *Ten Year Almanack,* in doggerel verse, the notable events that gave evi-

† *Journal of American Folklore,* XIII, 105–22.
* Damon, *Journal of American Folklore,* LIX, 530–31.

dence of God's wrath, such as storms, earthquakes, epidemics, northern lights, wars, crimes, and disasters. The Springfield Mountain accident he deemed worthy of record and set it down in the following lines:

> *At Springfield Mountains there was one*
> *Bit by a Rattlesnake alone,*
> *The poor Man he to death did yield,*
> *As he went home died in the field,*
> *He called for Help but none did go,*
> *'Til Death did prove his Overthrow.*
> *And all the Jury did agree*
> *His Leg was bitten as they could see.*

The Fisk text, brief and unballadlike though it is, is as near as we can come to a contemporary text of "Springfield Mountain." In his lengthy study Barry does not notice the Fisk text, but categorically says: "There is no evidence that the ballad is of earlier date than the second quarter of the last century," and furthermore holds that the Myrick and Curtis texts "belong to domestic tradition not traceable back of the year 1849." *

"Not traceable," however, by no means should be taken to signify "nonexistent." The survival of the text which Barry calls Myrick A and takes as the "Master Text" of the Myrick type carries some implication of the existence of the ballad prior to the date—April 30, 1849—affixed to the manuscript found in the old secretary belonging to Dr. Luther Brewer of Wilbraham. For whatever it may be worth, too, we have the implication of long previous currency in J. G. Holland's observation—in his *History of Western Massachusetts* (1855)— that the ballad "has been added to and modified, until the versions of it are numberless." The version printed by Holland, furthermore, like both the Myrick and the Curtis texts, which Barry distinguishes as belonging to "domestic tradition," is elegiac in its treatment, and like them preserves at

* *Bulletin of the Folksong Society of the Northeast,* No. 12, pp. 1–7.

its core the narrative details (except for the viewing by the jury) recorded in Fisk's 1765 doggerel couplets.

It seems therefore difficult to avoid the assumption advanced in Newell's attractive theory that "Springfield Mountain" flourished as a ballad elegy—despite the lack of documentary evidence to that effect—prior to the appearance of the first comic stage version in 1836. To argue the contrary is to be led into absurdity by reliance upon "documentary evidence." For it is impossible to believe that either George Andrews' "Love and Pizen" of 1836 or George Gaines Spear's "The Pesky Sarpent" (copyright, 1840) could have served as an original of the numerous elegiac texts. Folk singers may accept and transmit a stage version of a ballad. They may also merge it into already existing traditional texts until a new, hybrid version develops, as has clearly happened with "Springfield Mountain." But they do not take over a comic stage ballad and self-consciously remould it into a completely serious elegy in an entirely different and somewhat archaic ballad style.

Unpublished material in the Helen Hartness Flanders Collection at Middlebury College, Vermont, reinforces the view that the elegiac form of "Springfield Mountain" is much more prevalent in New England, and much more widely favored by New England folk singers, than Barry could have realized when, shortly before his death in June, 1937, he completed his lengthy study of the relatively few "Springfield Mountain" texts then available to him.* It should furthermore be noted that in Barry's own lists of texts the "Sally" and "Molly" texts, derived from stage influence, come largely from sheet music imprints, newspapers, periodicals, and songbooks of urban provenience, while the "Myrick" and "Curtis" texts more prevalently come directly from oral sources, and especially from those literate and indeed educated singers whom Barry

* Information from Miss Marguerite Olney, Curator of the Flanders Collection, who is unexcelled in her knowledge of the New England folk tradition.

prized as the most trustworthy preservers of genuine balladry.

Out of numerous interesting texts of the latter two groups, I choose for quotation here the Kennison text, first published in 1932 by Helen Hartness Flanders and George Brown, in *Vermont Folk-Songs and Ballads,* as recorded from the singing of Josiah S. Kennison, of Townshend, Vermont. In the early nineteen-thirties I heard Mr. Kennison sing this ballad, at one of the first ballad evenings which Mrs. Flanders conducted annually to the great pleasure and instruction of the Bread Loaf School of English, and my impression of the ballad has been colored ever since, I freely confess, by the remarkable austerity and force of Kennison's rendering. Sung though it was to the rather trivial "Butcher Boy" tune, the ballad imparted a definite sense of remembered tragedy, and for Josiah Kennison at any rate it stood on an equal plane with "Lord Thomas and Fair Eleanor," which he also sang on this occasion. The Kennison text stands for me as a good representative of the elegiac tradition that must have flourished before the stage versions transformed the ballad.

> *On Springfield Mountain there did dwell*
> *A handsome youth, was known full well,*
> *Lieutenant Merrill's only son,*
> *A likely youth, near twenty-one.*
>
> *On Friday morning he did go*
> *Down to the meadows for to mow.*
> *He mowed, he mowed all around the field*
> *With a poisonous serpent at his heel.*
>
> *When he received his deathly wound*
> *He laid his scythe down on the ground.*
> *For to return was his intent,*
> *Calling aloud, long as he went.*
>
> *His calls were heard both far and near*
> *But no friend to him did appear.*

They thought he did some workman call.
Alas, poor man, alone did fall!

Day being past, night coming on,
The father went to seek his son,
And there he found his only son
Cold as a stone, dead on the ground.

He took him up, and he carried him home
And on the way did lament and mourn,
Saying, "I heard but did not come,
And now I'm left alone to mourn."

In the month of August, the twenty-first,
When this sad accident was done.
May this a warning be to all,
To be prepared when God shall call.

Kennison's text resembles in many respects the 1855 Holland text, but its superiority over the Holland text and others that have interesting features is in the clear dramatic emphasis on the grief of the father, which points up with a distinctness not found in the Brewer manuscript (Barry's master text for the Myrick type) or in many other texts the tragic irony of "hearing" but "not coming." Thus the lonely midsummer death in a New England meadow gets a rather powerful accent.

Some degree of authenticity may attach to the Kennison text, Barry points out, by its use of the August 21 date, instead of August 7, 1761, as in the Holland text. August 21 is the date given for the accident in the contemporary diary record that Barry cites.* But this particular kind of authenticity is not the point here. I quote the Kennison text merely as an example of the standard elegiac form of "Springfield Mountain" on which the stage laid hands for its own exploitative purpose.

* *Bulletin of the Folksong Society of the Northeast,* No. 7, p. 5.

The course of this exploitation is easily traced, and of course
the first step in stage treatment, as might be expected, is to
eliminate the grieving father and to add a "love interest." The
ballad does not, however, become a romantic tragedy. It is
converted into comedy or, rather, straight burlesque. In 1836
George Andrews of the Tremont Theatre, in Boston, sang
"Love and Pizen, or, The Sad Story of Young Farmer Mazzard
and Sally Thomas." How this *divertissement* fitted into *The
Massacre, Or, The Malay's Revenge,* in which Andrews was
acting the part of Jotham Gam, is hard to imagine. Barry gives
a text * which he takes as representative of the Andrews song:

> *Farmer Mazzard had a son,*
> *A pious youth of twenty-one.*
> > *Ri ta too rallingly, too rallingly,*
> > *Too rallingly, too raillay.*
>
> *He loved a gal, Sal-lee by name,*
> *And for to love her was not to blame.*
>
> *One day while mowing in the field,*
> *A wiper bit him in the heel.*
>
> *Among the rest, Sal-lee was there;*
> *Oh, how she wept and tore her hair!*
>
> *And cried, "O Sam, why did you go*
> *Into that medder for to mow?"*
>
> *Sez Sam to Sal, "I thought you knowed*
> *That, spite of snakes, grass must be mowed!"*
>
> *Right here the pizen struck inside,*
> *And with one gasp, he straightway died.*

The tradition of irreverence has here begun its work, but
the burlesque elements are even more prominent in the Spear
text, which followed shortly after and became so popular that

* *Bulletin of the Folksong Society of the Northeast,* No. 2, p. 10.

Barry uses it as the master text of the now gigantic family of comic Springfield Mountain texts. George Gaines Spear served a stage apprenticeship under Andrews and worked the Springfield Mountain ballad story up into an entirely new ballad, called "The Pesky Sarpent," which he published, with words and music, in 1840.

The decorative front cover of this publication carries a lithograph presumably depicting Mr. Spear in the role of "Tommy Blake," as he sang and acted the little drama. Tommy Blake is bareheaded and barefooted. He is clad in white shirt and black pants. Dangling in his hands is the "sarpent," which he is showing to "Molly Bland," his sweetheart, who stands in front of the fireplace, arms upraised in horror. The scene is a New England kitchen with a window looking out upon the hayfield. Around this pictorial center runs an ornamental border, consisting of various kinds of farm implements. At the top of the border is a tiny inset which shows the hayfield, with Tommy mowing and the "sarpent" vindictively approaching him. Below this inset protrudes a bare foot, which is being savagely bitten in the heel by the two serpents whose twining bodies form the top part of the border. At the bottom of the decorative border, in the center, is a coiled "sarpent," head uplifted, forked tongue protruding, eye wickedly gleaming.

We lift the grotesquely realistic cover and find the text and tune of "The Pesky Sarpent: A Pathetic Ballad," as sung by Mr. Spear. The tune has been identified as the "Liggeram Cosh" known to Robert Burns, but more generally called "The Quaker's Wife" or "Merrily Danced the Quaker." It is the tune to which "Springfield Mountain" is now most commonly—and much too merrily—sung throughout the United States. The text is as follows:

> *On Springfield Mountain there did dwell,*
> *A comely youth I knew full well.*
> *Ri tu ri nu, ri tu di na,*
> *Ri tu di nu ri tu di na.*

One Monday morning he did go,
Down in the meadow for to mow.

He scarce had mowed half the field,
When a PESKY SARPENT *bit his heel.*

He took his scythe and with a blow,
He laid the pesky Sarpent low.

He took the Sarpent in his hand,
And straitway went to Molly Bland.

Oh, Molly, Molly, here you see,
The Pesky Sarpent what bit me.

Now Molly had a ruby lip,
With which the pizen she did sip.

But Molly had a rotten tooth,
Which the pizen struck and kill'd them both.

The neighbours found that they were dead,
So laid them both upon one bed.

And all their friends both far and near,
Did cry and howl they were so dear.

Now all you maids a warning take
From Molly Bland and Tommy Blake.

And mind when you'r in love don't pass,
Too near to patches of high grass.

Gone now is the "only son" of Lieutenant Myrick, whose untimely death the community bewails. Gone is the bereaved father whose failure to answer his son's call introduces a slight accent of tragic irony and thus saves some of the elegiac texts from lapsing into mere sentimentalism and didacticism. Gone, too, is the conception of sudden death, the sense of mortality in the midst of rural peace. In the Spear text, death is simply a little joke played by the pesky sarpent on Tommy Blake, who is clearly an ordinary "rube" or "hick," so ignorant that, instead of seeking help, he carries the snake indoors to show to his hick sweetheart. In this touch, especially, we feel the presence of theater-going Boston and the actor who is catering to an urban audience; we are very far from the rural sagacity that surely marked the pioneer inhabitants of either "downeast" or western New England. Then there is Molly Bland's rotten tooth, which turns her into caricature and her devotion into comic absurdity. The neighbors "cry and howl" instead of conducting a dignified funeral. And a sly salacious hint appears in the bedding of the lovers after their death and in the warning to maidens not to go near high grass when in love.

It is true that, since in the Spear version the story is extended and briskly dramatized, with the addition of a love story, the way was clear for what may be regarded as a development of the Springfield Mountain ballad. The development took place by the process of interchange between stage and folk that is generally familiar to ballad scholars but that has not yet been critically explored by them. Seemingly the first period of development occurred at a time when the comic Yankee was in vogue both in the theater and in newspaper and almanac humor, with a parallel tendency in the true folk tale of the period. The Spear version of "Springfield Mountain" was further popularized by Adoniram Judson Joseph Hutchinson of the stage group known as the Hutchinson Family. Judson Hutchinson's words, more decorous than Spear's, appear in *The Hutchinson Family's Book of Words*, 1851. The "lovers' colloquy," which supplies dialogue not achieved in Spear's text, is regarded by Barry as a collaborative effort "by folk and actors" to fill out the implied drama. But when George Handel Hill, the famous Yankee actor and singer, enters the process of change, the "development" moves still more strongly in the direction of burlesque. In his own person Hill is described as being the regular stage Yankee, with the long nose, receding chin, and speech traits attributed to the type. The Hill text—which may also be called the Derby text, since it was printed by George H. Derby in the humorous *Squibob*

Papers (1859, 1865)—introduces a deliberate parody of Yankee talk and Yankee ways. The satire is sharply emphasized by the substitution of "Zerubbabel" as the name of the youth, instead of the "Johnny" or "Tommy" of previous texts.

> *On Springfield mounting, thar did dwell,*
> *A likely youth, I knowed him well;*
> *Leftenant Carter's only son,*
> *A comely youth, nigh twenty-one.*
>
> *On Monday morning he did go*
> *Intew the meadow for to mow,*
> *And all ter once, he thar did feel*
> *A pizen sarpint bite his heel.*
>
> *Quick as he felt the sarpint bite*
> *He raised his scythe, with all his might*
> *He struck ter once a deadly blow,*
> *That lay the pizen creetur low.*
>
> *He tuk the riptyle in his hand,*
> *And straightway went tew Molly Bland;*
> *Oh! Molly, Molly here you see*
> *A pizen sarpint, what bit me.*
>
> *Zerubbabel, why did ye go*
> *Into the meadow for to mow?*
> *Oh! Molly Bland, I thought you knowed*
> *'Twas Daddy's field, and must be mowed.*
>
> *Then Molly Bland, she squatted down,*
> *And sucked the pizen from the wound;*
> *But oh! she had a rotten tooth;*
> *The venim soon affected both.*
>
> *Oh, then they ware all spotted o'er*
> *With all the colors that the sarpent wore,*
> *They laid them both upon a bed*
> *And they swelled up and di-ed!*

> *And when they had gin up the ghost,*
> *From Springfield Mounting they went, post;*
> *And they larfed and sung, as up they went,*
> *As chipper as if there wa'nt no pizen sar-pent.*

This is "stagey" in the same way that Lowell's Hosea Biglow of the Biglow Papers is bookish. The effect must have depended very heavily upon Hill's peculiarly personal manner. I would suspect that the last line, from its irregularity, was spoken rather than sung—for the final laugh.

Other comic effects were gradually added, the most notable of which appear in the well-known and now widely prevalent stammering version. But meanwhile, if we accept as significant the appearance of a text of the comic type in *Carmina Yalensia* (1867), the stage version, rather than the folk version, must have passed into college song, and therefore into a branch of the American oral tradition that has not yet been sufficiently studied by ballad scholars. One may infer—though the inference would have to await confirmation through documentary evidence if it survives—that the comic "Springfield Mountain" not only was transmitted far and wide by individual college graduates (who, like school-children of the past, have been faithful carriers of the oral tradition), but that it passed into the repertory of college glee clubs and social singing groups, and thus secured a continued audience and widespread dissemination long after it had been forgotten as a novelty of the stage.*

At any rate, the momentum given the burlesque versions of "Springfield Mountain" has been sufficient to make them dominant over the elegiac versions in the United States as a whole. But the ballad as thus carried is always more jest than

---

* For example, Dr. Edward D. Williams, of East Hampton, Mass., wrote Mrs. Helen Hartness Flanders, September 5, 1930, that "Springfield Mountain" had been adopted by his society (The Owls) in Burlington "about eighty years ago." The Owl Society, in 1930, was ninety-four years old. The Williams version is of the comic stage type and contains "one or two somewhat vulgar stanzas." (Letter in Helen Hartness Flanders Ballad Collection, Middlebury College, Middlebury, Vt.)

tragedy, and it is likely to be a degenerate form of the original stage texts. There was a possibility, no doubt, that "Springfield Mountain" might "develop" into a fully dramatized and serious ballad with some pretensions to tragic dignity, but even the best of the numerous texts that derive from the stage versions or the fusion of the stage and folk influence fail to attain the tragic level. They cannot shake off the flavor of the comic.

On the other hand, how far "Springfield Mountain" can go in degeneration is illustrated in John Lomax' "Ranch Haying Song" which he published in 1910 as a "cowboy song." * It is the "stammering" version. I quote a few stanzas:

> *A nice young ma-wa-an*
> *Lived on a hi-wi-ill;*
> *A nice young ma-wa-an,*
> *For I knew him we-we-well.*
>
> *This nice young ma-wa-wan*
> *Went out to mow-wo-wow*
> *To see if he-we-we*
> *Could make a sho-wo-wow.*
>
> *He scarcely mo-wo-wowed*
> *Half round the fie-wie-wield*
> *Till up jumped—come a rattle, come a sna-wa-wake,*
> *And bit him on the he-we-weel.*
>
> *He laid right dow-wo-wown*
> *Upon the grow-wo-wown*
> *And shut his ey-wy-wyes*
> *And looked all aro-wo-wound.*
>
> *"O pappy da-wa-ad,*
> *Go tell my ga-wa-wal*
> *That I'm a-goin' ter di-wi-wie,*
> *For I know I sha-wa-wall."*

* John Lomax, *Cowboy Songs and Other Frontier Ballads* (New York, 1910).

And forty years after the publication of Lomax' volume we find, in Alton C. Morris' *Folksongs of Florida* (1950), what appears to be the last remnants of George Hill's "Zerubbabel," seemingly fused with the stammering effect:

> *There was a young man, bubbawan, bubbawan,*
> *That I used to know, bubbawo, bubbawo,*
> *And he went right down, bubbawoun, bubbawoun,*
> *Across the field, bubbaweel, bubbaweel,*
> *On an oozi, oozi day.*

And so on through the Springfield Mountain sequence of events, with "bubba" used throughout as a prefix for the stammered echoes of the terminal rhymes. "Bubba" does not seem to be explainable other than as a garbled fragment of "Zerubbabel."

This sketch of Springfield Mountain history exemplifies, as perhaps no other single American ballad will, the triumph of burlesque over tragedy, and the extreme degenerative results of such triumph. The course of degeneration, in this instance, can be traced in detail, and also with some assurance.

With less assurance we can trace a similar tendency in other ballads of native origin. "Casey Jones" will serve as a notable example of a ballad of heroic death into which the comic note has intruded under stage auspices. Here again, despite claims to authorship and even to copyright, authenticity cannot be proved for any supposed original. A Negro named Wallis Sanders, of Canton, Mississippi, is the putative "author," but it has been held that Sanders used, in his "Casey Jones," the pattern of the railroad song "Jimmy Jones," which he had learned from a Kansas City friend before the Casey Jones wreck occurred and which had been in circulation for some years. Two vaudeville actors, T. Lawrence Serbert and Edward Newton, after hearing Negroes sing the Casey Jones ballad in New Orleans, made it into a vaudeville number and tried to get the song published, but without success. Meanwhile the Three Leightons put the Serbert-Newton version on the stage and, in 1909, published the song, which immediately became a popular hit. I can myself remember when the sheet music of this "Casey Jones" began to appear on the music rack of the upright pianos of those years, along with "School Days" and other popular songs of the period.

By way of brief analysis, let us observe that "Casey Jones," as generally sung, begins seriously enough on the theme of predestined tragedy, as the hero mounts to the cabin with his orders in his hand, to take his farewell trip into the Promised Land. He is a "brave engineer," admired by all valiant railroad men, who are aware that their dangerous occupation sets a premium on courage and resolution. The initial apostrophe to Casey Jones, sufficiently heroic in tone, implies that any trip undertaken by a brave engineer may be a trip into the Promised Land. There is no hint anywhere of the soft modern doctrine of "safety first." But this heroical strain, though maintained very well for two or three stanzas, begins to weaken a little with the semihumorous line, "Two locomotives are goin' to bump." By the time of the announcement of Casey's death to Mrs. Jones—which ought to give opportunity for a courageous or at least dignified assertion of grief—the heroic strain is lost in a comic-ironical emphasis on the marital adaptability of the bereaved wife—

> *Children, go to bed and hush your cryin'*
> *'Cause you got another papa on the Frisco line.*

In a version entitled, "Mama, Have You Heard the News," we get a comic emphasis in the very first stanza on the benefits of social security:

> *Mama, mama, mama, have you heard the news?*
> *Daddy got killed on the C-B-and-Q's.*
> *Shut your eyes and hold your breath,*
> *We'll all draw a pension upon papa's death.*

A less printable text that I have heard sung uses the stanza beginning "Casey said just before he died" to develop Casey's supposed last words into a ribald commentary on Evelyn Thaw, of the once famous Thaw case. The singer of this version, a gentleman of education and great name, had learned the song while he was a student at one of the Ivy Colleges.

Since we do not have any trustworthy record of such Casey Jones texts as may have preceded the stage version, we cannot know with certainty whether the corruption of heroism into comedy began with the Negro texts, or whether the stage is chiefly to blame. But certainly "Casey Jones" achieved its great popularity as a comedy hit, not as a lament over the death of a hero. The rollicking tune undoubtedly assists the process of comedy, and we all know that "Casey Jones" is commonly sung in a boisterously humorous manner. That the ballad of Jesse James is similarly affected by the tradition of irreverence seems apparent from the comment of Charles J. Finger, who observes, in his *Frontier Ballads,* that the ballad is "peculiarly suitable to gay and light moods, provided that the singer is conscious of an intense sympathy with the train robber. Special emphasis must be given to the words 'dirty little coward,' because Ford is always the subject of execration—a sort of super-Judas."

"Springfield Mountain" and "Casey Jones," as here considered, are of course only suggestive examples. A broader study would have to deal more exactly and thoroughly with the influence of the stage—and particularly, I believe, with the blackface minstrel show tradition—upon American balladry and folk song. If undertaken, such a study will inevitably reveal, I believe, that stage influence will account to a considerable extent for our preference for the sentimental and sensational in balladry; or else for the comic, with a very marked leaning toward burlesque in many notable instances; and along with these tendencies, a very weak sense of the tragic. The critical inquirer of the future may well wonder at our incapacity. Why do our national heroes—Washington ("Captain Washington, upon a strappin' stallion"), Lincoln, Andrew Jackson, and David Crockett—appear in folk song and folk tale only at the comic level and no other? Why do "The Jam at Gerry's Rocks" and "Little Joe, the Wrangler" stay, rather awkwardly, at the sentimental level? How could a great or at least a powerful, well-endowed people exist without a highly developed sense of tragedy? How could they march into battle to the tune of such comic songs as "Dixie" and "Yankee Doodle"? How could they, on the evidence of their balladry, find death by snakebite or death by train wreck an occasion for merriment?

Whatever may be said by the Spenglers and Toynbees of the future about our cultural condition, I would argue now that the cause for the prevalence of burlesque over tragedy, and of the tradition of irreverence in general, must be sought in the realm of metaphysics and religion. To say that the American preference for a humorous approach derives from frontier tradition is superficial, since it leaves out the urban theater, which, no less than backwoods cabin, farm house, plantation house, or the open range, has shaped our popular song and story. Both influences have operated on our culture, by a process of mutual and reciprocal interaction. But the cause of the stage preference for the sentimental and comic over the tragic remains to be accounted for. It can be accounted for only by assuming, first, that both urban theater and backwoods cabin were subject to the post-Renaissance influences that have dominated and shaped our general life; and, second, that, while the "frontier" was by no means sealed off from these post-Renaissance influences, as is often too romantically supposed, the theater was naturally more exposed to them, more sensitive to them, and therefore first reflected their impact.

The tradition of irreverence necessarily arises in a culture where the human impulse for reverence no longer has a worthy object—that is, in a culture where no person, institution, or thing is any longer sacred. In other terms, it is a culture from which the idea of divinity has more or less evaporated and in which, therefore, religion is no longer the arbiter of knowledge. That is what our society has been in process of becoming ever since the sixteenth century—slowly at first, but, since the beginning of the industrial revolution, with the accelerated speed observed and predicted by Henry Adams. We are now predominantly a secular society, ruled by science, theoretical, applied, and "social." In a society ruled by science tragedy becomes an impossible conception, since science must hold that events can be explained, and must essentially be explained, in terms of causes logically describable and logically knowable. The pity and terror that belong to tragedy by the Aristotelian definition are necessarily excluded from the skeptical, inquiring, analytical processes of science. And their exclusion by science means that in the long run they will be excluded from the arts, including the traditional oral arts, or else will be bootlegged in, under some disguise or other.

The tragedy of Sophocles' *Antigone* would be impossible in a completely secular society of the scientific regime. Antigone's burial of her brother, which represents both filial duty and an act of reverence to the gods, would necessarily seem incomprehensible, archaic, and backward to the typical scientist, behaving as scientist. As scientist, he would unquestioningly obey the tyrant of the state, and forget about filial duty and the gods. There could be no tragic conflict of duties—no choice to make between religion and the state. To this scientist, or to anyone accepting his views, the tragic revelation of the hero of the ballad "Edward" would be only symptomatic evidence of mental disorder. The fearful cry, "O I hae killed my fadir deir, Mither, Mither," could only mean to him the active presence of the Oedipus Complex. Edward would be no tragic hero, but only a social delinquent.

An absolutely complete secularization of society under thoroughly scientific auspices would of course ultimately mean not only the elimination of pity and terror (in the Aristotelian sense), and therefore of tragedy, but also of laughter, with the consequent elimination of comedy. It may be difficult to imagine a society that is both pitiless and humorless, yet that is the direction in which modern Western society has seemed to be moving. We are not yet there, and I trust never will be. The tradition of irreverence—which affects not only ballad-making, but speech-making, the drama, poetry, and prose fiction—nevertheless strongly suggests, in one of its aspects, that we are in some danger. For the tradition of irreverence, whether found in frontier humor and the mock-tragic ballad or elsewhere, may be theoretically taken to represent an intermediate stage between the old society which could both feel and express pity and terror, and the new order in which nothing will any longer even be funny.

But in another aspect the tradition of irreverence indicates that we are willing to be serious, or even tragic, if the seriousness and tragedy can be bootlegged in under the cover of humor. The humor arises ultimately from the ironical juxtaposition of dogma or idealistic promise with the harsh reality that was going to be removed or explained away, but quite evidently has not been. This juxtaposition, in the New England that saw the substitution of "The Pesky Sarpent" for the elegiac versions of "Springfield Mountain," would be, fundamentally, a juxtaposition of Emerson's too-reassuring but completely secular transcendentalism with the hard truth that secularism has no comfort to offer a young couple whose romance is ended by death from snakebite. More generally speaking, the tradition of irreverence acknowledges, in a wry sort of way, the imperfection of man and the inscrutable power of God. It is one of the disguises that a wholesome but endangered tradition puts on in order to survive. It is evidence that we are still alive in characteristic human terms and have not inwardly and really submitted, as much as is outwardly pretended, to the bleak neutrality of secularism. We may be in better health than we realize, if the condition of our balladry is at all symptomatic of social well-being. From the mother country, Great Britain, we draw our inherited stock of the old ballads and the models for many of our own later ballads. But during the period when we were "evolving" such ballads as "Springfield Mountain" and "Casey Jones," the old country produced nothing remotely comparable to these very characteristic American items. We are, then, that much more alive than the British are.

CURRENT ATTITUDES TOWARD FOLKLORE

I HAVE TAKEN the subject "Current Attitudes toward Folklore" because I find myself confused by the mixed results of the vast and far-ranging activity of the devotees of folklore. I number myself among the devotees, but I feel a little concerned to know how to direct my devotion so that it will count. Many others, I imagine, must suffer from a like confusion of mind, and therefore of purpose.

It seems worth while, accordingly, to try to set down the current attitudes, to define them briefly, and to estimate their relative fruitfulness.

It is somewhat difficult to analyze briefly a tradition of study and devotion that in America begins, let us say, with the majestic figure of Francis J. Child, and that now surrounds us with accumulating volumes of balladry and folk song, compiled and edited by very distinguished scholars; with the much more carefree promotional labors of Mr. John Lomax, Miss Jean Thomas, and similar enthusiasts; with the productions of hillbilly radio singers who also claim the title of folk singers, sometimes deservedly, sometimes not; and with a Negroid popular music that, whatever its original sources, now emanates chiefly from New York composers and is danced to by the season's debutantes. Such phenomena are highly miscellaneous. I can do the job of analysis only by a rather bold attempt at classification. I distinguish at least three prevalent attitudes; and I can imagine, and to some extent define, a fourth attitude which I would like to see prevailing over and directing the other three.

These attitudes I name as follows: (1) the Historical-Scholarly; (2) the Enthusiastic-Promotional; (3) the Commercial-Exploitative. For the fourth attitude I have no name. Perhaps it is not an attitude so much as a state of being.

The Historical-Scholarly is of course the most respectable of the four attitudes, and naturally is the only one that attracts prestige in the academic world. It is respectable because, in imitation of physical science, it views balladry, folk song, and folk lore as human cultural phenomena and therefore as a body of knowledge that may be collected, studied, classified, collated, and annotated. The cultural phenomena bear some relationship—though perhaps an uncertain and, it would almost seem, an illicit relationship—to literature. Louise Pound has pointed out how the scholarly confusion as to the relationship between ballads and literature has led to confusion and even outright deception in the textbooks of English literature. Although we have only a small scattering of ballad texts that can be dated as prior to the sixteenth century, the editors of college survey textbooks in English literature insist on regarding almost any ballad text as vaguely medieval. The ballad section of such a college book may therefore be sandwiched in anywhere—after *Beowulf,* perhaps; or in juxtaposition with Chaucer; or in that scholarly attic of odds and ends, the fifteenth century. A college student of such a textbook, furthermore, may never learn that the famous Percy text of "Edward" is a unique, somewhat dubious text and that the texts commonly remembered both in Great Britain and in the United States are markedly different from the Percy text.

Nevertheless the relationship, however undetermined, between literature and the ballads, gives a good academic reason for studying ballads as cultural phenomena and putting them in order—and also for rating them as worth an occasional (but only an occasional) Ph.D. dissertation, especially if the material investigated by the candidate is not of very recent origin. The historical scholar is most at ease when he can consider phenomena that belong to a culture safely remote in the past. He does not want to be confronted with lively, fluid phenomena, for that kind of phenomena make him nervous, and uncertain of his conclusions.

For all their magnitude and conceded excellence, the studies of Francis J. Child have been much to blame for this attitude of crusty scholarly diffidence. Child seems to assume, or is too often interpreted as assuming, that balladry is a dead phenomenon. He moves among his versions and variants with the kind of safety enjoyed by an archaeologist moving among his artifacts. Child is in fact a kind of archaeologist, with a mixture of the anthropologist and the specialist in comparative literature. Out of his attitude—which he never clearly defined, but which we can see at work—comes his obsession that he must finally and definitely establish the canon of English and Scottish ballads, fix the exact number to be admitted to the canon (it turns out to be 305), and reject all intruders and impostors. Ballad scholars know better now; but Child's eminent contemporaries in the ballad field, Gummere and Kittredge, follow his lead obediently. They excavate and comment the remains of balladry very much as Heinrich Schliemann and his successors excavated and commented the ruins of Troy—that is, as something all over and done with long ago. Kittredge in 1902 almost triumphantly announced that ballad-making was a "closed account."

The labors and great influence of these men to a large degree have determined the course of ballad and folklore studies until recent years. We pay tribute to their power when we gather in the character of a learned society, dutifully presenting papers which embody our researches, which inevitably put great emphasis upon *collecting*. By far the greater number of state and regional ballad publications follow the model of Child, even to his system of numbers and letters. Generally the effort of the collectors is first of all to see what "Child ballads" can be recovered, in text and music, and to get as many versions and variants of versions as possible—garbled and worthless fragments often being recorded just as dutifully as the best texts.

The enormous conservative value of such work is self-evident. We owe ballad scholars an immense debt both for the material that they have preserved and for the insight that they give us, through their accompanying studies, into the folk-tradition itself as a historical and cultural fact. But there, I am afraid, the value stops. The conservation after all is limited, even when it is extended to items outside the Child canon, for the ballads and folk songs thus recovered are conserved only as specimens in a museum are conserved.

Ballad scholarship seems to have had little impact upon our contemporary culture—nothing even faintly resembling the wonderfully quickening influence that Bishop Percy's *Reliques* and Walter Scott's *Minstrelsy* had upon the culture of the later eighteenth and early nineteenth century. Ballad scholarship as we now have it may conserve; but it does not *transmit*. A folklore that is really to count must transmit, in other places than graduate school seminars. Perhaps the Historical-Scholarly attitude, legitimate and valuable though it clearly is, has led us to an undue emphasis upon collecting *per se*. It has led to the tedium—almost the madness—of accumulating hundreds of only slightly different texts of "Lord Randal" and "Barbara Allen," to what end is not altogether evident. Worst of all, it diverts the devotees of folklore from other possibilities that might conceivably bear a fruit not commonly plucked from doctoral dissertations.

The Enthusiastic-Promotional attitude is, I suppose, in part a reaction against the excessive frigidities of historical scholarship. I have heard it said that a certain notable professor at an Eastern university, who edits ballad collections and directs ballad research, does not himself *like* ballads. If at some social gathering anybody begins to sing a ballad, he hurriedly makes his excuses and leaves the party. Perhaps he is only worn out with the subject. But perhaps his feelings, when a ballad is sung in his presence, are comparable to the feelings of a zoologist whose pickled frog suddenly starts to croak in the jar on the laboratory shelf.

At any rate, the Enthusiastic-Promotional attitude is the extreme opposite of the notable professor's attitude. It buttonholes you too familiarly and constantly to hearken to the croaking of almost any sort of ballad frog, alive or dead. It becomes a zealotry that threatens to cheapen balladry and folk song with too much unrestrained admiration. One mark of the Enthusiastic-Promotional attitude is attempt at popularization, frequently through books that drop the paraphernalia of scholarship and deliberately try to win an audience. For all their conceded merits, the collections of Mr. John Lomax and Mr. Carl Sandburg lean too much in this direction. The sin of Mr. Lomax in using composite texts, grievous in scholars' eyes, is of course disturbing. But much worse is Mr. Lomax' and Mr. Sandburg's foggy enthusiasm, which casts a very peculiar romantic mist over the whole subject of ballad and folk song and leaves us in doubt as to where we really are. Yet there is certainly some clear gain in the attitude I am discussing. The enthusiasts are really trying to transmit as well as to conserve, and if they overreach themselves at times, it is the defect of their good qualities. The attempt itself is healthy. But it is still not quite good enough, and the reason why it is not good enough is easy to find.

The popularizers try to win an audience—but what audience? They aim at the sophisticated urban audience, the audience with money enough to buy books and with a taste jaded enough to welcome for the moment (but only for the moment) the novel bit of antiquity, of local color, of "regional" quaintness. A moment before, the same audience welcomed Viennese light opera, or George Gershwin. Tomorrow it will welcome something else, and Lomax and Sandburg will be back numbers.

The situation is more clearly revealed when we turn to the somewhat weaker members of the tribe. Dorothy Scarborough's *On the Trail of Negro Folk-Song* and *A Song-Catcher in Southern Mountains,* for example, are the romantic adventures of a Columbia professor who happens to be collecting folk songs instead of early American glass. And, for another example, the books of Jean Thomas, seem deliberately to cater to the urban notion of balladry as "quaint." Such works involve a dangerous kind of condescension. They, too, have relatively little impact upon our culture as a whole, and what impact they do have is specious, in as much as they indulge in a theatrical display that reduces folk song to a kind of parlor vaudeville, a very minor form of entertainment, or at best a fleeting escapism.

The third attitude, the Commercial-Exploitative, needs little definition. At its best it may give us the finished professional performance of folk song, either by choral groups singing from a sophisticated part-song arrangement, or by the noted singer who includes a ballad or sea-chantey among the lighter, miscellaneous numbers at the end of a concert program. More rarely, we get an entire program of folk songs, but such a program, however delightful, is nearly always rendered by a trained vocalist who, though he sings folk song, is not in the true sense a folk singer. We may prolong this type of enjoyment by buying his album of phonograph records and, from this model, learn to perform our favorites, with or without the accompaniment of that popular but difficult instrument, the guitar.

I should certainly concede that the Commercial-Exploitative attitude, at its best, improves musical taste and lures us toward the much higher attitude that I would call Artistic-Exploitative. But the Artistic-Exploitative attitude, which could do much to enrich our culture, can as yet show only a scattering of serious devotees among American music composers, poets, and dramatists. The "idiom" of our folk music is occasionally exploited as a novelty in orchestral or operatic composition. It is rarely an organic part of an American composer's style and subject matter.

At its worst, the Commercial-Exploitative attitude gives us the hillbilly singer and his "band," from whom we get only the lower levels of folk performance and often no more than the straight "commercial." It is quite true—though too often forgotten—that the "Grand Ole Opry" of radio station WSM at Nashville, Tennessee, the great originator and popularizer of hillbilly music, began at the genuine folk level and that even in the later stage some of the hillbilly radio groups often perform genuine folk songs, along with the fiddle tunes which of course are entirely traditional. But commercial pressure is irresistible. The hillbilly singer is inevitably tempted to compose *new* songs—quasi–folk songs or frankly popular ditties—which will bring him royalties from phonograph records and music-sheets. Radio performances of hillbilly music (now called "country music") notoriously run to sentimental numbers, and hardly ever to the true ballad, the really convincing folk song. And, in another sphere, what has happened under the commercial auspices of New York, Harlem, and night-club orchestras and singers to the secular or sacred songs of the Negro is too obvious to need comment. It is, again, an exploitation that caters to the passing urban mood and has little to do with folk song as we know it in its traditional haunts. It represents a vulgarizing process.

All these attitudes have one characteristic in common. Their approach is *external* to the tradition and essential being of folk song and folklore. In one way or another they may conserve or embalm the folk product. They do not transmit it, except at great expense to the object transmitted. They cannot genuinely cherish it. To transmit the folk product effectively and to cherish it genuinely, the impetus must come from within the folk itself.

The fourth attitude (which I have spoken of above but cannot name) would draw its strength from within the folk tradition. It is a real question whether the transmission that it would foster can be much assisted by a self-conscious effort on our part. Yet such a transmission has been achieved in the past, and may be again. Why are the Danish ballads available to us in a more fully rounded, less mangled form than the English and Scottish ballads? Scholars tell us that the preservation may be partly due to the devotion of certain noble Danish ladies who took care to write down the ballads. But these ladies wrote down the ballads that they might be remembered, not that they might be "collected"; and, still more concretely, that such ballads might be better performed in Danish households. If we preserve ballads in order to learn them and perform them (as some of us in this very Society are doing today), then we join in the folk process—*we* become the folk.

How does it happen that the Confederate song "I'm a Good Old Rebel," though composed by a known author and indeed published soon after its composition, became a Southern folk song rather than a merely literary relic? Aside from its intrinsic appeal and character, it became a folk song because the author let his song go, to whoever would like it, for what it was worth to Confederates and others, not for what it was worth to a music publisher. We too may become contributors to folk song on one condition: we must be nameless, we must let the song go, we must set up no copyright claim.

The roots of the best attitude toward folk song, it seems to me, lie in such circumstances. If such views have merit, we ought to become cherishers by participation, in at least as much degree as we are cherishers by recording and collecting.

Perhaps we can also do certain things in a concerted way— things which will do good, or at least work no harm. We can strive to inculcate respect for folk song among those who already possess it naturally. We can strive to see that love of old song is not wholly replaced by love of new song. That means, certainly, that our schools should negatively refrain from some of their customary educational policies—especially their callous assumption that the first duty of the school is to weed out ruthlessly all elements of nonliterate culture and replace them by completely literate requirements. Yet I hardly know whether we dare risk the cherishing of folk song by the schools as a planned and definite part of the school program itself. The schools have been so guilty of diluting and vulgarizing what they attempt to convey that I am almost ready to say that they should not be trusted with this precious heritage. I am tempted to declare that I would rather risk leaving the preservation of folk song to the old, anonymous, accidental process, even under perilous modern conditions, than to give it a place in a curricular or activities program administered by the certificated products of our higher educational institutions.

The point is debatable. But undoubtedly our concern should somehow be directed toward the young folks rather than, as now, exclusively toward the old folks from whom we collect such interesting examples of folk song and folk tale. The young folks should have their part in all nonschool undertakings—festivals, fairs, entertainments, competitions—that strive to bring folk song into good respect.

Back of all this lies the soil in which the tradition is to be nurtured. The true cherishers of the folk tradition are, first, the family in its traditional role, securely established on the land, in occupations not hostile to song and dance and tale; and, second, the stable community which is really a community and not a mere real estate development. If we cannot cherish these, we cannot hope to cherish folk song, and probably we cannot long cherish the high forms of art that feed upon folk tradition. We may even prove ourselves ignorant of what life really is.

THE SACRED HARP

IN THE LAND OF EDEN

IN THE plantation country of Middle Georgia is a land
which ought to be, but is not, called Eden. Whatever one may
argue about the phantasmic impositions of automobile and
radio upon appearances, here there is little change in the essence of things as they were in other days. Small farmers, to
be sure, have invaded what was once only a land of great
estates, but this change is simply a more intimate mingling
of the old elements of the Southern tradition.

To the modern visitor, the noteworthy fact is that the tradition has here been preserved at the very time when there
has been the greatest temptation to depart from it. Perhaps,
in their conservatism, the folk of Eden have been armored
in nothing more formidable than innocence: but their innocence is now beginning to look like wisdom, or at the very
least like a rare fidelity to which time may give some reward.
The folk of Eden do not have to study much over what to
keep and what to abandon, because they know how they wish
to live. The town of Eden keeps some things, and the country
around it other things, but they do not make it their business
to disturb one another where their ideas of preservation do
not happen to coincide. Indeed, they do not particularly notice what they are keeping or make any great outcry pro and
con. Thus it happens that the land of Eden has kept alive,
almost unwittingly, the all-day singings which have been a
feature of life in the South since eighteenth-century times.

My tale here is not of the town, except as it good-naturedly
tolerates or ignores the slightly different customs that prevail

in the surrounding country. The all-day singings take place on the fringe of Eden's land and not in the town. In the town the churches have choirs of the regular sort that sit behind an elevated rail with a little velvet curtain. At intervals they dutifully rise to sing the hymns provided in decorous books published by church boards in Nashville or Atlanta—books from which zeal and musical vitality have been fairly well extracted by years of revivalism and musical professionalism in the church. The choir sings competently because it is made up of educated musicians with well-behaved voices. The congregation listens obediently because that is what it is supposed to do. When the service is over, they all go home to dinner without knowing exactly what is missing from the procedure to which all the people once said Amen—actually said it, did not leave it to a choir to intone. It would never occur to them that they have allowed improvers and reformers to deprive them of a musical tradition that was once native to their religion, and is now in the keeping of their humbler brethren, outside the church organization. To rediscover this tradition, one must forsake the neo-Gothic churches of the town, which reflect the fleeting prosperity of the New South and the taste of the Gilded Age, and seek out the plain rectangular "church houses" that stand beside lonely graveyards, in groves of pine or oak, in the midst of old plantation lands now sometimes tilled by tenants from North Georgia or Alabama.

Here the "old timy singings" still flourish, as they did a century ago. Upon question, the townsfolk of Eden may talk about them a little—half-condescendingly (because one is used to hearing Walter Damrosch or Lily Pons on the radio), and half-wistfully (because the old music is still in their blood); but they rarely attend the singings in any numbers. They have not yet got around to reading George Pullen Jackson's account, in *White Spirituals of the Southern Uplands,* of "the lost tonal tribe of America"; and they are therefore as ignorant as urban America of the nature of the choral art that flourishes at their very doors: the tradition of the "shape-note" singers

that once swept the rural South, after a fleeting residence in
New England and the West, and that seems to be the original
source of the Negro spirituals.

Many of the Eden-folk had seen the "shape-notes" in the
older hymnbooks, in the days when even the churches had to
yield to the old-fashioned method; but they had forgotten the
singing "classes" that were once taught to associate the tones
of the scale with the shapes named "fa," "sol," and "la," and
thus developed a remarkable facility at a kind of *a capella*
religious singing. They could hardly be expected to know
what Dr. Jackson had gone to such labor to discover, that the
"Fa-sol-la- Folk" used a method of music reading that derived
from Elizabethan England and sang from books like *The
Southern Harmony* (1835) and *The Sacred Harp* (1844),
which garnered up some of the noblest and most ancient
strains of folk and art music in combination. The Eden folk
did know, however, that old tunes like "Amazing Grace" had
a power to move them far beyond the polite dilutions offered
in modern hymnbooks. They answered a stranger's questions
tolerantly but vaguely. Yes, there were singings at Cedar Valley and Salem, but they hadn't been there in years. Dinner-
on-the-grounds, of course, was something anybody could rel-
ish— Lord, what dinners there used to be! If we wanted oldtime singing, why not go to the Negro churches, where one
could hear all those Negro spirituals that people up North
kept talking about?

But Mr. Knowles, the barber, knew all about the white
spirituals. By practice and preference he was of the old "four-
shape" school, and a devotee of the *Original Sacred Harp*.
Systematically, he had started out to master every one of the
609 tunes in that great collection—a "new edition" of a work
dating back to 1844. Yes, he had learned to sing by the "four-
shape" method: *fa, sol, la* for the first three notes of the
scale (triangle, circle, square); and *fa, sol, la* again for the next
three; and *mi* (a diamond) for the seventh if you ever needed
it. But he had learned the "seven-shape" system too, which

went *do, re, mi, fa, sol, la, ti, do,* with a different shape for every note, And he had even learned the round notes, he was careful to remind me, for I should know that his preference for "shapes" was no Hobson's choice. Mostly he had figured it all out for himself, just as he had spelled his way through the Bible.

From a drawer beneath the hair tonic and shaving mugs he took out a well-thumbed copy of the *Original Sacred Harp,* and from another drawer a pitch pipe and a tuning fork. This was the way one sang. One set his pitch pipe for whatever the key-signature was, and sounded "fa." Then it was easy to go right ahead, because the shape of the notes told you exactly what sound to make. If you used a tuning fork, of course, you often had to work up or down, and it was harder to hit the key. The book fell open at "The Morning Trumpet," which Dr. Jackson has earmarked as the probable original of a famous Negro spiritual. Could he sing this one by way of illustration, I asked. Well, he didn't know that song, but he would try. He didn't have to noddle his head over new songs, like some church pianists he had seen. Let's see—this song was a minor—F sharp minor. He set his pitch pipe, blew a thin strain, and then went through the plaintive old air without missing a single note. It was a convincing exhibition of sight reading. The church choir, I fancied, would have noddled their heads considerably over "The Morning Trumpet," which fazed Mr. Knowles not at all. This was the music I wanted to hear.

Very good, he said, the singing was to be at Cedar Valley, the last Sunday in April, as it had always been. The Cedar Valley people sang in the old-fashioned way, out of *The Sacred Harp* only. They permitted no departures, and they used no instruments of any kind, not even a tuning fork or a pitch pipe. For this strict orthodoxy they suffered a little, Mr. Knowles thought, for if the leader did not watch, he would set the tune too high. The Cedar Valley folks disdained pitch pipes to their hurt. Nevertheless they were fine folks and fine singers, right down to the very children. They were not like the "new way" folks at Salem (though these were good singers too) who used "seven-shape" notes and had a new book every year; they stuck to the *Sacred Harp*. We must be sure to go.

II

So we went, and a fine Sunday morning it was, with the sun bright on the cotton plants and the peach orchards. The hard-paved highway turned into a sand road that wound past deserted Negro cabins and half-plowed fields, red with sour grass plumes or brown with sedge where the earth lay fallow. We passed Hog Crawl Creek, a muddy rivulet, and presently, there among the pines, with a grassy clearing in front, was Cedar Valley Church. It was a small white building with rickety front steps. A little beyond showed the bare sand, and marble or wooden headstones, of the burying-ground. Already a school bus, a few automobiles, and a mule wagon were drawn up in the shade. Men and boys lounged on the steps of the church. Women sat in the cars, chatting and waiting.

A huge man, who but for his horn-rimmed spectacles was the image of girt John Ridd in all his brawn, turned from the Model-T Ford where he was talking with some new arrivals and came to greet us.

"Oakes is my name." He extended a great hand, rough from plow and ax. "I see you all are strangers here. We are mighty glad to have you."

Yes, we came from Tennessee, but were living at Eden for the winter.

His blue eyes twinkled speculatively, but he suppressed the desire to question these foreigners who came from so far North that they might as well be Yankees, and welcomed us heartily.

Yes, this was the place where the old-timy singing went on. When he took this church—hit was a Missionary Baptist church—he kept up the old singing because he was used to it where he came from, over in Clay County, Alabama. The old songs were the best. They tetched you right thar (he motioned

toward his heart), but the new songs only got into folks' feet
and made them want to dance. But songs were anyhow mostly
better than preaching; better, at least, than the new-fangled
sermons that had too much starch in them, all filling and no
real body of the gospel. Not so many folks could sing by the old
way as there used to be. At a burying now, it was sometimes
hard to find anybody to set a tune. Still, a lot of people always
came to Cedar Valley on this Sunday—people from all around,
from Macon, even from Atlanta. Wouldn't I lead them in a
lesson, he added, courteously?

No, much obliged, I could not. I liked the singing, but came
only to listen.

Well, there were many such. But we must jine in when the
singing began. And now wouldn't we step out and meet some
of the folks?

Particularly there were Mr. and Mrs. Dunn. He was a stocky
man with a drooping flaxen mustache and she a slender, wistful woman, a good farmer's wife. They were eager to talk and
anxious to make the visitors feel at home.

Like Brother Oakes, they came originally from Alabama.
Mr. Dunn wanted to go back, but Mrs. Dunn was against that.
She didn't want her children to have to hoe that rocky ground,
as she had had to do. But this was a good country. They lived
near Vienna, twenty miles away. (Pronounce it Vīenna.) Their
farm was really a five-mule farm, but now, times were so bad,
they were plowing only two mules. And so I was from Tennessee? And my wife from Ohio? Ohio was too incredibly far
away for comment, but Mr. Dunn said he had always wanted
to go to Tennessee. His father, after he had fought in the Confederate War, had always talked so much about that fine Tennessee country. And two of his seven sons had been selling
Bibles up in Tennessee—the same two that had been going
to Miss Martha Berry's school at Rome. One of the boys was
here now—the only one, out of all seven, who liked the Sacred
Harp singings. He never missed a singing anywhere—he had

even been known to hitchhike in order to get to a singing—
and he was really responsible for their coming today.

We talked on, as the sun drew higher and the crowd increased. People came in all sorts of vehicles: mule wagons
with chairs and planks for seats, a buggy or two, a couple of
"Hoover carts," automobiles of fairly recent models, school
buses, open trucks, and many Model-T Fords and ancient
Chevrolets. There were many more young people than old.
The girls wore their lipstick and rouge with an air. Their hats
and dresses were in the spring fashion or not far behind. People had on their Sunday clothes, which might be unobtrusively
patched or darned; but nobody wore overalls. A few of the
older men wore the broad-brimmed black hats and string ties
of another day, but among the women there were no old-
fashioned shawls and bonnets. They were a handsome, hearty
race, unconquered by depression or modernity; and the children, running numerously to and fro, were the handsomest
and most neatly dressed of all.

As ten o'clock came near, Brother Oakes began to get wor-
ried. There was a shortage of books. In the past they had depended on old man H——, who regularly appeared with an
armful of "sacred harps," some to lend, some to sell. He was
not at the Unadilla singing last Sunday, a voice said. He must
be sick then, said another, for he was never known to miss a
singing. Brother Oakes went through the crowd and returned.
There were nine books, he said. That would do to begin with
—everybody come in!

The people filled the rude wooden benches, and the singers
gathered at the front around the pulpit. For the singers there
were benches at the sides and a bench or two facing the congregation, so as to form, with the front benches, a hollow
square, four sides for the four parts of the songs. There were
many more men than women. As the singing got under way,
late arrivals came up from the rear or entered from the side
door. Before long, at least forty singers were engaged, and the

volume of tone, a little unbalanced at first, swelled to majestic proportions.

A few of the singers were oldsters, of sixty and upwards. A much larger number were in their hale fifties. There were several young men and a few young girls. One tiny girl of about ten years sat on the front bench and sang from her mother's book. In the rear of the singers a few men joined in at times; they had no books but they knew some of the songs by heart.

"The lesson will begin," announced Brother Oakes, "with Number Fifty-nine." (For this ancient ritual still keeps the procedure of the eighteenth-century singing school; it speaks of "lesson" and "class.") "Not all of our friends are here. Some are missing that have always been on hand. But we have enough to make a show. Now everybody jine in as we sing these songs of Zion, and if you ain't got a book, open yore mouth and make a noise anyway."

He peered at his book and hummed under his breath to set the pitch, leaning over to let the others try it with him. And now he had the pitch. To right, to center, to left he swept his hand, and the groups of voices in turn proclaimed the pitch. Then with the downward stroke of his hand they went through the tune together, singing the syllables, *fa, sol, la,* and calling to life the ancient shape notes that told singers how the tune went. Without a fumble they syllabled the tune; and the pines outside, and the plowed fields, and the throng of folk on the rough benches heard again the ritual of fa-sol-la, kept for them in hard times and good, by men and women who knew how to worship in song. *The Sacred Harp,* many-voiced and strong, was sounding again in the land of Eden.

The tune first chosen was much like a dance-song tune that could have come from an English green in the time of Henry VIII, the king who loved music and himself knew how to set or make a tune. But here it was sung slowly. It was a good stately tune, and when the fa-sol-la-ing had ended, Brother Oakes adjusted his glasses and looked around. "The words," he said; and they sang the words: "Brethren, we have met to worship, And adore the Lord our God. . . ."

Brother Oakes was a good leader. He tolerated no dragging. He swept all along—singers and crowd alike—with the strong trumpet of his voice carrying the air and the bulk of his great body that put out a commanding arm to wave us into the deep rhythm of the antique spiritual music. He knew words and tune by heart. He could fa-sol-la the tune with hardly a glance at the book. The songs of *The Sacred Harp* were a life that he lived, burningly and familiarly. Chosen by him, the songs went beckoning into the woods and fetched the people in. And they came in, leaving no bench unfilled, clustering at the doors and beyond.

The next song was in a minor key—a solemn and plaintive echo, with as much strength as mournfulness in it, of times when the songs of the faith had not brightened up into the persevering optimism of the exclusively major modes. When it was finished, Brother Oakes prayed for a blessing in the Biblical language whose seventeenth-century idiom was not far removed from his own colloquial English. After the prayer, the customary committee was appointed to call up the leaders of the lessons in their due turn. Brother Oakes then led in his third song, "Farewell, vain world, I'm going home," and presently another leader took charge.

By dinnertime nine leaders, besides Brother Oakes, had done their part, some spiritedly, some haltingly, but even the weakest with plausible correctness, and all with dignity and fervor. It was a point of courtesy for the committee to call up all who could lead or were ambitious to lead, and to compliment the veterans and the guests from far off by calling on them first. Brother B—— of Macon, the second to appear, had a slight air of the professional. In his neat business suit he looked like any Rotarian; but he had a musical earnestness and expertness that no Rotarian ever dreamed of. He beat time with a pencil, and in the complicated "fuguing songs" that he selected he waved up this or that part like the conductor of an orchestra. He was so accurate in hitting the pitch that succeeding leaders, if they felt a little uncertain, leaned over and deferred to him in their efforts to strike the right tone. In general the songs were astonishingly well pitched. Only twice were there false starts; both times, the pitch was too high. One or two of the leaders were old gentlemen whose quavery voices were well-nigh lost in their beards. One of the younger men was obviously frightened and shaky. The most self-assured and even was a girl of nineteen or twenty, whose rouged lips and smart spring dress might have nominated her for the ranks of the jazz singers and crooners; but she led the difficult old music like a veteran.

III

The choice of songs included one or two familiar hymns, other much less hymn-like tunes that might be called the classics of the shape-note tradition, and a general sprinkling of the "fuguing tunes" that required the parts to follow out contrapuntal figures. The selections fully revealed the richness of *The Sacred Harp* collection and the good taste and varied inclination of the leaders. The device of rotating leaders was itself a revelation of the sturdiness and good sense of these musical democrats. There must be no true singer who could not lead, and no leader who could not in turn give way and enter the ranks.

Of the thirty-four songs sung during the two-hour morning session, four were in a minor key.* Perhaps the prevalence of the major modes indicated that the old folk were surrendering to the modern prejudice against minor scales, which dominates the newfangled and heretical school of the "seven-shapers," with their more jigging and conventionally harmonized tunes of "gospel hymn" flavor. Their performance in general was

---

* Not really in a "minor" key, but undoubtedly "modal." But in 1933 I knew nothing about Dorian, Mixolydian, and other modal scales, and Dr. George Pullen Jackson, my authority, was himself just beginning to explore them.

beyond the powers of the average church choir. In the morning they sang thirty-four songs; in the afternoon they would sing at least as many more, a total of seventy or eighty songs during the day. Some of the singers, of course, were *Sacred Harp,* or shape-note, devotees who frequented the singings that go on through the Middle Georgia neighborhood from early spring till fall; a few no doubt attended the Sunday afternoon "classes" held occasionally at Cedar Valley. But many had had no practice since last year's singing at this place. Yet they must be ready to follow a leader who could choose anything he pleased from the five-hundred-odd pages of *The Sacred Harp.* And they must follow, too, not merely some simple tune for which the harmony could be "faked," but music in which the four parts were written on separate staffs and had to a considerable degree their own melodic patterns. If the song were not familiar, they must take it at sight; but they could do this (as they would have explained to the novice) because of the shape-notes, which from their contour as well as their position told what the tone was. If anybody were rusty and uncertain, the preliminary fa-sol-la-ing would set him straight.

The voices blended best, it seemed, and the musical effect was best, during this fa-sol-la-ing. Sometimes the tone was queerly balanced, though never exactly discordant, when the words began. The discrepancy came partly, I suspected, from a mechanical difficulty. To save printing space, the words, in *The Sacred Harp,* are distributed too compactly and awkwardly through the four staffs. The men who sing the "lead" (tenor), which is on the third staff, must glance up to the first staff for the first stanza of the words, while continually glancing down at the third staff to hit the tune.

The tonal effects were not what a trained chorus leader would seek to obtain. These singers were not trying to please an audience with a fine balance and blending of tone. They knew nothing about "artistic effects." But they were singing to please themselves, to enjoy the music, to feel their own emotions in song. Hardly ever did they need the leader's admonition to "keep together." The deep organic surge of the music and everyone's hand-beat sufficed for that. The powerful accents carried them along irresistibly. But there was no soft pedaling, no shading. Each musical democrat simply opened his mouth and let his feelings find utterance in unrestrained vocality. The singing was at its best when it reached its fullest volume. The rich bass and tenor of the men dominated nearly always. There were fewer women's voices; and these few gave the chorus a quality that might have seemed harsh, or even offensive, to an ear accustomed to a different tonal balance. The women's voices, too, separated a little stridently from the vocal mass. They had none of the sweet liquidity of the traditional soprano. They were not, in fact, sopranos at all, or altos; but theirs were the high "treble" (pronounced "tribble") and the lower-voiced "counter" parts —the old terms for the parts sung by women.

To an unaccustomed ear the strangeness of the effect was increased by the peculiar intonation given to the words themselves. The word utterance of these folk (like the way of most old-fashioned singers in the South) was partly a sliding around and to the words intoned, and partly an orotundity and a separateness of one word from the next. It was the opposite of the intonation of trained singers who, in their zeal for pure tonality, obscure consonants and merge syllables so as to make words indistinguishable. To the Sacred Harpers the music was much, but not everything. They sang the words as well as the music. They believed in the words and loved the old figures of speech. They were happy to think that they "were marching through Immanuel's Land to fairer worlds on high," or that "somewhere their troubles would be over." Little wonder that at such singings the Sacred Harpers were often moved to tears. The singing was an intense personal experience; it was poetry and religion united in music. The words meant what they said, for the Sacred Harpers were like ballad singers, to whom the ballad is as much story as song. Perhaps their manner of intonation was itself traditional and went back no telling how far, to some time when music was in truth wedded to immortal verse.

The "folk" quality of the songs, or at least the folk-like quality, was recognizable enough. Not only did one hear borrowings from secular music—a song set to the tune of "Robin Adair" or "Long, Long Ago"—but the melodic patterns continually ran in the direction of folk music. The songs were often pentatonic in scale; in the fa-sol-la-ing one rarely heard the "mi" of the seventh. Their musical style drew one's mind back to the great camp-meeting days, from which songs improvised and remembered found their way into collections like *The Sacred Harp*. As for Dr. Jackson's argument that the Negro spirituals derive ultimately from the white spirituals, I thought as I listened that no one acquainted with the controversy between those who argue for a white origin and those who hold out for an exclusively Negro origin could remain unconvinced in the light of the Sacred Harp performance. Songs like "My troubles will be over," "Oh, who will come and go with me," and "On Jordan's stormy banks I stand," were remarkably like Negro spirituals, but they were demonstrably older than the recorded versions of the Negro spirituals that resemble them. They had been created in the heyday of the shape-note choral art and had been kept alive by the obscure devotees of *Sacred Harps* and *Southern Harmonies*. Doubtless the Negro had adapted them in his peculiar way, but he had first of all taken his songs from the source where he had got his Bible, his plow, his language.

Indeed, the music, I thought as I listened, was something whose influence every native Southerner has subconsciously recognized, even when he has not experienced its direct force. The Sacred Harp people were keeping alive "native" American music which had made itself felt in unacknowledged ways upon many of the songs, secular and sacred, that reflect an indigenous American experience. The townsfolk of Eden had neglected or lost this tradition, but at least they had not gone

out into the woods and tried to educate the Sacred Harp people into a progressive contempt for their good old music. Now
it had lasted so long that it might become new-fashioned. One
could cheerfully agree with George Pullen Jackson's argument
that the "cult of listening silence" encouraged by radio and
the philanthropic patronage of orchestral and operatic performances might lead only to a sterile musical culture; but
the Sacred Harp tradition, which was only a part of the larger
shape-note tradition with its thousands upon thousands of
Southern devotees, gave the living experience of music itself.

IV

As the singing went on, the congregation swelled in numbers. There was a little casual coming and going, but its in-
formality did not mar the dignity and intense spirit of participation that charged the little church room. Now and then
girls looked back, smiling and whispering, and went out to
join their beaus. Late comers edged through the crowd and
found places. But the *Sacred Harp,* with its many-voiced harmony, was lord in that place. The grave, attentive men in
their Sunday suits, the women in their modest finery, the
children quiet and a little awed, were borne with the choral
music, their souls feeding deep on its archaic splendors. To
them it was "the most beautiful music in the world." Near
the front, where there were still not enough books to go
around, one saw hands on the backs of benches softly rise
and fall, and open and close, keeping time as students of the
Sacred Harp are taught to do. One could see an old man's
eyes close and his lips move, as he joined in some familiar
chorus and thought perhaps of boyhood days, when first the
singing-master came to the settlement from which the sound
of pioneer axes and the noise of war had not long departed.

As the time drew near twelve o'clock, Brother Oakes again
arose. "We have time for one more song before dinner," he
said. "Turn to 528. And I like it tolerable peart. I like it the
way the brother led us just now. I never did care for a song

to be drug out. When I was a boy I plowed with oxen, and when I got hold of an old blind horse I thought I was flying— I never went back to oxen. I never like to hear a song drug out."

"Oh, For a Heart," his last choice, was a sonorous minor setting of verses by Wesley. He led it vigorously. His eyes looked far off, hardly ever at the book. The song ended. *The Sacred Harp* was closed and put away.

We went out with the throng into the sunshine. The grove was full of vehicles and people. Everybody was shaking hands. There were more people outside the church than had been in it. Many of them were young folk, doing their courting while the elders sang. Our own car, we found, was occupied by two such couples, who laughingly made way for us.

Many were the invitations to stay for dinner. Surely we weren't going right now, when the fried chicken and sausage and pie and cake were being set out, from baskets that the women had cooked all day Saturday to fill. But we were the mysterious strangers, the unaccountable folk from a long way off, who must say farewell too soon, far too soon. We left the Sacred Harp folk under their pines, where in a moment the preacher would ask the blessing of the Lord upon the bounty that His hand and His earth, despite man-made hard times, had given His people; and went on our way with the strings of the *Sacred Harp* still vibrant in our minds, and saw the cotton springing up, the peach trees in full green, the grain already nearly ripe for harvest in the land of Eden.

THE ORIGINS OF OUR HEROES

Mr. DIXON WECTER'S admirable study *The Hero in America: A Chronicle of Hero-Worship* is the fruit not only of one man's contemplation and sound scholarship; it is also the fruit, and might be called the epitome, of the most remarkable period of retrospect and self-examination in our national history. In the years from the publication of Beveridge's life of John Marshall (1919) to the present we have tried in hundreds of books, monographs, and literary articles to say what we think our history is; and beyond what officially passes as history, to say also what traditions we inherit; what our national and regional peculiarities are; what our folkways are, too, in particularized detail and in the large; and, as in the focus Mr. Wecter invites us to use, who are true heroes, and why.

This recovery of the American past has been both systematic and nostalgic. Undoubtedly the graduate schools have led the way and prepared the foundation. Their vast researches are supposed to be objective, but sometimes one can detect in them a passion not quite concealed, a fervor so irrepressible that it makes even *ibid.* and *op. cit.* look like partisan terms. Biographers and historians, amateur and professional, have exploited their materials, and, for better authority, even the writers of historical fiction have aped their methods, until we now find footnotes and bibliography in the best-selling novel, as in the dusty monograph. One is surprised, indeed, not to find a scholarly apparatus appended to the historical picture strips that compete for public favor with Popeye and Joe Palooka.

In the same period, American literature and the study of

152

it have gained enormously. The American historical novel has been triumphantly reborn. To assure us that it is really historical, the authors sometimes provide us—as Kenneth Roberts has done—with painstaking monographs about the unreliability of their predecessors and, in contrast, the trouble they have been put to, in order to set the record right. Ballad, folk tale, folklore have been hunted out of their wilderness lairs and caged, in book and phonograph record, no less for the benefit of the scholar than for the hungry sophisticate of the cities, who very often may be a Harvard undergraduate with a guitar. The arts everywhere have felt the influence of retrospection. Music, drama, painting, architecture, even fashions in dress and cookery, revive the American theme.

Against this overwhelming tide, the efforts of the "debunking school" of the nineteen-twenties now seem trivial and almost pathetic. The Marxists, swept by the same flood, have shrewdly attempted to ride it. They have hoisted Lincoln's effigy to the masthead and invoked other sanctions and symbols from the American past. Their championship of the past cannot be accepted as sincere, since, once in power, they would lose no time in obliterating all traces of the past. But it is a testimony to the prestige of Lincoln's name that even the Marxists seek to invoke its magic. As never before, we are emphatically and affectionately self-conscious toward our history.

It is necessary to say all this in order to describe Mr. Wecter's book. He has evidently absorbed the works of his predecessors. Despite the limitations suggested by his title, his book is most of all summation, deft and well-balanced, of the thought of the period. His chapters on Washington, Jefferson, Lincoln, Lee, and other heroes, though they hark back to earlier attitudes, are in essence reviews of what our generation has learned about the American past. One could not imagine any better book to recommend to an inquiring European who might want to find out just what kind of nation he has become involved with under the postwar arrangements. For the American reader, the pleasure and value of Mr. Wecter's book would have to be differently described—it is old acquaintance brought to mind; and if that reader is addicted to Americana, he will marvel at Mr. Wecter's ability to make the old acquaintance new.

Mr. Wecter's main business, nevertheless, is not with historical narrative as such. His real subject is the "secular religion" of hero-worship in the United States, and how it works, and what it reveals about us as well as the heroes. In this connection arises the only quarrel that a critic could reasonably work up with him. The issue is whether the method he uses—which is essentially the method of the historical scholar—enables him to do justice to his real subject.

Like Carlyle, to whom he refers, Mr. Wecter accepts as "hero" the great man who is the type of his age and his people, who both makes the times and is made by them, and who, though embodying the ideal of a particular era, lingers on permanently as a national tradition. This definition admits the Man of Letters and the Prophet to the pantheon of heroes no less than the military chieftain or the purely mythical folk hero. Although Mr. Wecter offers us no American examples of the hero as Man of Letters or as Prophet, he does follow the Carlylean principle to the extent of giving us the Hero as Inventor (Edison) and as Aviator (Lindbergh), as well as the Pilgrim Fathers, the Embattled Farmers, the Frontiersman, and the like, along with Washington, Andrew Jackson, and Lee.

If hero-worship is indeed a "secular religion," then is the historian, as historian, really competent to deal with it? Is it any of his business, if he is going to insist on remaining a researchist? Our great men, or "heroes," attract reverence not merely from the facts of their careers, which may often be in conflict with legend, but from folk-interpretation of facts, or addition to facts. Mythologizing is an essential part of the hero-making process. Mr. Wecter recognizes its importance, but does not quite know what to do with myths, other than to annotate them. He announces, it is true, a kind of philosophy of American hero-worship. As a nation, he says, we have too large a habitation, containing too many "interchangeable places," to find collective unity in loyalty to place-traditions. Instead, we seek our emotional center in the Flag, the Declaration of Independence, the Constitution; and, most of all, in our "heroes" who have become "institutions," "talismans," "great gods of the tribe." "Our folk attitude toward our greatest heroes," he writes, "approaches the religious."

Mr. Wecter does not speak to this text systematically and convincingly. He has a divided interest, which might be stated thus: (1) in the pure myths, considered as strictly cultural data; (2) in the wider mythologizing process which treats facts selectively or, by some exaggeration, gives them the dramatic power of fiction; (3) in historical perspective in general; (4) in the crowd-responses which, in so far as they condition the careers of our "heroes" and their after-fame, suggest the nature of crowd psychology in the American democracy.

To Mr. Wecter the myths seem always data in the study of crowd responses. They hardly ever acquire an elevation equal, in his mind, to the recital of facts established by historical research and set in historical perspective. Again and again he says, almost wistfully, things like this: "In the making of American legends the Puritan Fathers are often praised for contributions not very well deserved—such as religious liberalism and democracy in government—but slighted as pioneers both in State control of business and the quite different cult of idealizing the merchant prince." To Mr. Wecter myths are falsifications, exaggerations, distortions, which are interesting for the states of mind they reveal, but are otherwise a little regrettable. He is a brilliant social historian, and if it had been his announced purpose merely to study our great men, our various beloved and popular characters, in order to determine by this means our social and political preferences, there could be no objection to his view of myths. But his subject is American heroes, American hero-worship. In the study of that subject the myth is all-important; it is indeed a truth which may tell more than facts.

Probably Mr. Wecter has stretched the term *hero,* or used it metaphorically, all the while meaning really to say *great man, statesman, popular leader.* A more serious concern with the nature of myth itself might have strengthened his book considerably. With a better understanding of myth, Mr. Wecter might have improved his now inadequate chapter on the frontiersman. He might also have detected some of the curious ways in which the methods of historical research are used to rationalize historical myths, especially those of sectional origin. For example, the Lee of his book is "The Aristocrat as Hero"—a bookish creation, the product of recent biography, which has been engaged in rationalizing, by approved scholarly procedures, the "gentle" Lee of the New South myth; and this invented personage is emphatically not the *General* Lee to whom the unreconstructed Old South gave its fierce devotion.

In the case of Lee, as elsewhere, Mr. Wecter cites "myths" to illustrate the nature of the crowd's irrational "worship," but turns generally to "facts" in order to frame his own sober judgment of the hero's place and worth. He does not perceive, apparently, that "facts" can be used to rationalize a myth, no less than to explode it. The Parson Weemses of our day are often enough gentlemen who, like Mr. Wecter, have spent much time in the Huntington Library, and like him have consulted many authorities in person or by letter. One who reads his list of acknowledgments and finds the names of Thomas J. Wertenbaker, Carl Van Doren, Carl Sandburg, Ernest K. Lindley, H. L. Mencken, Howard Mumford Jones, and various others of that ilk, is entitled to wonder whether Mr. Wecter never knew that he was consulting some of the greatest partisans and slickest myth-makers of our day,

Part IV

THE SOUTH

⊁⊱

WHY THE MODERN SOUTH

HAS A GREAT LITERATURE

For a thematic text I ask you to consider a famous
passage from Vergil's second "Georgic":

> *Felix, qui potuit rerum cognoscere causas,*
> *Atque metus omnes et inexorabile fatum*
> *Subjecit pedibus strepitumque Acherontis avari.*
> *Fortunatus et ille, deos qui novit agrestes*
> *Panaque Silvanumque senem Nymphasque sorores.*
> *Illum non populi fasces, non purpura regum*
> *Flexit et infidos agitans discordia fratres,*
> *Aut conjurato descendens Dacus ab histro,*
> *Non res Romanae perituraque regna; neque ille*
> *Aut doluit miserans inopem aut invidit habenti.*
> *Quos rami fructus, quos ipsa volentia rura*
> *Sponte tulere sua, carpsit, nec ferrea jura*
> *Insanumque forum aut populi tabularia vidit.*

Vergil, like us lived at a time when republican institutions
had been undermined by those who were responsible for up-
holding them. Skepticism and materialism were destroying
religion. A New Deal, headed by a dictator on the make, was
pretending to restore the republic but was actually subverting
it. Foreign and civil war had produced economic and adminis-
trative chaos. The urban proletariat was being bribed into
complacency by a program of bread and circuses. Veterans of
the Roman armies were being subsidized. Tax burdens were
enormous. Armies of occupation had to be maintained in
various parts of the world, yet the threat of war in the direction of what is now Germany, the Balkans, and the Near East

remained continuous. Since these, Vergil's circumstances, were much like ours, I trust I may be pardoned if I offer a free modern paraphrase of Vergil's Latin rather than a literal translation:

> Happy (no doubt) is the man who believes that science has the answer to everything, and so thinks that he no longer need fear anything—such as hell, which must be a mere superstition, or even death itself.

> But blessed, too (if not happy), is the man who knows that the God of his fathers is still manifest in the fields, woods, and rivers. That man does not have to cater to the urban masses of New York and Detroit. He does not need to beg favors from Roosevelt or Truman. He has nothing to do with the jealous and traitorous schemes that split our parties in fratricidal strife. He doesn't spend his time worrying over where the Russians will strike next, or about Washington politics, or over whether the French or British cabinet will again have to resign. He may be one of the "have not's," but he doesn't envy the "have's." He just knows that country ham and fried apples are mighty good eating, especially when they come off your own land; and that "parity prices" don't have anything to do with their essential goodness. Knowledge of such things is his safeguard against the tediousness of bureaucrats, the madness of Washington, and statistics.

My answer to the question, "Why does the modern South have a great literature?" could easily hinge upon Vergil's deliberate contrast between two words, *felix* and *fortunatus*. To understand that, we must understand the two kinds of knowledge that Vergil associates with the intellectually "happy man" (*felix*) and the "blessed man" (*fortunatus*). But we cannot understand Vergil's meaning until we have examined our own condition of knowledge.

The man of our time who "knows the causes of things" is of course the scientist. We generally turn to the scientist for explanations of physical or social phenomena. We do not any longer ask a philosopher for explanations, and least of all a novelist or a poet—that is, if a public policy that will cost us money and trouble is to be based upon the answer. We live under the rule of scientific expertism. The President does not dare send a message to Congress, nor does Congress dare pass a law, without at least going through the motions of consulting scientific experts and bolstering up the "program" with an array of statistical information that they have compiled.

The Church itself—especially the Protestant church—no longer relies exclusively upon Scriptures and church doctrine. It still reads "lessons" from the Holy Scriptures as a part of its ritual, but the commentary upon the Scriptures avoids the Church Fathers and draws heavily upon social science. The Cole Lectures at Vanderbilt University, for example, were founded as religious lectures, to be delivered by clergymen. But in this, the seventy-fifth year of Vanderbilt University, those Cole lectures, offered under the auspices of the Vanderbilt School of Religion, were given by the famous white Russian sociologist Pitirim Sorokin. He was assisted by two or three prominent ministers who, if they are not as good sociologists as Sorokin, are just as sociological-minded.

So the official, the really valid answer to my question, "Why does the modern South have a great literature?" ought to come from modern science, which is supposed to know the answer to everything. I do not expect the physicist or chemist to deal with it, since as yet there does not seem to be a physics or chemistry of literature. The answer must come from the social scientist. Since literature is somehow or other related to the cultural condition of a people, I turn hopefully to the sociologist, for he makes it his business to deal with all cultural matters whatsoever.

My question contains two assumptions, which are implied in the terms "modern South" and "great literature." I hasten to explain that by "modern" I mean "contemporary" and perhaps a little more—in point of time, the South of the past thirty years, but also the South which in various ways seems consciously striving to be "modern." By "great literature" I mean "great" in the sense of being generally accepted by distinguished critics as of highest quality and most serious import.

One of the Southern writers thus accepted is William Faulkner of Mississippi. Suppose, then, I turn to sociology and ask whether it can account for the appearance in Mississippi, of all places, of William Faulkner, in the three decades between 1920 and 1950. My question has a corollary which I believe I am entitled to state: Can sociology also explain why William Faulkner, or some novelist of comparable stature, did not appear, during this period, somewhere north of the Ohio—say, in Massachusetts or Wisconsin?

For convenience, I shall seek my answer in the statistical tables assembled from various sources and approvingly published by Howard W. Odum and his associate, Harry Estill Moore, in a compendious book entitled *American Regionalism: a Cultural-Historical Approach to National Integration.* The authors are sociologists of unchallenged eminence. Their book is a synthesis of information gathered from many fields of inquiry over a long period. I assume that it is authoritative and reliable.

The focal point of my inquiry is the decade from 1920 to 1930, for if any cultural factors determined the performance of William Faulkner, they must have been the factors prevalent at about this time, when the new Southern literature was beginning to emerge. No figures are available in this book for the previous decade, but I believe we may safely assume that the decade from 1920–1930 is good enough for our purpose, since that was William Faulkner's formative period.

Now in the formative period of William Faulkner—and, if you wish, of his contemporaries—what cultural factors, exactly, were at work in the Southern scene?

I am very sorry to have to report to you that during William Faulkner's formative period the cultural factors were extremely forbidding in the State of Mississippi. I can hardly see how Mr. Faulkner survived, much less wrote novels. On the evidence of Mr. Odum's tables, culture was at a very low ebb in Mississippi—so low that, if I had only these tables to depend upon, I would confidently assert, as a devoted follower of sociology, that a William Faulkner in Mississippi would be a theoretical impossibility; and that, if he emerged at all, he would have to originate in, say, Massachusetts, where the cultural factors were favorable to literary interests.

Here is the picture. In Mississippi, in 1920, the per capita wealth, as estimated by bank resources, was under $250, and Mississippi, in this respect, was in the lowest bracket in the nation. In Massachusetts, on the other hand, which was in the highest bracket, the per capita wealth by the same measurement was $1,000 and up.

In this decade, too, Mississippi had a very small urban population. In 1930 it was less than 20 per cent despite a small recent increase. Mississippi was almost entirely rural, while Massachusetts was just the other way—90 per cent urban. Most of the South was nearly as rural as Mississippi. The point is important. It has often been thought that cities foster the literary arts, while the country does not. Lack of cities has frequently been assigned as the reason for the lack of a flourishing Southern literature.

As to "plane of living" (Mr. Odum's term) Mississippi by 1930 was about as low as a state can get. "Plane of living" in Mr. Odum's terminology refers to a composite figure calculated from per capita income, tax returns, residence telephones, ownership of radios, and the like. Well, Mississippi by this standard was on a plane of living described as 15 to 40 per cent of the national average—but much nearer to 15 than to 40 per cent. It was in the low bracket. In comparison, Massachusetts was in the high bracket, 70 per cent and above.

Mississippi was in the lowest bracket in nearly everything as compared with Massachusetts and most of the Northern, Midwestern, and Western states. In ownership of automobiles per farm, it was 26.5 per cent as compared with Massachusetts' 61.9 per cent. In average value of farms Mississippi was in the lowest bracket, except for the Delta, which was in the next to the lowest bracket. In "farms with water piped into the house" Mississippi offered a pitiful 5 per cent in comparison with Massachusetts' grand 79 per cent. Mississippi farmhouses were almost without plumbing fixtures. Mississippi spent only a lean seven and a fraction cents per capita for libraries, the lowest expenditure in the nation, while Massachusetts, home of the Pilgrim Fathers and of Harvard University, spent $1.18 per capita, the highest in the nation. Mississippi was in the lowest bracket, too, in expenditures for public education. Only Georgia was lower. And Massachusetts in this respect was of course very high, though not quite as high as New York.

Mr. Odum offers no tables in this book as to religious belief, but we all know that Mississippians in the 1920's were mostly conservative, true-believing Christians rather Fundamentalist in tendency. On the other hand Massachusetts, except for its Catholic population, would certainly be rather heavily liberal, progressive, skeptical, as to religion, and perhaps even atheistical. If liberalism in religion is an index of cultural welfare —and it is often so regarded—then Massachusetts during this period would again be in a very high bracket, despite its Catholic Irish and its Italians, and Mississippi would be rated very low by modern standards.

We need not continue with Mr. Odum's interesting tables. By every cultural standard that the sociologist knows how to devise, Mississippi rates low in the national scale during William Faulkner's formative period. The only bracket in which it would stand high would be in ratio of farm tenancy to population. Its proportion of farm tenants would be very high —but that fact would put it low in Mr. Odum's cultural ratings, for he would take it to indicate a bad economic condition and hence a bad cultural condition.

So it would go for all the Southern states at the time of the emergence of the new Southern literature. All would rank low by the sociologist's measurements. The highest-ranking one would be North Carolina, which has long been heavily industrialized and is reputed to be fanatically liberal, and which, interestingly enough, has not contributed nearly as profusely to the new Southern literature as have Mississippi and other Southern states.

But we are perfectly familiar with the picture of the South that has been built up during the past three decades. It has been dinned into us—and into the nation—through newspapers, magazines, books, moving pictures, radio broadcasts, political speeches, and quasi-religious preachments that we are a backward area in an otherwise progressive nation. We have lacked everything, it seems, that makes Massachusetts and Wisconsin great: educational facilities, factories, libraries, hospitals, laboratories, art museums, theaters, labor unions, publishing houses, accumulations of wealth, high dams, electric power, agricultural machinery, birth control. Some of these material deficiencies have been corrected during recent years, but the South is still "backward" in most of the categories named. "Backward," however, is one of the mildest terms used to describe us. In more common use are such terms as "bigoted," "intolerant," "reactionary," "ignorant," "uncivilized." We have been reproached for being lynchers and Ku-Kluxers; for living in the past rather than in the future; for passing anti-evolution laws and electing to office Huey Long, Bilbo, Talmadge.

Nevertheless, we have produced William Faulkner, and the literary intellectuals of Harvard University are reading Faulkner, studying Faulkner, writing essays and books about Faulkner. To find a novelist comparable to Faulkner in all the Northeast they have to go to more backward times and read Henry James.

Let us look at some of the queer conjunctions of events that ought to be illuminated by the sociologists.

In 1925 the Dayton trial took place in Tennessee. In the light of the famous Monkey Law, Tennessee was immediately judged to be one of the most notorious spots of cultural depravity in the whole world. But in those same years the Fugitive group of poets emerged in Tennessee and soon, broadening their activities, became the Southern Agrarians. The same cultural factors that produced the so-called Monkey Law must surely have operated upon the Fugitive-Agrarian writers. Did this condition of cultural depravity produce them? At any rate, the influence of this group now seems to have become so pervasive, even in the civilized North, that the defenders of Northern civilization have been thrown into a virtual panic. A flood of articles, many of them denunciatory, has suddenly appeared in the literary magazines. The most hysterical of all, written by Robert Hillyer, former professor of poetry at Harvard, though primarily directed at Pound and Eliot, wildly accused Allen Tate, Robert Penn Warren, and others of this group of organizing a kind of conspiracy to use the prestige of the national government in order to advance their "idiom." * This foolish charge might be interpreted to mean that Mr. Hillyer belatedly waked up to the fact that his own folks in the North liked the writings of the uncivilized Southerners better than they liked the writings of Mr. Hillyer and his party. Naturally, that was upsetting to a Harvard man.

But we do not have to stay at the high level of symbolist fiction, modern poetry, and the new criticism to get comparative examples. How did it happen that the State of Georgia, a very backward state, which has distressed the liberals by steadfastly keeping the Talmadge regime in power, also produced Margaret Mitchell, whose *Gone With the Wind,* as a book and as a movie, has won and kept the attention of the whole world?

How does it happen that Kentucky, the home of feudists, night riders, and julep-sipping colonels, produced that marvelous phenomenon, Jesse Stuart? How does it happen that that same Kentucky, with cultural factors of very low grade by Mr. Odum's indexes, produced Robert Penn Warren,

* Robert Hillyer, "Treason's Strange Fruit," *Saturday Review of Literature,* June 11, 1949.

whose most recent novel has shaken the seats of the mighty and, incidentally, won just about every award that it is possible for a novel or a movie to win?

Examples might be multiplied indefinitely. I must now strive to answer the original question—in scientific terms if possible; in other terms if science fails.

The cultural factors described by Mr. Odum either had a causal influence on William Faulkner or they did not.

If they did have a causal influence, we must, under the rigorous impulsion of sociology, reach an astonishing conclusion: namely, that the way for a society to produce a William Faulkner is to have him born in a thoroughly backward state like Mississippi, of a chivalrously inclined, feudal-minded, landed Southern family that was ruined by the Civil War and later dipped, not very successfully, into modern business. In other words, a prevalence of rural society, devoted to cotton-growing, afflicted by sharecropping, rather poverty-stricken, conservative in religion and politics, prone to love the past rather than the future, chockful of all the prejudices and customs of the South—that is what it takes to produce a William Faulkner.

Contrarily, a prevalence of material progress, great wealth, modern institutions such as libraries and art museums, factories, industrial gimcracks, liberalism, science, political radicalism—that is the way not to produce a William Faulkner. If it were otherwise, Massachusetts and Wisconsin by this time would have produced not one but a couple of dozen William Faulkners.

This conclusion may be discomforting to all who argue that material improvements, liberalism, industrialism, science, and so on are what Mississippi and the South need to attain a high culture. If the appearance of a master artist is an indication of a high culture, they are wrong. Our sociological study clearly indicates either that material improvements, liberalism, industrialism of the order and scale prevalent in Massachusetts are not necessary to produce a master artist;

or else—horrible thought—that these factors have a negative, blighting effect, and prevent his appearance. And without master artists, especially literary artists, how can you have a high culture? I am not the one who proposes that test of a high culture. Our friends of the North have insisted upon it. The British, the French, the Italians, the Germans for centuries have held that view. For a hundred years, too, it has been said, over and over, that that test, above all, was the test the South failed to pass.

The critics of the South might perhaps feel more comfortable if they could argue that Mr. Faulkner's writings are in some sense a reaction against the backwardness of his Southern origin and situation. But there is not a solitary hint of such a reaction against backwardness in his novels and stories. Whatever Mr. Faulkner may be against, he is not in his novels against the so-called backwardness of the South. In his novels he has not advocated or even implied an advocacy of any social reform. He does not rush around issuing pronouncements and indictments. He does not join propagandist movements.* He doesn't even write literary criticism.

All the same he is as completely Southern as Shakespeare is completely English. So, too, in their various ways are his Southern contemporaries whose works the nation has been reading. They, too, have emerged from backward Southern states in which the cultural factors, by Mr. Odum's ratings, were most forbidding. We must then conclude that the way to produce a John Ransom, an Allen Tate, a Robert Penn Warren, a Julia Peterkin, a Stark Young, a Eudora Welty, a Thomas Wolfe, a Jesse Stuart, an Elizabeth Roberts, is to have them be born and grow up in a backward Southern community that loves everything that Massachusetts con-

---

* True in 1950. But *not* true of the post–Nobel Prize Faulkner. In this essay I am taking Faulkner at the current estimate of 1950 and the years just previous. I offer no estimate of my own but merely use Faulkner as an example. Here I will add that Faulkner the storyteller is a man to take seriously. As a commentator on public affairs Faulkner is ignorant, gullible, and sophomoric.

demns and lacks nearly everything that Massachusetts deems admirable and necessary. Let us concede that some of the Southern writers have been more openly sensitive to Northern criticism of the South than Mr. Faulkner has been and that the sensitivity has affected their writing. But the literature of social protest, represented in the North by such men as Theodore Dreiser, Sinclair Lewis, John Dos Passos, is so uncommon among the distinguished Southern writers of our day as to be hardly worth comment. At its substantial best— the new literature of the South is not a literature of protest but a literature of acceptance which renders its material as objectively and seriously as any great literature has ever done. It also displays a sense of form, a vitality, a grace, a power, and often a finality of treatment that are remarkably scarce in American literature elsewhere.

But suppose we take the other horn of the dilemma. Suppose the cultural factors described by Mr. Odum did not operate in a causal way upon Mr. William Faulkner and his contemporaries. Where are we, in that case?

In that case, I should say, we are nowhere as social scientists. The social scientist must necessarily hold that human phenomena result from causal factors which may be broadly described as heredity and environment. At present he tends to favor environment over heredity, because heredity inevitably gets you into matters of race, and under present circumstances the social scientist does not enjoy discussing race and heredity together. At any rate, unless the social scientist can prove that cultural factors, mostly environmental, do determine human phenomena, his statistics have no more value than crossword puzzles, and he is not entitled to give expert advice on our social arrangements. If the sociologist admits that, because of its very "backwardness," the South produced a William Faulkner, he is in an uncomfortable plight, because that is something he didn't intend to prove. If he admits, on the other hand, that William Faulkner developed regardless of the backwardness or even in spite of it, he is still in a painful plight, because he must then admit that the cultural factors affect some people but not others, especially not high-class literary artists like William Faulkner—which is a very damaging admission.

Or else he must break down and say that, perhaps, after all, he has not yet been inclusive enough. There must be some cultural factors that he left out; but if he can get a large financial subsidy from the Social Science Research Council, he will assign a squad of graduate students to the job, and start punching cards and running the calculating machines, and in a few more years he will have some more indexes to round out the picture. . . .

But I believe we have reached the point where we can dispense with his services. Let us turn back to Vergil, who knew a lot about people and society, as all great artists must.

Vergil's "happy man" who "knows the causes of things" is really a philosopher, not in any way like our modern experimental scientist. His knowledge, which includes a knowledge of science, results from a very lofty intellectual effort that lifts him far above human passions and fears. This knowledge is a sublime, most admirable attainment, and in Vergil's day it was not in conflict with poetry. In fact, the passage under discussion is thought to be a tribute to the Roman poet Lucretius, whose *De Rerum Natura* is perhaps the only completely successful "scientific epic" ever written. The happiness associated with this knowledge, however, must be considered a state of intellectual being so very sublime and abstract that few could ever attain it. In our day, it would be almost impossible for a modern experimental scientist to attain it, since he is a specialist and cannot in one operation combine the functions of philosopher, scientist, and poet. Whatever happiness the modern scientist attains is a negative rather than a positive state. His knowledge does not so much exalt him as it dissociates him, because it is exclusive and special rather than inclusive and general. This characteristic has made modern science the enemy rather than the friend of poetry and other literary arts. And any literature that accepts modern scientific knowledge as being an ultimate and complete knowledge is certain to be an incomplete, distorted literature.

But there is another kind of knowledge, which makes men "blessed"—for so I translate Vergil's *fortunatus*. It is the knowledge enjoyed by Vergil's countryman. In the context of the passage I have read, Vergil says that if he cannot have the high philosophic knowledge that makes men "happy" (*felix*) he would next choose the knowledge that makes men "blessed" (*fortunatus*). This is a stage lower than the very highest knowledge, but it is very admirable and desirable, and it, too, is a high form of knowledge. It rests upon traditional religion—or, in Vergil's exact language, "the rustic gods, Pan and old Silvanus, and the sister Nymphs," which I have freely translated "the God of his fathers." It is a knowledge that possesses the heart rather than a knowledge achieved merely by the head—a knowledge that pervades the entire being, as the grace of God pervades the heart and soul. In the phrase of Allen Tate's famous poem "Ode to the Confederate Dead," it is "knowledge carried to the heart." Negatively, it relieves the individual from the domination of the mob, the insolence of rulers, the strife of jealous factions, the horrible commotion of foreign wars and domestic politics, the vice of envy, the fear of poverty. Positively, it establishes the blessed man in a position where economic use, enjoyment, understanding, and religious reverence are not separated but are fused in one.

The picture in Vergil is idealized, of course. Nevertheless, that is the kind of knowledge that the South has faithfully cultivated throughout its history. Devotion to such knowledge, knowledge "carried to the heart," is the dominant characteristic of Southern society. Through the influence of Thomas Jefferson and his great contemporaries, it has been woven into our political institutions.

Devotion to this knowledge, I would contend, is the great,

all-pervasive "cultural factor" for which the sociologists have
neglected to provide data. Therefore they cannot account for
William Faulkner and other writers, and their diagnosis of
Southern society is untrustworthy.

Furthermore, in viewing Southern society as "backward,"
they make a false and misleading assumption. In number and
size of cities, in number of factories, in number of farmhouses
with modern plumbing, the South may be "backward" as
compared with a national average calculated from such data.
That does not mean that Mississippi or any other state is, for
that reason, socially, culturally, intellectually backward. In
terms of the standard I have proposed, I can easily argue the
contrary and assert that Southern society in the 1920's and
1930's was the most "advanced" in the United States. If "in-
dexed" according to the quality and consistency of its literary
performance, it would be indeed very advanced.

But I prefer to describe the South of the past three decades
as, on the whole, a traditional society which had arrived at a
moment of self-consciousness favorable to the production of
great literary works. A traditional society is a society that is
stable, religious, more rural than urban, and politically conservative. Family, blood-kinship, clanship, folk-ways, custom,
community, in such a society, supply the needs that in a nontraditional or progressive society are supplied at great cost by
artificial devices like training schools and government agencies. A traditional society can absorb modern improvements
up to a certain point without losing its character. If modernism enters to the point where the society is thrown a little out
of balance but not yet completely off balance, the moment of
self-consciousness arrives. Then a process begins that at first
is enormously stimulating, but that, if it continues unchecked,
may prove debilitating and destructive in the end.

Greece in the fifth century B.C., Rome of the late republic,
Italy in Dante's time, England in the sixteenth century, all
give us examples of traditional societies invaded by changes

that threw them slightly out of balance without at first achieving cultural destruction. The invasion seems always to force
certain individuals into an examination of their total inheritance that perhaps they would not otherwise have undertaken.
They begin to compose literary works in which the whole
metaphysic of the society suddenly takes dramatic or poetic
or fictional form. Their glance is always retrospective, but
their point of view is always thoroughly contemporary. Thus
Sophocles, in his *Oedipos Tyrannos*, looks back at an ancient
Greek myth, but he dramatizes it from the point of view of a
fifth-century Athenian who may conceivably distrust the leadership of Pericles. This is what I mean by the moment of self-
consciousness. It is the moment when a writer awakes to realize
what he and his people truly are, in comparison with what they
are being urged to become.

Such a writer is William Faulkner, and such are many of
his Southern contemporaries. In sixteenth-century England
there was also a kind of William Faulkner—a country boy
from the insignificant village of Stratford, handicapped from
the beginning by his ridiculous countrified name, William
Shakespeare. That he also had a country accent, not unlike
a Southern accent, seems apparent from what the printers
have left of his original spelling. He did not have a college
education. In the words of his rival and friend, Ben Jonson,
he had small Latin and less Greek. But whatever new learning he needed he readily acquired, perhaps in the very process
of composing poems and plays. And all the time he had—as
Ben Johnson never did—that second kind of knowledge that
Vergil praises, that knowledge "carried to the heart," which
London and university education could not give, but which
he inherited by natural right through Stratford. Ben Jonson,
a city boy, schooled by a famous master, William Camden,
could never get out from under the weight of his learning.
Jonson was always more the critic than the poet, more the
adapter and copyist than the original dramatist. But Will

Shakespeare, the country boy from a backward region, became one of the world's incomparable originals. London alone could never have produced him.

Prior to the Civil War the entire United States, in greater or less degree, was a traditional society. But the decision of the North to force war upon the Confederacy and the subsequent victory of the Northern armies threw the traditional society of the North into a state of disequilibrium so profound and so rapid in its development that Northern society has never recovered from the shock. The moment of self-consciousness that I have described could therefore not be utilized except by scattered individuals like Henry James, who had to flee to Europe to get his bearings. The Northern writer had scant opportunity to consult the knowledge in the heart that was his original right. The Northern triumph over the South meant the unchallenged rule in the North of science, industrialism, progressivism, humanitarianism. For Northern writers this rule was disastrous, since it meant that the kind of knowledge chiefly recommended to them was the kind that accomplishes material results—the limited, special knowledge of the scientist and technologist. The result has been that the works of the great Northern writers tend to be all head and no heart. Or else they bear the marks of a lamentable conflict between head and heart. Out of the schism between head and heart arises the literature of realism, of protest, of social criticism. Or else a literature all too evidently determined to be artistic, no matter whether the art has any real subject matter to exhibit.

Among Northern writers, therefore, a rich subject matter and a sense of form rarely go together. Sinclair Lewis has an excellent subject matter, but as to form he is still a cub reporter with a good memory, hacking out copy to catch the two-o'clock edition. Dreiser impresses us with the mass of his enormous case histories, but they are written in laborious prose and have apparently been organized with a meat saw and a butcher knife. On the other hand, Thornton Wilder has a beautiful, though somewhat precious, prose style, but he has no subject matter for the prose to use. One notable instance of a contemporary Northern writer in whom subject and form support each other perfectly is the poet Robert Frost; but Robert Frost rejects the orthodox modern knowledge of the progressive North and adheres to rural New England, which preserves the remnants of its old, traditional society. Beyond these selected examples, the North shows a hodgepodge of experimentalists, propagandists, plausible but empty Book-of-the-Month Club specials, a vast number of scholars and critics, but very few writers of first rank who are not injured by the fearful imbalance of Northern civilization. The Northern writer cannot trust the knowledge in his heart, even when he has it, because he has allowed his civilization to discredit that knowledge. There are too many people looking over his shoulder as he writes—too many college professors, social welfare workers, atomic scientists, pressure groups, librarians, editors of slick magazines, impatient publishers, and seductive subsidizers.

In the South this destructive process has been slow to take hold. Defeated and ravaged in war, the South put up fierce underground resistance to the Reconstruction and thus emerged at the turn of the century, poor in money and what money will buy, but rich in what money can never buy, in what no science can provide, for the South was still a traditional society, injured but very much alive, and by this time wise and experienced in ways of staying alive. The advocates of a New South of industrialism and mass education, though eloquent and powerful, and heavily backed by Northern money, were not able to alter the traditional South very much. So it was not until the latter part of the Roosevelt administration that the South began to receive the full shock of modernism.

What the future offers, I do not know. In the immediate past it seems obvious that Southern writers have not generally been confused by the division between head and heart that is the great problem of Northern writers. The case of Thomas Wolfe offers an interesting exception to the general rule. From traditional sources Thomas Wolfe inherited a remarkably rich subject matter, but he was utterly incapable of reducing it to coherent form and without the aid of his editor, Maxwell Perkins, might never have been able to publish even the somewhat formless books that he did publish. I suggest that his trouble was that he had been taught to misunderstand with his head what he understood with his heart. Thomas Wolfe had a divided sensibility which very likely resulted from his education at Mr. Howard Odum's citadel, the progressive University of North Carolina, and from his subsequent unfortunate experience at Harvard.

But most of our abler Southern writers, unlike Thomas Wolfe, seem to be born in possession of an endless store of subject matter and also a sense of the form that belongs to the subject matter. I do not know how to explain this except by saying that the person who is born of a traditional society, if he is not corrupted, will act as a whole person in all his acts, including his literary acts. The truth of experience that fills his emotional being is not at war with the truth of his intellectual judgments, but the two, as he writes, are one. His apprehension of his subject matter, which is intuitive and comes from "knowledge carried to the heart," moves hand in hand with his composition, which derives from his intellectual judgment, his sense of fitness and order. Thus an act as cold-blooded as deliberate literary composition must be is redeemed and assisted by the warm-blooded knowledge of the heart. It is natural for a Southern writer to compose that way, as it is natural for him to ride a horse with his whole heart as well as with his controlling intelligence.

It is also natural for him to see men in their total capacity as persons and to see things in all their rich particularity as things and to understand that the relationships between persons and persons, and between persons and things are more complex and unpredictable than any scientific textbook invites one to think. He needs no literary critic to tell him that, for his traditional society has already taught him to look at the world in such a way. It has also impressed upon him that the world is both good and evil. Toward nature, toward his fellow creatures, toward the historic past, he has learned to exercise that piety which Mr. Richard Weaver, in his book *Ideas Have Consequences* has praised as the virtue most needed in the modern world.

Thus it is that in the moment of self-consciousness the Southern writer is able to bring to bear, not only his personal view, but also the total metaphysic of his society. He is therefore unlikely to indulge in the exaggerations and oversimplifications that are the mark of a divided sensibility. For him the people in the bend of the creek are not only sharecroppers representing a certain economic function. They are complete persons with significant personal histories. In fact, they are Joe and Emma, who used to work on old man Brown's place but left him for reasons well known. The banker is not merely a banker. He is Mr. Jim, whose wife's mother was somebody's grandmother's double first cousin.

The difference between Southern and Northern writers is the difference it would make if Sinclair Lewis instead of Robert Penn Warren had written *All the King's Men*. In Sinclair Lewis' hands that same material would take on the exaggeration and oversimplification that we are familiar with in Mr. Lewis' novels. Willie Stark would be the caricature of a demagogue—he would be Babbitt recast as a politician. Hunks of satirical realism would be relieved by chunks of humor in the style of the sports page. Mr. Lewis could not achieve the intricate complexity of Mr. Warren's design, in which every seeming elaboration proves in the end to be, not an elaboration after all, but a supporting element of the grand scheme. Nor could Mr. Lewis achieve the ethical meaning of Mr. Warren's narrative. Mr. Lewis cannot do such things because he cannot use the knowledge of the heart, if he has it. He cannot use it because he belongs to an antitraditional society

which gives its allegiance to a different sort of knowledge.
Perhaps Mr. Lewis is in rebellion against that society; but in
his novel about Willie Stark we would never be able to discover just why Willie Stark misbehaves. Willie Stark would
of course misbehave in Sinclair Lewis' novel, but it would be
only misbehavior, not evil behavior, not sin. For Sinclair
Lewis, as for most Northern writers, evil and sin were abol-
ished by Grant's victory over Lee at Appomattox, since which
time the North has proceeded on the assumption that there
is no defect or irregularity in human nature and human affairs
that cannot be remedied by the application of money, science,
and socialistic legislation. Therefore, in reading Mr. Lewis'
novel about Willie Stark we would inevitably feel that there
was no defect in Willie Stark that could not be remedied by a
visit to a psychoanalyst or an amendment to the United States
Constitution. But it is quite different in the novel that Mr.
Warren has written about Willie Stark. We are there confronted with the ancient problem of evil and its manifestations. We must contemplate the imperfection of man, for
whatever it is worth of good and bad. For Willie Stark, for
the Compsons of Faulkner's novels, for the characters bad or
good of most serious Southern novels, there is no remedy in
law or sociology, and no reward but the reward of virtue and
the hope of heaven.

The point of this discourse is a difficult one. I hope, in seeking to bring it to your attention, that I have not overstated
it. At any rate it is the point I would be most anxious to make
at this time before any group of Southern writers.

In summation I would say: study your art, all you can. It
is indispensable, and no opportunity should be lost to master
it. But it is not really the gravest problem, since whatever can
be studied can surely be learned. The gravest problem is how
and where to apply the art, once it is learned. No textbook, no
school, no writers' conference can solve that problem for you.
You only can solve it. To solve it you must become aware of
the difference between what you think you know, and what

you really know. The latter, what you really know, in your bones as much as in your brain, is what I mean by "knowledge carried to the heart." Only that will lead you to your real subject and release you from the false knowledge that brings imitation, subservience, and distortion.

For you as Southern writers that great problem—the problem of discovering your real subject—is easier to solve than if you were Northern writers. But even for Southern writers it is more difficult than it was thirty years ago. The regime of false knowledge has invaded us and threatens still heavier invasions. Therefore, as writers, we have not only a private interest to defend but also a public duty to perform. What that duty is I surely do not need to say, this morning in the State of Mississippi, which in 1948 cast its electoral vote for Thurmond and Wright. I trust you will understand that I have been attempting to define not only a principle of literature but also a principle of life. Out of the knowledge carried to the heart let us defend it, as the true source of virtue and liberty.

IN JUSTICE TO SO FINE A COUNTRY

ONCE, YEARS AGO, a Southern historian beckoned me aside and led me to a room some distance from his own office. "Look!" he said. There was exultation in his voice and much grim purpose in his exultation. An enormous machine occupied about half the room, and a graduate assistant was feeding punch cards into it. With inhuman noise and precision, the machine was sorting the cards. The historian closed the door upon the noise and, with a kind of Stonewall Jackson glint in his eye, explained. Documentation, he said—*mere* documentation—would never convince the North. Mere argument was futile. But if he could say, in a footnote to his forthcoming publication, that the figures in his statistical tables had been achieved by the assistance of a card-sorting machine (he would carefully cite the machine's name and model), then the Yankees might hearken to both his documentation and his argument. The machine, a guarantee of his "objectivity," would remove his work from the area of suspicion that a study originating in the South would normally occupy.

Mr. Jay B. Hubbell, in his monumental new work, *The South In American Literature,* makes no citation to a machine, and, indeed, is praiseworthily spare as to footnotes. He is optimistic, however—and perhaps with good reason—in his assumption that an objective, scholarly history of Southern literature can at long last be achieved and can be accepted on its objective merits. "The best living Northern and Southern historians are now so nearly one in their interpretation of the place of the South in American history," he writes in his Foreword, "that it is often difficult, by internal evidence, to distinguish the Northern historian from the Southerner."

Then he adds, perhaps with some mixture of apprehension and hope: "That unfortunately is not quite the case in American literary history. And yet it seems to me, today, three-quarters of a century after the end of Reconstruction, it should be possible for a scholar who is a native of the South but has lived and taught in the North and West to view the writers of the South from a national point of view." For *national* read *objective,* and you have the key to Mr. Hubbell's apprehension, which is inescapable under the circumstances. Mr. Hubbell knows, as every Southerner does, that "objectivity" has not generally been conceded to the Southerner unless, in his judgment of things Southern, he accepts and proclaims the Northern (i.e., "national") interpretation of Southern things. And Mr. Hubbell as literary historian has not the slightest intention of yielding in that direction except as the said Northern (i.e., "national") interpretation can be "objectively" established.

Old experience as well as the impact of recent events would prompt me to be somewhat less hopeful than Mr. Hubbell apparently is about the chances of his fine book's being accepted as something belonging to "the national point of view." Yet certainly he has achieved his aim with great effectiveness. *The South In American Literature* is a triumph of the scholarly-historical approach to the intricate problem of Southern literary history. And since a method is nothing without a master hand to wield it, the book is also a triumph for the distinguished Professor Emeritus of English at Duke University, who now crowns long years of devotion to teaching and research with a massive and conclusive work that scholars and critics alike can hardly fail to admire and treasure. It is the first book of large scope and high quality ever to be published on the subject. It has forerunners, but no true predecessors. Montrose J. Moses' work of nearly half a century ago is hardly to be compared with it. And though Parrington, in 1927, did much to establish a climate of opinion hospitable to the claims of Southern literature, his work is colored by a

narrow social thesis and is fragmentary and at many points
poorly informed or misinformed. Aside from these two works,
Southern literature until now has been something to be
gathered at hazard from scattered, multifarious, and often
partisan sources—something discoverable, to be sure, in regular histories of American literature, yet squeezed almost into
the proportions of mere crack-filler by the devout necessity of
allowing large space to Emerson, Lowell, Longfellow, Whittier, and other deities and demigods of the "national point
of view"; or else something too much enlarged upon by defensive and overenthusiastic Southern partisans—partisans
to whom Mr. Hubbell shows no more favor than he does to
their Northern counterparts.

Coming thus before us, a just, definitive, and thoroughly
matured accomplishment, *The South In American Literature*
will not very soon be paralleled. Undoubtedly it will be sup-
plemented and extended, as it should be in time, to cover the
literature of the twentieth-century South, to which Mr. Hubbell, by way of epilogue, devotes only a brief but interesting
discussion. It is surely enough achievement, indeed all that
could be asked of one scholar, to bring order out of disorder
in this history of pre-twentieth-century Southern literature.
Only one adjective seems adequate to describe it, and that is
an adjective seldom applied to the publications of research
scholars. I would call it a noble work. And when I say that
both the South and the nation owe Mr. Hubbell a very great
debt, I mean the words both as an expression of plain truth
and of warmth of feeling. Mr. Hubbell might have elected an
easier, safer subject and stood in high honor. That he chose to
give twenty years to the perilous path marks him as no less
than heroic. I hope we may take his choice and its result as
augury of times changing for the better.

It would be hard for me to imagine any just complaint
being made against *The South In American Literature* by
scholars in general, though there may be quibbles and cor-
rections bearing on minor details. A possible complaint by

literary critics may, however, arise. A literary critic (one may anticipate) preoccupied with literary excellence as a great determining principle, may find no virtue in Mr. Hubbell's inclusiveness. What gain is there, this critic may ask, in exhuming the remains of writers of meager literary value—say, Beverley Tucker, William Wirt, John Esten Cooke—or of the subliterary Augusta Evans Wilson? Or, if the critic takes the extreme position frequently attributed to the New Criticism, he may even question the validity of Mr. Hubbell's historical approach to the undeniably major authors.

Mr. Hubbell's answer is, to choose a phrase, that "the pattern of literary culture in the Southern states" has its importance. My answer is that while, in his insistence upon excellence, the critic seems to take a sound and impregnable position, it does not seem to follow that, because Poe was a greater poet than Timrod, the latter should be dismissed from examination; or that, because the South produced no Dante, we should forget all about Edward Coote Pinkney; or that, because John Esten Cooke is no Thomas Hardy, I should therefore throw away my cherished copy of *Surry of Eagle's Nest*. Furthermore, a criticism that essays entirely to exclude historical circumstance weakens to that extent its own avowed claim for the supremacy of art as a "form of knowledge" and thus exposes itself to the risk of degenerating into mere aestheticism. Once historical circumstance enters art— and it always does, despite claims to the contrary—it becomes an organic part of that "knowledge" which the critic claims for literary art. The relevance or irrelevance of the historical factor is then to be determined from the particular instance. If the critic accepts Dante's exile from Florence as a historical fact relevant to a discussion of *The Divine Comedy,* he can hardly, with consistency, deplore as irrelevant a biographical inquiry into the facts of Poe's famous "dissociation."

As literary historian Mr. Hubbell must at any rate assume the relevance of historical circumstance. The literary critic is under no compulsion to read the book, but I think he will ignore it at his peril. More than a hundred authors, major and minor, are treated in the 879 pages of Mr. Hubbell's historical discussion. The bibliographies—indispensable to scholars and teachers—occupy another 80 pages. Each of the six grand divisions begins with chapters, executed with admirable succinctness and clarity, that deal with historical background, the state of education, books, reading, and similar topics. Other chapters, interspersed among the material devoted to authors, deal with phenomena related in one way or another to literary culture. Many of these, correcting as they do the stereotyped and often wholly false conceptions of Southern life, will be revelations to the uninformed and will astound many persons who have considered themselves quite well-informed. Mr. Hubbell's chapters on *The Virginia Gazette* and *The South Carolina Gazette,* for example, may be surprising even to Southerners; and incidentally they support Mr. Hubbell's claim for the literary importance of Colonial newspapers. Mr. Hubbell is greatly to be thanked, also, for carefully working over the myth—popularized by Mark Twain, in ignorance and malice—of the influence of Walter Scott upon the "chivalrous" tendencies of the South. He dispels the myth—and dryly asks why the popularity of Scott in England, France, Germany, and elsewhere did not beget "chivalrous" tendencies in other societies. The conditions of authorship come into frequent consideration—especially the relationship between Southern author and Northern publisher. And so, most illuminatingly, does the question of libraries, public and private—including the libraries built up by the literary (or debating) societies, which often numbered more volumes than the libraries of their parent colleges.

These chapters of more or less straight history give the book a rich perspective and, by establishing the variety and complexity of the Southern scene, correct the oversimplified interpretations under which for many generations the South has groaned—yet done little but groan. The pattern of variety is reinforced in the discussion of individual authors, in which

Mr. Hubbell rather deliberately maintains a matter-of-fact narrative procedure. Generally he begins with a skillfully handled array of biographical material, which blends easily into a development of the author's literary career and includes a judicious "placement" of his work, whether with reference to contemporary issues and modes or to some more general pattern. Mr. Hubbell gives much space to biographical detail for a very good reason. "The historian can assume on the part of his readers some knowledge of Irving or Lowell; he cannot when he is writing about William Wirt or Hugh Swinton Legaré." For a similar reason, Mr. Hubbell is chary of criticism; his task is mainly historical and expository. He avoids the temptation to enlarge upon the minor authors. Thus William Dawson, colonial Virginian and gentleman-poet, gets three paragraphs, followed by a brief sample of his not very impressive verse. But George Tucker (1775–1861)—"one of the best and one of the least-known Southern writers of his time"—is redeemed from neglect in an interesting twelve-page chapter. Major authors, of course, receive extended consideration. And Mr. Hubbell's prose, always lucid and straightforward, is on the whole an excellent vehicle for his large task. He avoids flourishes. Some of the dryness commonly attributed to scholars he may have, but none of the characterless abstraction that is their frequent vice. In the long tale of Southern literature and the varied life from which it stems—a tale so often animated by tense issues and darkened by frustration and misunderstanding—it is a relief not to be smothered by the lush pontifications of a Van Wyck Brooks or to have to stay on guard against the seductions of Parrington's sometimes deceptive rhetoric. To let the subject speak for itself is the best kind of magnificence. That is what Mr. Hubbell achieves.

To call *The South In American Literature* a triumph of historical scholarship is to say also, in some measure, that it is, within its limits, a triumph of the graduate school method —a method often abused and its abuses rightfully deplored. The modern graduate school, with its seasoned researchists,

its aspiring candidates for the higher degrees, its endowed library and its special collections of rare books and manuscripts,
is as new a feature of Southern life as the hydroelectric dams
and four-lane divided highways to which it is in principle
anthithetical. Without the resources and organized activity
of the Duke University Graduate School and similar institutions, Mr. Hubbell's work could hardly have attained its present degree of accuracy and completeness; and perhaps it could
not have been accomplished by any one author. Inadequate
treatment of Southern writers by Northern historians, Mr.
Hubbell says, has often been due to the difficulty of finding
materials—a difficulty now at least partly surmounted. Mr.
Hubbell's bibliography abounds in citations to theses, published and unpublished, originating at Duke or other Southern universities, and to articles and distinguished books that
owe much to the discipline and resources of the Southern
graduate schools. The volume, as Mr. Hubbell readily acknowledges, is thus to some degree a distillation of a concerted
effort that has gone on, with rich results, for the past twenty-
five years or more. The master hand, nevertheless, is Mr.
Hubbell's, and his historical summation of Southern literature now easily takes its due place alongside the notable
works of Owsley, Sydnor, Coulter, Woodward, Simkins, and
others that derive from a similar concert of forces in Southern
departments of history.

The graduate school or scholarly-historical method works
best in Mr. Hubbell's hand when applied to a subject in which
no severely troublesome critical issues arise. It does very well
for William Byrd, whose career and works call for little more
than clear expositing. It does admirably, too, for neglected
minor writers like Grayson or James Legaré; for Jefferson,
Madison, and other political writers; and, by and large, for
all writers whose importance derives chiefly from their con-
nections with the tragic divisions of the nineteenth century
—say, from the beginning of the quarrel over slavery up to
the "New South" period. But for Poe, as might be expected,

the method falls short of complete adequacy, although Mr. Hubbell very soundly develops the main aspects of Poe's career as an isolated artist and, in sketching the peculiar history of Poe's reputation, roundly rebukes the literary historians, particularly those of New England, for their obtuseness toward him. "One of his chief claims to our attention," Mr. Hubbell notes, ". . . is that his writings have forced us to broaden our conception of our literary tradition beyond what it would have been if the old New England point of view still dominated our national literature." That Mr. Hubbell does not, after all, say just how the art of Poe broadens our conception of literary tradition is evidence, no doubt, of a weakness in the historical method where Poe's case is involved. In the extensive and interesting chapter on Simms the historical method works excellently—up to a certain point. In his praise of Simms's fiction, however, Mr. Hubbell puts Simms down as very largely an early "realist," an antisentimentalist with gusto but little art. It is a plausible estimate, but it fails to take into account Simms's debt to oral tradition and his role as interpreter of the Southern colonial frontier. Yet I would not altogether blame Mr. Hubbell for the defect, although it appears again in his somewhat conventional treatment of the humorists of the old Southwest. For our regular historians have so far failed to amend very much the prevalent misleading accounts of the Southern colonial frontier; and for most professors of British and American literature, the oral tradition of the South remains a mysterious, unapprehended subject.

Such defects are, however, the defects of an organically strong book and do not much affect its obviously great value. That value in its most general aspect would surely be in the long-range steadying and reinforcement it can give to the best in our literary criticism, the best in our scholarship, and, in immediate application, the best in educational instruction at *all* levels. *The South In American Literature* shows no disposition to set scholarship and criticism at odds. It moves, rather, toward ending the uneasy divorce, amounting at times to open warfare, that has marked their recent relationships. Mr. Hubbell has opened his mind to the modern literary critics and added their insight to the inductive explorations and guarded deductions of scholarly science. I should think the insight of the critics would be fortified by some reciprocation on their part.

In fact, on most of the great central issues, Mr. Hubbell, following his own method, arrives with fair consistency at approximately the position taken by Allen Tate. If Mr. Hubbell does not say precisely in what respects Poe "broadened" our literary tradition, he nevertheless does assert in his own terms that Poe is "Our Cousin, Mr. Poe"—a Southerner by affiliation and principle. Mr. Hubbell's matter-of-fact observation that Poe "was too much the pessimist to share the optimism of Emerson and Lowell" parallels Mr. Tate's view that Poe "represents that part of our experience which we are least able to face up to. . . ." Throughout his book, without flinching or evasion, Mr. Hubbell faces calmly the same grave and troublesome problems that Mr. Tate discusses in "The Profession of Letters In the South," and in most respects the "objective" scholar agrees in his "findings" with the "subjective" estimates of the distinguished poet and critic. Doubtless Mr. Hubbell would reject Mr. Tate's rather despairing concession: "We lack a tradition in the arts . . . we lack a literary tradition. We lack a literature." He would offer this volume as proof to the contrary. But as to the peculiar estate of the Southern author in the past—as to causal factors, social and sectional, operating upon him from both North and South, as to misunderstandings, injustices, false vanities, shortcomings, and handicaps only recently mitigated—on all that, Hubbell and Tate could not have much to quarrel about. With some amendment of terms, Mr. Tate's essay would parallel Mr. Hubbell's position on certain great contentions—notably on the old and shopworn thesis that the South's "lack" of a literature must be attributed to its slaveholding economy, or the new, but similar thesis that social barbarism and "back-wardness" are to blame.

Mr. Hubbell's position is firm and perfectly clear. American literature has not been a "national" literature exactly; it has been "an aggregation of sectional literatures." The nine-teenth-century North nevertheless assumed "nationality" for its own product and rationalized its assumptions through such fictions as the one mentioned above, about the putative effect of slavery upon literary culture. Mr. Hubbell, soberly but relentlessly, traces the effect of this and other Northern fictions, together with the defensive Southern fictions they begot, upon Southern literature. Sometimes, by closing the channels of publication and appreciation, Northern fictions have acted as direct obstacles to Southern endeavor; some-times, more subtly, they have operated as a kind of editorial censorship. Mr. Hubbell traces out all this, most carefully. He also deals directly and frankly with the fictions themselves.

Perhaps "phantasms" would be a better term than "fic-tions." Early in his book Mr. Hubbell explains that the mo-tive behind much Colonial writing was "a desire to correct British misconceptions of American life." He quotes a passage in point from Robert Beverley's *History and Present State of Virginia* (1705):

> And this I should rather undertake, in Justice to so fine a Country; because it has been so misrepresented to the com-mon People of *England,* as to make them believe, that the Servants in *Virginia* are made to draw in Cart and Plow, as Horses and Oxen do in *England,* and that the Country turns all People black, who go to live there, with other such prodigious Phantasms.

The phantasms that impede British-American understand-ing have been hard to quell. I think nobody will deny that they still persist in latent or active forms. It is even harder to quell the phantasms that affect the relationships of North and South, which now are not only deeply planted in sectional habit but are also involved with entrenched political and economic interests. Indeed, one particular phantasm, passing under the name of "desegregation," has lately been declared to be associated with the official foreign policy of the United States. For the confrontation of phantasms, Mr. Hubbell is as stout a champion as has come forth, and he has the great advantage of not having to assume the role of champion. He is the personification of historical scholarship, one primary function of which is to rout phantasms. Whatever historical scholarship can do to that end, Mr. Hubbell has done. By way of shrewd counterstroke on the slavery issue, he has even devoted some chapters to the doings and writings of Lowell, Emerson, Harriet Beecher Stowe, and John William De Forest. The counterstroke, of course, is objective scholarship, no less. And Mr. Hubbell has the further advantage, as scholar, of not having to take the defensive attitude that for a century has been one of the greatest Southern afflictions. The prestige of contemporary Southern literature and the present fairly tolerant temper of both scholarly and critical opinion are also in his favor. All such circumstances make it possible to hope that his book will everywhere receive the generous welcome that it deserves but that it could hardly have received if it had appeared in any previous generation. At any rate it will be a hard book to get around—about as hard to get around as the Appalachian Mountains, which, if you can't fly over, you must generally go through.

MR. CASH AND THE PROTO-DORIAN SOUTH

MR. W. J. CASH'S *The Mind of the South* is, I believe, the first book of its specific title in our history. It proposes to interpret the phenomena of Southern life and history in the light of the peculiarities of the Southern mind, to which Mr. Cash ascribes a perfectly rounded, distinct, and definite character: *the* Southern mind, not *a* Southern mind or *some* Southern minds. That is not all. With comparatively little reservation, this book argues that the phenomena of Southern life and history *derive* principally from the peculiar set of this mind. The South was what it was, and is what it is—more or less regardless of external persuasions and compulsions—because Southerners have become fixed in certain ways of thinking and feeling. In his determination to uphold this thesis, Mr. Cash differs very much from the Southern liberals, who, I imagine, share his views as to what ought to be the course of things in the South. He concedes that there are indeed many Souths of a kind Howard Odum can describe; but the many Souths have only one mind: "a fairly definite mental pattern, associated with a fairly definite social pattern—a complex of established relationships and habits of thought, sentiments, prejudices, standards and values."

The unique convenience of this thesis is self-evident. If Mr. Cash's delineation of the Southern mind will stand up under close inspection, then Southerners from now on will be spared much agony. Instead of vainly striving to answer the incriminating questions asked of them, with horrible directness, by the extraordinary question-askers who inhabit the rest of the United States, what a blessing if the harassed Southerners could simply say: "If you please, just read Mr. W. J. Cash on this subject."

What a blessing indeed! Oh, dear Cousin from South Carolina or Virginia or Alabama or, yes, Texas, think of the times when you have been paralyzed by a question from some inoffensive-looking little lady from New York State or from some handsome intellectual-looking gentleman from Boston, in English tweeds. And what did you say, Cousin, when they asked you that? Did you change the subject? Did you hem and haw? Did you employ the Retort Courteous or the Lie Direct? Did you tell one of those evasive anecdotes that you keep in stock for just such occasions? Or did you, alas, try to *explain*—knowing all the while that some things can be known, experienced, practiced, but simply cannot be explained; and knowing too that the question ought never to have been asked in the first place, and that you would never have dreamed of asking it, had positions been reversed? I am sorry for you, Cousin, if you tried that method.

But perhaps you counterattacked, with furious shot and shell, and swept the field with your superior conversational firepower? Oh yes, we all know that method. The ladies cherish it, especially. I can see Miss A—— and Mrs. B—— in action, right now! The trouble is, it silences the questioners but doesn't persuade them. But don't tell us, Cousin, that you were so unworthy as to use a kind of reply that I dread to mention, and am ready to apoligize for mentioning. Surely you didn't say that; while the *poor whites,* being still illiterate, do, sure enough, indulge themselves in the peculiarly uncivilized way referred to in the question, all forward-looking Southerners (of whom you, naturally, are one) take the view (held, naturally, by your progressive-minded questioner) that the Past is *past,* and such "problems" will soon be solved by Programs, and while you admit that in certain respects, nevertheless and but also and as our great President so wisely has said. . . ?

Guilty Wretch—you would never have said *that* if your

revered father were alive and in hearing. You would not say it now, in a thousand places we all know. Then why, to the Yankee?

If Mr. Cash's book, however, answers those ugly questions, or even conveniently diverts them, our troubles are over. If he has succeeded, with honor, in the difficult undertaking, then let us get about the business of laurels and rewards. Let the Southern governors stop their futile worrying about freight rates long enough to declare a day of general thanksgiving, and let all the Confederate states proceed to erect suitable monuments to W. J. Cash, in those appropriate public corners not yet pre-empted for the Revolution, the War Between the States, the Race Horse, and the Boll Weevil.

But if Mr. Cash's book does not, with honor, thus succeed, and if in course of discussion he takes the role of the Guilty Wretch, then boys, you know what to do—we will meet, fellow-Ghouls, on Harpe's Head Road, at midnight sharp!

Actually, *The Mind of the South* is a short cut to historical interpretation, and "mind" is really a metaphor. Mr. Cash is principally interested in traits and circumstances that have made the Southern people, at various crises in their history, a people "of one mind" and that have acted continuously to keep them "of the same mind." He is trying to isolate and describe those elements, whatever they are, that render understanding among Southerners immediate, spontaneous, intuitive; that bind them, whatever their incidental differences, as members of a family are bound, so that they are conscious of a mutual interest that needs no definition and is beyond argument; and that, finally, rest upon principles of life, unquestioned, amounting to axioms, rather than on the series of pragmatic adjustments, capable of easy rationalization and also capable of quick change, so characteristic of modern life.

With some justice Mr. Cash apparently thinks that if this mysterious "mind" can be abstracted and studied, he has the key to Southern history and much else besides, including the oddities that trouble all modern investigators, such as lynching, racial antagonism, the pride of poor folk, and the like. Having this key, he seems to think that he can discard or minimize the investigations of historians. In fact, he does discard them to a large extent. His book is not documented. He rarely gives "proof" for his assertions. His discussion is a long analytical reverie or meditation not unlike Count Keyserling's studies which used to excite us so much; but much superior in quality, especially in its frequent matter-of-fact passages.

If the Southern "mind" can be isolated and described, can it then be conditioned, manipulated, controlled like any individual mind? I am constrained to think that Mr. Cash has some interest in this possibility. Much more than half of his book is devoted to the Southern "mind" from about 1900 to the present. This is the period during which the South has most wryly disappointed the prophets of modernism, by refusing to change its mind. Mr. Cash (knowing that "mind" as he does) can say that "its power over the body of the South would remain tremendous, even conclusive, and would exhibit itself with great distinctness." In other words, let planners and reformers be warned. Mr. Cash, who really would like to believe the contrary, sees that the disguises assumed by the South or imposed upon it by the New Deal are very superficial. The same old South is there, often most formidable when it is least vocal. And so he chides the Roosevelt administration for its stupidity in certain of its approaches. For example, the famous report on Economic Problem Number One was received "not only as an unnecessary attempt at trouble-making but as a gross affront to the section." Mr. Cash would have known better. It would be easy to predict the strategy of a reform movement that would retain Mr. Cash as expert adviser.

In abstracting the "mind of the South" from the body with which we are so familiar, Mr. Cash encounters two difficulties that he never fully surmounts. First, there is no accepted terminology for the science he would practice. He must fall back on an eclectic mixture of terms grabbed up from anthropology, Greek myth, sociology, politics, literature. To describe the object, he must depict it in such terms as to create a fiction—or something certainly not recognizable as truth by the persons to whom he would apply it. Sister Caroline and Uncle Charley would not know what the man is talking about; and if they did know, they would be more outraged than were Southern chambers of commerce by the Roosevelt report. Second, he cannot after all succeed in abstracting it. This "mind" cannot be viewed apart from the solid circumstances that are its "body." Mr. Cash no sooner starts to describe the differentiae of the Southern mind than he falls headlong into history—and there we have him!

"Proto-Dorian" and "the savage ideal" are his favorite phrases of characterization. These terms evidently stand at the center of his meaning, and must be carefully examined.

The "Proto-Dorian convention" is Mr. Cash's name for the complex of attitudes that I have listed above, and still more particularly, for a significant feature of this complex: the fact that it all but obliterated class distinctions and has prevented class consciousness (in the modern sense) from developing even under present conditions. I do not claim to understand the word itself, *Proto-Dorian.* My dictionary gives it as an architectural term. The slaves of course might be thought of as "helots," but the Old South was certainly anything but Dorian, or Spartan. Perhaps the word is Menckenese, surviving from the days when Mr. Cash wrote for *The American Mercury.* Anyway, Mr. Cash uses it primarily to describe the paradox, so troublesome to social historians, under which, in the Old South, aristocracy and democracy not only flourished blithely side by side but fused and rendered each other mutual support. Mr. Cash's explanation of this crux is that Negro slavery, with its corollary, strict racial distinction, supplied the means of harmony between two theoretically opposite principles.

If the plantation had introduced distinctions of wealth and rank among the men of the old backcountry, and, in doing so, had perhaps offended against the ego of the common white, it had also, you will remember, introduced that other vastly ego-warming and ego-expanding distinction between the white man and the black. Robbing him and degrading him in so many ways, it yet, by singular irony, had simultaneously elevated this common white to a position comparable to that of, say, the Doric knight of ancient Sparta. Not only was he not exploited directly, he was himself made by extension a member of the dominant class—was lodged solidly on a tremendous superiority, which, however much the blacks in the "big house" might sneer at him, and however much their masters might privately agree with them, he could never publicly lose. Come what might, he would always be a white man. And before that vast and capacious distinction, all others were foreshortened, dwarfed, and all but obliterated.

The grand outcome was the almost complete disappearance of economic and social focus on the part of the masses. One simply did not have to get on in this world to achieve security, independence, or value in one's own estimation and in that of one's fellows.

Hence it happened that pressure never developed within the enclosing walls thrown up by the plantation, that not one in a thousand of the enclosed ever even remotely apprehended the existence of such walls. And so it happened, finally, that the old basic feeling of democracy was preserved practically intact.

Before making this deduction, Mr. Cash sketches the origins of the paradox. The man of the Old South, viewed as a type, had in him a great deal of frontier tradition, indistinguishably mixed with all he got from the plantation tradition and with whatever he got, too, from the yeoman farmer tradition (which Mr. Cash consistently underemphasizes or just omits). The colonial gentry (whom throughout the book he insists on calling "the Virginians") were, Mr. Cash quite correctly argues, a much more homespun lot than the Williamsburg Restoration and the Colonial Dames would have us imagine. The frontier in fact lasted in almost its original form in the South down to 1860 at least and was just as great a conditioning element as the plantation. Although "the Virginians" exerted some "artificializing influence," they too had to meet frontier requirements. The distance between them and the "common whites" was not great, in material reality. And the "manners" of the Old South (which Mr. Cash is never tired of praising) operated to diminish social distance, too, since they did not encourage undue hauteur on the part of the great person and did not call for obsequiousness and servility from the less great. Furthermore, the whole South was kin, and blood counted for more than material condition. The great planter might have near cousins in velvet or in leather breeches, who might be in Texas or Arkansas, or right across the hollow. Above all, the society was based on land—the cultivation of land, the possession of land, the love of land, among great and simple alike. Possession and love of land was in fact the goal toward which the frontier moved. So we have as the typical man of the Old South, "a simple rustic figure."

"This simple rustic figure," writes Mr. Cash, "is the true center from which the Old South proceeded—the frame about which *the conditions of the plantation* threw up the whole structure of the Southern mind." (Italics mine.)

To get the Proto-Dorian convention, then, we take this simple rustic figure and add the "ego-warming" notion of the superiority of white man over black. Thus we wipe out "economic and social focus on the part of the masses" and eventually create the Solid South.

To extend the picture, remember that "the conditions of the plantation" by the middle of the nineteenth century, not only had fixed the plantation type itself, but had made the plantation master the type to which all aspired. Or so Mr. Cash! All Southerners, whether transplanted "Virginians," new-rich cotton snobs, yeoman farmers, or "common whites," shared the same culture and adhered to the same fundamentals of belief and conduct. The code of honor, with all its familiar features; adoration of woman; chivalrousness of manner and outlook; pride of person, conceded to all alike and defended by all alike, by direct satisfaction and personal violence if need be; pride of ancestry, which, Mr. Cash says, became "an obsession, informed with all the old frontier inheritance of brag"; and yet, with all these, a prevalent democratic temper which destroyed class feeling and obscured, according to Mr. Cash, the true nature of the paternalistic pattern under which the planters were—quite unconsciously, he admits—"exploiting" white men as well as Negro slaves; and above all a sense of complete unity, of belonging to one great Southern clan, which obscured old differences between states and parts of states—all of these characteristics were implanted everywhere, no less in the poorest than in the richest.

Then, as the abolitionist attack gained force and war broke out, the patterns of belief, far from weakening, became more fervently entrenched, unity became intense, loyalty to the South became a cardinal principle. At last, out of the supreme ordeal of war, "the masses had brought, not only a great body of memories in common with the master class, but a deep affection for these captains, a profound trust in them, a pride which was inextricably intertwined with the commoners' pride in themselves. They had tried these men under difficult circumstances and had found them bold, dashing, and splendid, and, as a rule, neither overbearing nor, in the field, careless of the welfare of their following; above all, able, fit to cope with the problem in hand and to cut through to the common goal if anybody could."

In this summary it would be impossible to present every facet of the Southern mind as Mr. Cash reveals it in his intricate exposition. But, in contrast to his wise and glowing account of the state of things at the close of the War, I must not neglect to notice his shallow, almost obtuse treatment of religious tendencies. In the religious department he is de-

cidedly Menckenesque. He notes, correctly, the prevalence
from 1800 on of evangelistic religion, which thrust aside the
old deism and the old Anglicanism. But this evangelistic religion to him is a completely vulgar phenomenon—an entirely
crude Calvinism, presided over by a tribal Jehovah, and im-
planting everywhere finally a grievous Southern version of
Puritanism. Later on, it is nothing more than vulgar Fundamentalism, stupidly interfering, at Dayton and elsewhere,
with the march of progress. Its effect on the Southern mind,
Mr. Cash says, is twofold: first, it strengthens still further the
unity of the South, by linking with the cult of the Confederate
soldier and defining the Southern people as a Chosen People,
suffering nobly under adversity; but, second, it splits the
Southern psyche; for although the innately hedonistic South
would not give up the pleasure principle, the new Southern
Puritanism condemned all conviviality; and hence the festive
fiddle was laid away, and men took to furtive bouts with the
jug and the cards.

This is a trashy way of discussing the greatest of all issues,
indeed the ultimate issue. But Mr. Cash is quite content thus
to repeat the trivial booing at religion which we heard so much
in the 1920's, and he probes no further. In fact, he seems rather
malignantly satisfied to have it that way, because he immediately proceeds to link his characterization of Southern religious tendencies with "the savage ideal." And he defines the
savage ideal as "that ideal whereunder dissent and variety are
completely suppressed and men become, in all their attitudes,
professions, and actions, virtual replicas of one another." Reconstruction was, in truth, a rape more stupid and cruel than
the rape of Poland; he concedes that. But evangelistic religion,
added to other causes, made the South, he would argue, into
a society governed entirely by taboos and repressions.

> The final great result of Reconstruction . . . is that it
> established the savage ideal as it had not been established
> in any Western people since the decay of medieval feudalism,

and almost as truly as it is established today in Fascist Italy, in Nazi Germany, in Soviet Russia—and so paralyzed Southern culture at the root.

These are terrible words—terrible, as suggesting the contempt of Mr. Cash's heart for the role of religion in the South; terrible, for what they imply as to the future he would desire. But it is not the first time I have heard this pronouncement. Clifton Fadiman, that bright fellow of "Information, Please" and self-styled propagandist for democracy, has announced over the radio that he, too, would put the South of former days in the same class with Nazi Germany. If Fadiman will say it, then I know it is a fashionable sentiment in New York. And does Mr. Cash, who holds that even the modern South has not changed its mind, mean to imply that the modern South is also in essence Fascist? What a sentiment to offer a South which, as I write, is being celebrated in the newspapers as exceeding all other sections in its enthusiasm for aid to England if not for war!

But perhaps he does not really mean it. Reconstruction, he says, returned the South to frontier conditions, threw all classes back on a common ground of suffering and privation, entrenched white supremacy, once more obliterated "economic and social focus on the part of the masses," and indefinitely postponed the working of Marxist principles in the Southern scene. The Proto-Dorian convention wedded the Savage Ideal. The Southerner, by our author's account already naïve and unanalytical, already heedless of "intellectual culture," already prone to make personal judgments, became more that way than ever.

Then came the New South. To Mr. Cash, the New South program of industrialization and education was a vast enthusiastic folk-movement, presided over by the Southern "mind." To industry and public education, he says, the South transferred the sentimentalism and solidarity of the Lost Cause. The thing worked, for a while. The South underwent large physical changes and got some modern improvements. Then, with the Depression, came another lapse into Proto-Dorianism. The New Deal intervened, though clumsily, and partly saved the day. But Mr. Cash is skeptical about final results. His review of the operations of the New Deal in the South is the most shrewdly realistic part of the book. His final remarks may possibly be characterized as temperate:

> Proud, brave, honorable by its lights, courteous, personally generous, loyal, swift to act, often too swift, but signally effective, sometimes terrible in action—such was the South at its best. And such at its best it remains today, despite the great falling away in some of its virtues. Violence, intolerance, aversion and suspicion toward new ideas, an incapacity for analysis, an inclination to act from feeling rather than thought, an exaggerated individualism and a too narrow concept of social responsibility, attachment to fictions and false values, above all too great attachment to racial values and a tendency to justify cruelty and injustice in the name of those values, sentimentality and a lack of realism—these have been its characteristic vices in the past. And, despite changes for the better, they remain its characteristic vices today.

By way of objection to Mr. Cash's general line of argument, I should say, first, that his terms are too simple and are entirely inadequate for his ambitious task. But once he is committed to them, he must see the thing through. The logical devil of consistency forces him to apply them where they will not apply and tempts him to omit much that should not be omitted. "Proto-Dorian" is a pretty rhetorical figure and might do to adorn a casual illustration; but it is rhetoric, and farfetched rhetoric at that, and certainly does not provide a good foundation for an interpretation of three centuries of Southern history. "Savage ideal" is effective vituperation, but again is only rhetoric, empty of substantial content, except such as Mr. Cash arbitrarily supplies. The really marvelous intricacy of his book is a tribute to his ingenuity; but it is a false intricacy, since it bears no true relation to the intricacies of his subject, and derives, instead, from his attempt to apply a purely rhetorical definition to a stubborn and unwieldy body of facts. *The Mind of the South,* a book brilliantly executed, abounding in miscellaneous passages full of insight, and enormously instructive even in its errors, is nevertheless, as a whole, a tremendous demonstration that there is no short cut to historical interpretation. The mind of a society cannot rightly be allegorized into a personality and then praised or blamed, as above, for rigidly distinguished virtues and vices.

It is true that Mr. Cash's method, inadequate though it is, and in essence sophistical, does often lead him into direct encounter with formidable truths. Let us praise him for his discovery of the paradox of aristocracy and democracy in the Old South (of which, more later); for his emphasis on the paramount importance of the frontier; for his honest admission —rare, in recent interpretations—that the South has not had "class feeling," even when industrialization most threatens to produce it. And even while withholding complete praise, let us salute him for his acknowledgment that the race problem is central to an understanding of the Southern situation. In this connection, Mr. Cash is discerning enough to reject, as absurdly false, the common contention that lynching is a specialized pursuit of "the white trash classes" and is due to "economic rivalry," or else is a kind of hellish diversion with which backward Southerners enliven their dull lives. Mr. Cash knows better than that, and says so. He recognizes that rape or the danger of rape is the ultimate fact behind the prevalence and persistence of lynching. On the other hand, I regret to say that he surrounds and colors even this realistic view with a sickly goo of Freudian psychology, such as will be found in the book called *Caste and Class in a Southern Town,* by Dr. Dollard of the Yale Institute of Human Relations.

But, to continue with the objections, the great defect of Mr. Cash's procedure is his failure to give the context at points where the context is of decisive importance. Again, this is a defect of method. He omits the context, that is to say he omits the history, when he cannot adapt it to his account of the

Southern mind as such. These omissions are gross, and they seriously impair the validity of his study.

A minor omission, but a typical one, is his failure to give the context of the Southern defense of slavery during the ante-bellum period. As I read Mr. Cash, I get the impression that Harper, Dew, Fitzhugh, and Calhoun arose more or less spontaneously, in answer to the demands of the Proto-Dorian convention, rather than in answer to the attacks from the North —which attacks, it is true, Mr. Cash does actually mention, but casually, rather as if these attacks did not really matter. But the attacks from the North, that is from the Abolitionists, are here the main part of the context, and the historical interpreter who omits them is talking nonsense. Yet the omission is not, after all, very surprising in a writer whose occasional citations, I notice, refer rather exclusively to such writers as Gerald Johnson, Broadus Mitchell, and others of the North Carolina school. Or in a writer who is so far gone as to admit, into the gaps left by the omission of nonprogressive historians, such puling bits of malice as Henry Adams' famous sneer at Rooney Lee. My impression is that Mr. Cash's interpretation of Southern history is deeply colored by the reading he did in the gay, emancipated 1920's, when Gerald Johnson and Broadus Mitchell were still the wonder of our stage, and when many young Southerners, struggling with *The Education of Henry Adams,* learned something they had never before known—the sneer.

Among major omissions I put Mr. Cash's failure to do anything at all with the yeoman farmers of the South, whom, again, he mentions but quite evidently knows nothing about. Yet these yeoman farmers, at the very time when the Southern "mind," in Mr. Cash's account of it, became fixed and unified, outnumbered and outweighed all other types. Mr. Cash has not read, or has ignored, Frank L. Owsley's recent monographs which prove that the yeoman farmer rather than the planter or "poor white" was the dominant figure by 1850 if not before, even in supposedly big-plantation areas. If Mr. Cash had taken this material into reckoning, he might have felt less free to write those cruel sentences in which he depicts the "fine gentleman" as patronizing the "common white"—"in such fashion that to his *simple eyes* [my italics] he seemed not to be patronized at all but actually deferred to, to send him home, not sullen and vindictive, but glowing with a sense of participation in the common brotherhood of white men." The truth is that the "simple eyes" of yeoman farmer or "common white" quickly detected any mere affectation of democracy, and retorted with considerable roughness if the occasion demanded. It was no community of gulls and simpletons that in Tennessee itself overthrew the Andrew Jackson machine with an uproarious smash; or that in the Deep South elected to office such men as Jefferson Davis, Bob Toombs, Alexander Stephens, John C. Calhoun.

But here we come to politics, and to another major omission. In Mr. Cash's account of the mind of the South, politics does not exist, except as a kind of rhetorical picnic; and as for political theory, he simply does not notice it. "The politics of the Old South," he says, "was a theater for the play of the purely personal, the purely romantic, and the purely hedonistic. It was an arena wherein one great champion confronted another or a dozen, and sought to outdo them in rhetoric and splendid gesturing. It swept back the loneliness of the land, it brought men together under torches, it filled them with the contagious power of the crowd, it unleashed emotion and set it to leaping and dancing, it caught the very meanest man up out of his tiny legend into the gorgeous fabric of this or that great hero."

Such De Quincey–like rhapsodies constitute about the sum total of Mr. Cash's observations on Southern politics. I would not have thought it possible to leave *that* subject out, but Mr. Cash has done it. The political history is not there, nor is the political theory—those high and bitterly argued contentions as to the nature of man in relation to the state, and the nature of the state in relation to man, which sank deep into Southern blood and bone, established states and governments, and had certainly much to do with the scheme of Southern life. It does not fit Mr. Cash's psychograph of the Southern mind. Let the historians toil if they want to; Mr. Cash is looking the other way.

And while omitting politics, he makes a good job of it, and all but omits economics, until he comes far up into the modern scene. As I have already indicated, he does not omit religion, but he might as well have done so, since his account of it is a journalistic caricature. He complains that the South is divorced from its own intellectual leadership; but says nothing of the powers external to the South, economic, journalistic, and educational, which intervene between the South and its own leadership and indeed make native leadership impossible unless it operates in terms approved elsewhere. He is uneasy about the Southern economy; but never speaks of the problem that engages Walter Prescott Webb, in *Divided We Stand,* of the concentration of ownership and control of Southern resources in the hands of the North. There are more such omissions, and there are also some small inaccuracies, but it would be tedious to go on.

And probably it is quite wrong to chide Mr. Cash for sins in respect to historical substance. His work is not of the substance but of the spirit. He is writing poetically and should be answered poetically. Although he says in his preface that he intends to disabuse our minds of the "legends" of both the Old South and the New, and put truth in their place, he only substitutes the Cash legend of the Proto-Dorian South for the legends that he finds inadequate. And he should be answered thus, legend for legend. This is a complex task, however, since he sets up not one legend but two: the Proto-Dorian legend, which accounts for Southern characteristics and toward which he is critical; and the legend of the North, of progressivism and liberalism, toward which he is entirely uncritical. The second legend is implied rather than delineated. But it is the more powerful for being thus hidden.

What would the results be if, using Mr. Cash's method I should attempt to construct a legend, paralleling his, of an Anti-Dorian North, as it looks to the simple eyes of an intolerant, violent, woman-worshipping, nonanalytical, passionately personal, exaggeratedly individualistic, racially conscious, sentimental, unrealistic common white like, say, myself? I cannot write the book, of course, but I can dimly visualize its outline. Am I to suppose that this Anti-Dorian North possesses those admirable qualities the antithesis of which, in the mind of the South, Mr. Cash deplores?

Very well, then, the mind of the Anti-Dorian North is *tolerant:* e.g., John Brown of Ossawatomie, Garrison, Thad Stevens, Walter Winchell, Mayor LaGuardia. It is *nonviolent:* Aaron Burr, John Brown again, the opponents of the Fugitive Slave Law; Abraham Lincoln; John Lewis and the C.I.O.; the Marxists, *et alii.* It is *not woman-worshipping,* but—what is the antithesis anyhow? The Bayard Taylor type, perhaps? The inventor of Mother's Day? Jim Fisk? Or could it be the Feminists? This is a little puzzling, but let us proceed. It is *analytical,* very analytical: to be sure, there is Emerson the Transcendentalist, with his "Trust thyself, every *heart* vibrates to that iron string"; and no doubt the Abolitionists again; and those princes of abstraction, the northern Irish, especially the Fenians; and President Grant and associates; and Jimmy Walker; and Mrs. President Roosevelt. It is *anti-individualistic,* or *collectivist:* say, the New England or the Ohio farmer; Thoreau and Whitman, notably; Henry Ford, of course; and to crown our miscellany, Babe Ruth, Whistler, Ben Franklin, Westbrook Pegler. It is *antisentimental:* Longfellow, Whittier, Eddie Guest, James Whitcomb Riley, Edna the Millay, and all the movie people. It is *racially unconscious:* of course, the Northern people (99 and 44/100 per cent, anyhow) commonly and freely admit the Negro to their front doors, their dinner tables, their marriage altars, and so forth, don't they? And then, to these selective indications, we should add, I suppose (since what are virtues in the South must be vices in the North) that the North, unlike the South, is possibly *not* proud, *not* brave, *not* honorable, *not* personally generous, *not* loyal, and so on.

It looks like a hard thing to say. Intolerant though I am, I don't believe that I am mean enough to go on with it.

Instead, let us return, if possible, to realities. So far as Mr. Cash's description of the South is near the truth, it is a description not of a mind but of a traditional society, establishing and then maintaining with remarkable loyalty the institutions and mores that flow from convinced adherence to democratic principles. It might be better, following the example of the Fathers of the Republic, to say republican principles, but that term is not understood nowadays. I mean to say that the South— at the time when Mr. Cash holds that its mind was fixed—was as complete a realization as we have any right to expect, of the kind of society that Jefferson visualized—the society in which democracy could flourish and maintain itself without artificial stimulation. John Adams of New England, together with many other men of that day in all parts of the Republic, agreed fully, with only relatively minor amendments on matters like property, suffrage, and governmental devices. The Hamiltonians, of course, thought otherwise, being anxious to import the imperialistic English notions of finance and industry; but they were beaten and did not begin to recover strength or prestige until the 1860's. Southerners themselves from time to time made amendments in their political views, especially in the years of the slavery controversy when Calhoun took the lead. But they never modified their beliefs as to the kind of society that must be the necessary basis of democracy; and indeed only wished to go on and perfect and enjoy it.

A necessary feature of such a society is the paradox that so intrigues Mr. Cash: that it should be "individualistic" and yet be capable of social unity, indeed of a high degree of collectivity; that it also raise up leaders—the natural aristocracy of virtue and talent, in which both Adams and Jefferson believed —yet leaders who would have no will to do harm to the demo-

cratic principles and who could not, in fact, "exploit" their
followers or induce servility in them because both the tone
and the circumstances of the society would forbid that; that,
in Mr. Cash's own words, "economic and social focus on the
part of the masses" should disappear, not only without in-
jury to their liberties but even with positive access of liberty;
that there should be nonrigid divisions or orders of society
("classes," in a sense) without any real infringement of personal status—without "class consciousness." Unless a society
can achieve this paradox, which after all is nothing but a
highly desirable state of social, economic, and political equilibrium, it can hardly support democracy, in anything but
name. The distinction of the American experiment in government and its success up to a certain point arise from the
fact that the society to be governed was in such a state of equilibrium, not a perfect one, but good enough for practical purposes. This equilibrium, in the early years, existed in the
United States at large, not only in the South. It was an equilibrium founded upon rural occupations, widespread ownership of land as of property in general, and, of course, a frontier
which, in Professor Edgar Thompson's phrase, allowed an
economy of "open resources." Nevertheless, the most important single feature of this economy was probably the farm.
The plantation positively did not, of itself, create the equilibrium, but was itself held in check and made to conform
by farm and frontier. We may reasonably make this inference
because we know (Professor Thompson has recently reminded
us of this) that the plantation was a world-wide institution,
and that, in other countries than the United States, it did not
foster such an equilibrium and did not work in harmony with
democratic principles. (In Mexico and South America the
plantation evoked no democracy and no Proto-Dorian convention!)

But there is Negro slavery, which raises new questions and
encourages Mr. Cash to set up his Proto-Dorian myth. We all
know its history. Negro slavery was with us before the Revolu-

tion and before the true, or Jeffersonian, revolution. While our traditional, democratic society was achieving its equilibrium, slavery remained, a vestige from colonial times. At first it was not a very disturbing factor, and sentiment existed, in both North and South, for checking and removing it. Doubtless it would have been checked and removed, but for the entrance of disequilibrizing forces. In the North these were the new interest in manufactures and the rise of militant Abolitionism. In the South they were the invention of the cotton gin and the rapidly increasing demand for cotton fiber by Great Britain, which was selling textiles to its expanding imperial market. The North was lucky, and was not "caught." The South was unlucky, and was "caught"—that is, discovered by the pietists with an "anachronism" on its hands, which though affording a supply of controlled labor, nevertheless was an intrinsic domestic danger and a focus of perilous national controversy—a weapon, in fact, which the analytical, dispassionate, impersonal, nonviolent, unsentimental brethren of the North could and ultimately did drive to the heart of the South.

The situation was very complex, because this slavery was not just slavery. It was African Negro slavery, and therefore raised both the slavery question and the race question. The North took the romantic position that the complexities did not matter; it was willing to risk any disequilibrium that might result from abolishing slavery, especially since all the risk would be borne by the South. The South took the realistic position that the risk was too great, and was not to be thought of. The South knew that it could not maintain its society in the desired equilibrium unless the alien element, now vastly enlarged, could be strictly controlled. And if it could not maintain the equilibrium, it could not maintain democracy for white people. That was the position of the South from 1820 to 1860, and from 1860 through the Reconstruction, and is the position of the South today. It is a perfectly honest and realistic position.

But we are not arguing the race question here. I have given this outline merely with the purpose of impeaching Mr. Cash's wild claim that "white supremacy" is alone or chiefly responsible for what he calls the Proto-Dorian convention. Let us admit that the presence of the Negro, slave or free, enforces a more deep and ever-present concern among Southerners for preserving the traditional society that I have described. But the Negro is not the determining factor, he is the disturbing factor. And those who, like Mr. Cash, argue the contrary are talking the most dangerous kind of nonsense. For it is not possible to absorb the Negro into white society in full and equal status without tearing that society to pieces and completely, perhaps convulsively, changing it. And without status in that society, the Negro's democratic political status would be only a cruel and dishonest fiction, worth nothing to him. Those who close their eyes to this inexorable fact—and I regret to say that there are Southern leaders, among them congressmen and college presidents, who are thus obtuse—are the potential authors either of social degradation or of murderous mischief on a scale that, I should suppose, they would shrink to contemplate.

But dishonest fictions, not only in the case of the Negro, but in all conceivable situations, seem to be the order of the day. Long ago the North said, in effect, that it would risk disturbing the equilibrium of its own traditional society if it could use the industrial revolution to amass a general total of wealth and improvements, which, if they should turn out to be ill-distributed, either could be actually redistributed in some way or other, or else could be pooled and used to purchase benefits for all. The North has argued that it could do this, and yet remain democratic.

We now see before us some of the results of that choice. The near future, doubtless, will disclose more results. We keep the fiction of democracy, but behind the fiction, what do we see? The strongest central government we have ever known; the most elaborately restrictive and regulative laws; a continually increasing tendency of the government to call for and indeed to exact unanimity of opinion, to brook no criticism, to demand almost servile obedience. The Democratic party itself, still invoking the name of Jefferson, has taken these steps, using the idea-men of the North as its Dorian knights and the Southern politicians as its willing helots. In short, once society was thrown into disequilibrium —as it was thrown by the industrial regime—it became necessary to institute the rule of force, exerted at every point of our lives, in order to maintain even the semblance of democracy. And thus, in very truth, we arrive at the Savage Ideal (I thank Mr. Cash for the words)—"that ideal whereunder dissent and variety are completely suppressed, and men become, in all their attitudes, professions, and actions, virtual replicas of one another." And now, too, with war shaking the whole world, what prospect is there that this savage ideal will quickly relax its hold upon us? We will keep the name of democracy, and may keep the hope of it. But we have already in large measure flung away the substance of it and will not easily recover it.

The South, Old or New, was not a friend to the savage ideal. Not only could the South never have imagined or understood Hitler's Germany or Stalin's Russia; it could not have understood even the England of Chamberlain and Churchill; and, I strongly suspect, does not now understand the America of Roosevelt. Those who sincerely wish to comprehend the true basis of the democracy that they profess to defend will do wrong if they neglect to study the first principles which the South mastered long ago.

And now, fellow-Southerners, Proto-Dorians, the moon is setting, and the Fiery Cross is burning low. You all know what we came out here for tonight, and let's get through with it. You all have heard what Mr. Cash has had to say, and I have tried, the best I could, to make plain to you what it means. Now what do you say? Shall we use the gun or the rope? Or ride him on a rail? Or just turn him loose?

Before you make up your minds, I want to read you a piece that's printed here on the back of Mr. Cash's book. It says he was born in old South Carolina, where my Grandma Patton's folks came from, back in Andrew Jackson's time. It says he went to Wake Forest College. I seem to remember that's where your Uncle Charley used to send his boys— Ain't that so, Stonewall?

I say, turn him loose. I'm glad to see you all agree with me. Mr. Cash wrote that-there book for the Yankees anyway. It's about as much as they will ever understand.

And now we'll all go back to my house and see what the women-folks have got spread out for us. We hope you'll give us the pleasure of your company, Mr. Cash. Stonewall, don't forget you left that jug in the hollow beech tree.

SOME DAY, IN OLD CHARLESTON

O*N WEDNESDAY last,* said the South Carolina Gazette, *four large transport ships sailed up Cooper River for Straw-berry with the heavy baggage of His Majesty's troops, which are to be employed (in conjunction with the forces of this Province) under the command of Lieutenant Colonel James Grant in the approaching campaign against the Cherokees.*

Outside, on King Street, a distant rhythmic clangor intruded among the ordinary traffic noises. We ignored it, for we were trying to hear, within the sheltering walls of the Charleston Library Society, the noise of "waggons" carrying heavy baggage from Cooper River to Strawberry, and thence to Monck's Corner, where the Highland Scottish troops of Grant's command were assembled, and the bagpipes doubtless were playing. The large bound volumes of the *South Carolina Gazette* for 1760 and 1761 were open before us, and we were both taking notes. For that was the trade between us, between husband and wife, that if I would go with her to the various gardens at certain times, she would go with me to the Charleston Library Society at certain other times.

Right now it might be April 6, 1948, in the United States in general, and even on King Street, but inside the Charleston Library Society building it was March 21, 1761. The *South Carolina Gazette* said so. We did not want to be interrupted.

Yesterday morning—now that must have been March 20, 1761—*the troops began their march from Monck's Corner to Fort Prince George on the Keowee River.*

From the fort as advanced base Grant would raid the Cherokee towns hidden among the mountains. Grant was a Scot, probably of an ex-Jacobite family, but like most British officers he believed that Indians armed with rifles could be defeated by regulars armed with muskets, if the regulars kept formation and volleyed by platoons upon command of an officer waving a sword. . . .

The noise on King Street was getting louder. There was a lot of thumping in it, which we tried to tell ourselves was the drums of Grant's expedition, moving up from the Congarees to Ninety-Six. "The behavior of the troops during their stay in Charles-Town has given the greatest satisfaction to the inhabitants," said the *South Carolina Gazette.* The officers of the army had given a theatrical entertainment the week before—had put on a comedy and a farce, in the Council Chamber.

But everybody was leaving the reading rooms and going to the door. Even the librarians were going—even Miss Mazyck and Miss Bull. Then how could we forbear?

So we came out into the fine spring sunshine of present-day Charleston, and from the lofty stone porch of the Charleston Library Society we looked down as from a reviewing stand upon the approaching military parade. Recalled from March 21, 1761, and not unmindful of April 12, 1861, we entered without any great jolt into the concerns of April 6, 1917— no, April 6, 1948—and looked down upon King Street, feeling very proper, safe, relaxed, and patriotic, in the company of the lady who was looking up genealogies, the boy who was reading romances, a casual tourist or two, and Miss Mazyck and Miss Bull. It was (we at last remembered) a day called "Army Day." We had read about it in the *South Carolina Gazette*—no, the Charleston *News and Courier*—while we were eating breakfast at a grill recommended by Duncan Hines. There would be a parade of army and navy units, and airplanes overhead, including jets, and after the parade there would be a patriotic address by the inevitable successor of Lieutenant Colonel Grant.

It was a good parade, and we thoroughly enjoyed it, at least the military part of it, and no doubt we enjoyed it the more

because of the amiable confusion that always comes over the
visitor to Charleston, who can never be quite certain whether
at a given moment he is participating in the ardors and pleas-
ures of the seventeenth, the eighteenth, the nineteenth, or the
twentieth century. After all, troops had been marching along
King Street and other Charleston streets for a long, long time
—say about 250 years, to get a round number. It was so easy
to get mixed up and see redcoats, or kilts, or blue-and-buff,
or Confederate gray where the uniform of the day was actually
khaki. One had to make an effort to remember that the column
obeyed the orders of someone whose name was in the morning
newspaper, and not of Craven, Chicken, Cornwallis, Tarleton,
Moultrie, Nathanael Greene, Beauregard, Hampton, or Sherman.

The column of 1948, if the evidence of the eyes could be
believed, was mostly in khaki, mostly in the undistinguished
drab that properly belongs to the mechanical twentieth century. Its weapons were modern, and it had no horses or horse-
drawn "waggons." but only the self-propelled, often fantasti-
cally odd vehicles of up-to-date mobile warfare. And far above
the column—far above the Georgian façades and West Indian
verandas of Charleston—whizzed the bomber groups and jet
planes of the war in the air. But in its fundamental aspects it
was like all military parades from Julius Caesar to Eisenhower.
It was a ceremonious procession stepping to martial music, carrying flags and deadly weapons—a reminder, cast into a form
as ritualistic and devotional as the ceremonies of a church, that
the processes of government, laboratory science, liberalism,
and expertism must be depended upon sometime, somewhere,
to reach a breaking point, at which breaking point the army
takes over and the ancient battle begins once more. For this
reason a military parade has a certain order and decorum that
are traditional and unalterable.

This one was traditional up to a point. It was led by a company of paratroopers in helmets and half-boots. Soon came the
Marines, in red and blue, and a unit of sailors who looked

unhappy as sailors always do when marching as infantry. The thin crowd that fringed the street looked on in silence.

But now the crowd stirred, as another band rolled its drums and burst into music, and another column of infantry appeared. At its head, floating beside the Stars and Stripes, was the blue flag of South Carolina, with its palmetto tree and crescent moon. What was the regiment? The folds of the flag, drooping in the quiet air, hid part of the numerals. It was the One Hundred and—something—Infantry. From the back of the porch, near the door where the librarians stood, a Charleston voice spoke softly but firmly, and also, I thought, a little correctively: "The Washington Light Infantry." An old regiment, then, disguised in modern numerals, modern khaki. A regiment that had fought in the Revolution, at the Cowpens with Morgan, at Eutaw with Greene. But now—absorbed into anonymity—it was the One Hundred and—something—Infantry. The crowd handclapped merrily; a few cheers drifted up, half-apologetic.

Then here came another palmetto flag, and another South Carolina regiment, another One Hundred and Something. More cheers, that threatened to become yells, louder handclapping, a little tumult of excitement, amid which I thought I heard the corrective voice say: "The Sumter Guards." The names and even the old numerals (where there were numerals) of the old state regiments were wiped out, I remembered, during World War I, when it seemed safer for democracy to revise the old system and merge everything into the national lump. The regular regiments and divisions got the lowest numbers; the state or "national guard" regiments were renumbered in the hundreds; and the "national army" or drafted regiments were numbered in the three hundreds.

And now came the miscellaneous units of reservists, and after them the Citadel band, and after the Citadel band, the young cadets of Porter Military Academy. These were Charleston's own, and they were well received by the crowd. It was not until later that we learned why the Citadel cadets did not march, but sent only a band. They were having term examinations at Citadel, and only the band was allowed to join this parade.

Thus far, all had been traditional, all was in order, and just about what one would expect in a military parade in Charleston—a certain spirited smartness of appearance, combined with due restraint; a notion of doing well once more what had been done well many times in the past; a sense of a present occasion moved not only by its own energy but by the merging and supporting energies of all that had gone before.

But now, suddenly, there was more music, with a saucy blare in its horns and drums and a continuance of the parade that almost amounted to an interruption.

It was a band of youngsters not in uniform but in civilian dress. At the head of the band a girl dressed up in the stage costume of a blue devil turned dizzying cartwheels on the pavement of King Street. Up went the little devil's heels and around she went cleverly on feet and hands. And behind her pranced a whole squad of drum majorettes. They threw their knees high to the beat of the drums. They tossed and swung their batons, twisted hips and bodies, nodded their heads under their grotesque shakos. They simpered brassily, their girlish features frozen in a Hollywood smile. With them, not far behind the comely blue devil, trudged a youth carrying a large sign with the legend: NORTH CHARLESTON HIGH SCHOOL. They were received in silence, though eyes followed them and the agile blue devil as they passed on. There were a few half-suppressed titters, a few remarks in undertone along the sidewalk, and soon we drifted away as the end of the column came in sight. It was over, and we could go back to the files of the *South Carolina Gazette,* or we could adjourn to Middleton Gardens. Middleton Gardens seemed the better choice. We felt an urgent need to return to the seventeenth century and get our bearings once more. We had not counted on seeing the naked legs of drum majorettes on King Street, in old Charleston. Pathetic they might be in their juvenile insolence, in their parading of a new American convention that was not Charleston's, that could not possibly have been thought up in Charleston. But they were formidable, too.

Later on we brought our problem of disorientation to the attention of a Charleston friend. His family name is not Pinckney or Huger or Rutledge, but it is a Charleston name. For convenience let him be known here as Mr. Charles.

Out of deference to us, Mrs. Charles had moved the dinner hour up from the regular 2 P.M. to 1:30. It was dinner, not lunch, and we had ample time to talk before Mr. Charles had to return to his office on Broad Street and we to the Library Society.

There is no really proper moment for introducing a question about North Charleston into an after-dinner conversation in an old Charleston home, and we never would have succeeded in introducing it if Mr. Charles himself had not prepared the way. The conversation somehow turned to the Carolina Yacht Club, of which I knew he had long been a member. Did he still go boating as of old? Well, he still was a member, still had a boat—he said "bo't" in the Charleston English that is so odd and so charming to non-Charleston ears. Mr. Charles still had a "bo't," but he went sailing less often than of old. Formerly you just went to the bo't-yard, hoisted sail, and put right out with no delay. Now you had to go to the "yacht basin" and work your "bo't" slowly out through a lot of congestion, by a devious route, before you could do any sailing. It was too much trouble.

Things were not exactly what they used to be. For years and years Mr. Charles and his family had moved out to Sullivan's Island during the hot season, to get the sea breeze. It was very nice there, and they, like other Charlestonians, had always enjoyed their simple cottage and the relative seclusion of that summer colony. Now a large tract on Sullivan's Island was about to become a "state project," and their ancient privacy was threatened with invasion by the multitude.

The portraits of Mrs. Charles's Colonial and Revolutionary

ancestors were there on the wall. In particular there was a gentleman in a stock, with excellently powdered hair, who might have been Mr. Charles himself dressed up for a masquerade. In times past this gentleman and others like him had faced and solved, over and over again, the problem of the invasion of privacy, and still worse problems. They had known what to do about "state projects." They had a theory about such matters and had applied it with astonishing skill. Old Charleston was the physical evidence of their success. I looked this gentleman in the eye and put my question: "What about North Charleston?"

The gentleman in the stock did not change countenance. Neither did Mr. Charles. When you have been fighting intrusions with considerable success for nearly three hundred years, you do not quail before a North Charleston. Mr. Charles, smiling a little, explained the situation carefully, without the least air of irritation or patronage, as if my question were the most natural question that could arise in after-dinner talk.

During World War II there had been, he said, a vast development in connection with the Navy Yards and such things. A lot of people came in. They brought their families and settled down. So a small new city grew up over there in the direction of Cooper River. The Charleston Chamber of Commerce thought all that development a good thing because it brought new business to Charleston.

And that was the kind of thing Mr. Charles had believed in, too, in his younger days. But he had found out, long ago, that although business expansion looked good on paper, in practice it didn't mean that Charleston folks like himself were any better off. There would be more business, yes, but there would be more competition. So what happened was that you just worked harder than ever—harder than you ought—without getting any real increase of benefits.

As to North Charleston, he had expected it would more or less fade out after the war was over. But a lot of those people had stayed on. They didn't have war jobs any longer, but they got up things to do—dry-cleaning shops, garages, all sorts of little makeshift establishments. Perhaps some of them just lived off the government. And now it looked as if North Charleston were going to be a permanent thing. They had a population of some thousands, and yes, they had a high school. People had come from all around—not from South Carolina so much, not even from the South maybe, but from all over the United States. They hustled and made a lot of noise. They had begun to say that the future belonged to them, not to Old Charleston. They had even been known to say that they of North Charleston had the better right to the name *Charleston*. They wanted to assume the name—to drop the "North" part —and to let Old Charleston slide into a subordinate role, let it be the decaying suburb of a new city.

At this point Mr. Charles smiled again, as if to say that all occasion for gravity had passed, once the claims of North Charleston had been actually stated. He neither refuted nor supported the claims. He just stated them. There they stood in all their nakedness. That was what one noticed about them mainly, in Mr. Charles's sitting-room, as it was what one noticed about the drum majorettes during the parade. The flesh and the devil are doubtless ineradicable elements of human life, but when they suddenly appear as an accent in a parade or a program, one can see how stripped they are of any but the crudest meaning. Their inappropriateness is the signal of the power they propose to exercise—if they can gain power.

Back at the Charleston Library Society, or walking in Middleton Gardens, or elsewhere in Old Charleston, it was hard to have much faith in the boldly asserted claims of any other Charleston. If anything were going to swallow Old Charleston, it would have to display more capacity for destruction than any other natural or human force had yet been able to exert upon the ancient city. For from the beginning, through storm, siege, revolution, earthquake, flood and fire, and drastic social and economic changes, Charleston had remained distinctly

Charleston, and nobody had ever found a way to nickname it or advertise it as anything but Charleston.

Its Library Society, its colleges, schools, churches, orphanages, its St. Cecilia Society and other organizations had histories that reached back continuously into its remote past. The names on the rosters and at the heads of its organizations were the names that had been in such places since colonial days. Continuity of family, of family life, and family position —irrespective of economic status—was in fact a great distinction of Charleston among old American cities; for elsewhere that continuity had been generally broken by one cause or another.

With this continuity Charleston had a stability that expressed itself in the pattern of its streets and the conservatism of its architecture. The map of Charleston in 1948 was not substantially different from the map of Charleston two centuries before. If John Stuart, whom George III in 1763 appointed superintendent of Indian affairs for the South, could have returned in 1948 to seek his home, he would have found it at 106 Tradd Street, just where he built it in 1772—for a brief occupancy, as it happened, since the Revolution ejected him, as a Tory, rather speedily from his new house.

Not that Charleston had not changed from time to time in its own way. It had changed, but generally only by some mysterious process of adaptation that kept it still Charleston. Some might argue that this was all accident—might say that it was due to Charleston's unfavorable position as a seaport, or that kind of thing. But there must have been, surely, a strong element of deliberate choice in Charleston's process of adaptation to the new. As a seaport city, Charleston was necessarily an entrepreneur that had to give a great deal of consideration to its material concerns. In process of looking after its material concerns, if it had chosen to do so, Charleston at any time could have wrecked its Georgian houses, torn down its enclosed yards, junked its handsome iron gates, and gone in for

Victorian gingerbread, bungalows, imitation Greek revival, imitation English cottage types, functional architecture, or whatever might happen along. But it had not done so. Eighteenth-century Charleston had made just enough concessions to take advantage of the more desirable modern improvements. No more. And there it was. Among older American cities only its neighbor, Savannah in Georgia, approached that condition.

The secret of Charleston's stability, if it was any secret, was only the old Southern principle that material considerations, however important, are means not ends, and should always be subdued to the ends they are supposed to serve, should never be allowed to dominate, never be mistaken for ends in themselves. If they are mistaken for ends, they dominate everything, and then you get instability. You get the average modern city, you get New York and Detroit, you get industrial civilization, world wars, Marxist communism, the New Deal.

Historians, noting that the ante-bellum South was in a sense materialistic, in that it found ways of prospering from the sale of cotton and tobacco, and relied heavily upon slave labor, have had the problem of explaining why that same South developed a chivalrous, courteous, religious, conservative, and stable society quite different from that which obtained in the also materialistic, but more industrialized, rational, idealistic, progressive North. Frequently they have explained the paradox of Southern society by saying that the "aristocratic" planter was somehow able to dominate the coarser, more acquisitive elements of Southern life and, through some mysterious exercise of prestige, to persuade these elements to accept his "code" of chivalry, courtesy, religion, conservatism. But the historians have mistaken effect for cause. The planter's "aristocratic" leadership was the result, not the cause, of a general diffusion of standards of judgment that all the South, even the Negro slaves, accepted as a basic principle of life. Mr. Francis Butler Simkins, in his book *The South Old and New,* has taken securer ground than the average historian when he notes that the South at the outbreak of the Civil War was almost the only truly religious society left in the Western world.

That old, religious South set the good life above any material means to life and consistently preferred the kind of material concerns that would least interfere with and best contribute to the good life. Its preferred occupations were agriculture, law, the church, and politics—pursuits which develop the whole man rather than the specialist, the free-willed individual rather than the anonymous unit of the organized mass. It had other preferences which, like those named, represented the metaphysical choices of a traditional society. Books could be, and have been, and ought still to be written about these metaphysical choices; but with reference to material means of existence, such as money, one could clinch the discourse by pointing out the traditional attitude of the Southern Negro toward work and wages. If you paid the Negro twice the normal wage for a day's work, you did not get more work from him—that is to say, more devotion to work within a given period, with increased production as the result. Not at all. The Negro simply and ingenuously worked only *half* as many days or hours as before—and spent the rest of the time in following his conception of the good life: in hunting, dancing, singing, social conversation, eating, religion, and love. This well-known habit of the Negro's, disconcerting to employers and statisticians, was absolutely correct according to Southern principles. The Negro, so far as he had not been corrupted into heresy by modern education, was the most traditional of Southerners, the mirror which faithfully and lovingly reflected the traits that Southerners once all but unanimously professed.

That had been the idea in Charleston too. It was what Mr. Simkins in his book, perhaps being misled by his historical predecessors, had called the "country gentleman" idea. But Charleston, which had always been urban, always a town or a city of counting-houses, warehouses, factors, bankers, financial agents, and the like, was not a city of country gentlemen, exactly. It had agreed with the country gentlemen and with others of every sort, including the Negro, on letting the relationship between work, wages, and life be determined by the metaphysical judgment indicated above. That was what made Charleston Charleston and not "The Indigo City" or something of the kind.

But now here were the drum majorettes, representing North Charleston.

Perhaps they were, after all, the most formidable invaders that Charleston ever had to face.

What is a drum majorette? The word is not in my copy of *Webster's Collegiate Dictionary.*

A drum major, however, can easily be defined. A drum major is the leader of a band of music. Not its leader in a musical sense, not its musical director. The drum major is the leader of the band for purposes of marching and parading while band music is being played. As such he fills a utilitarian as well as an ornamental role. He marches in front and center of the band as it marches and plays, and with his baton he marks the time and signals for marching evolutions like "column right," "column left," "countermarch," "halt," "forward, march." His baton is not a mere foolish ornament; it is an instrument of direction. Formerly the drum majors of military and quasi-military bands were always as tall as could be obtained, no doubt because drum majors might be better seen and followed as they wielded their batons. Tradition also prescribed that they should be of tremendously military aspect, however ornately uniformed; and severity and precision, rather than drollery, were the essential thing. But, since a band of music is itself a kind of flourish, a gallant addition to the business of systemized killing and being killed, the drum major was permitted his individual flourishes even in strictly military bands. He could exhibit a certain amount of skill at twirling and tossing his baton if he did not abuse his official military capacity in doing so.

Now a drum majorette is or ought to be a female drum major. It must be allowed that such a role *can* be undertaken by a girl or woman, provided the drum majorette performs the useful as well as the ornamental duties of a drum major. It would be supposed that a drum majorette would be uniformed like the members of the band.

When a drum majorette is not so uniformed, is in fact largely without clothes, a new element has entered, and it is time to ask what is happening. When a band is led not by one but by a squad of drum majorettes, all equipped with batons and all equally unclad, you know exactly what is happening. The real function and use of the drum major have been ignored in favor of an exciting display which has nothing to do with music or marching or ceremony. An occasion has been exploited for purposes that will not bear examination. The drum major has turned into a follies girl, a bathing beauty, a strip-tease dancer. The baton, once used to give commands to the band, becomes the ornament by which the drum majorette attracts attention to her charms. The band, less and less important, gets along the best it can and becomes, in fact, a jazz orchestra accompanying the drum majorette dance.

To put it in other terms, the modern regime has performed one of the abstractions typical of its sway. It has abstracted the spectacular and ornamental features of the drum major from his complete role, and made that abstraction dominant to the point of extinction of all other features. The next logical step would be to abandon the band and to substitute a sound-truck playing phonograph records—a sound-truck which could be preceded by and followed by and covered with a large company of drum majorettes, all twirling batons, all as little clothed as the censor would allow.

The abstraction is so alluring that even college presidents, to say nothing of the public, do not perceive its meaning, which is as completely immoral and ruthless as can be. But it is not the bare flesh of drum majorettes in their quasi-march

—really a dance—that is per se immoral. It is the misuse of the ceremony of gallantry, implied in all march music, that is immoral in itself and that is symptomatic of a deeper immorality. Drum majorettes came into style, I believe, in high schools and colleges that had become addicted to professionalized athletics of the modern kind. The old amateur athletics, particularly football, was an exhibition of valor that once naturally deserved the kind of encouragement supplied by band music, especially martial band music. The new athletics systematically exploits the gallantry of youth for purposes confessedly material. It has put the schools and colleges in the business of commercial entertainment. The drum majorettes are an advertisement of that entertainment, a lure to the admission gate.

Communities that accept such perversions of the beautiful and the gallant are no longer communities in any true sense. They have passed into a state of disequilibrium and social instability that makes them extremely dangerous. If they do not know what use ought to be made of beauty and gallantry and, still worse, do not care what use is made of these so long as impressive material results are obtained, there is nothing to stop them from perverting and using as an instrument of power anything that can be so perverted and used. They are mobs, made vastly more dangerous than the ordinary spontaneous mob because, though spiritually mobs, they retain the rational organization supplied to them by science and education, and can thus use chaos itself as a form of power. The mob leaders always excuse the mob acts, of course, by proclaiming wondrous distant goals some day to be attained. Their proclamations are to be found in such documents as the Communist Manifesto, the Atlantic Charter, and the reports of the President's committees on education, civil rights, and the like. But always, inevitably, these mob leaders and mobs are so preoccupied with and dominated by the abstractions they create as means to an end that they never reach or even approximate the distant goal. They merely exert the power derived from the original abstraction, which becomes an end in itself.

The terrible results of this process are visible throughout the world. Everywhere one looks there are ruins—the ruins of societies no less than the ruins of cities. Over the ruins stream mobs led by creatures no longer really human—creatures who, whether they make shift to pass as educators, planners, editors, commissars, or presidents, wield batons, dance dances, and flaunt their naked abstractions with exactly the same inappropriateness and destructiveness as does the drum majorette.

Is Charleston gulled by the drum majorette and her parallels? I have no way of knowing. But things move very rapidly in our time, and doubtless we shall soon know the event. If any agent of abstraction rolls over and possesses Old Charleston, then something will be gone that money could not buy and that money can never restore, either through private philanthropy or Federal subsidy. And if Charleston should perish, strong and subtle in resistance though it has been in the past, can other communities which with varying success have fought the same fight also continue to stand? All face the same foe, and the foe is stronger, is pressing harder than ever.

Part V

REGIONALISM AND NATIONALISM

STILL REBELS, STILL YANKEES

AT A MEETING of Southern writers in Charleston during
the autumn of 1932, Laurence Stallings looked belligerently
around him and expressed an ardent preference for a "Balkanized America." "What I like about Charleston," he said,
"is that it has resisted Abraham Lincoln's attempts to put the
country into Arrow Collars. If the South had won the War,
the country would have had lots more color."

The rebelliousness of Mr. Stallings need not compel us
to suspect him of being an unreconstructed Southerner disguised as a man of letters, who was looking for artistic reasons
to justify what arms and politics once failed to secure. Discontent with the uniformity of America is common enough.
What is not common is the knowledge that this uniformity,
a byword ever since James Bryce looked at the American com-
monwealth through the spectacles of the Gilded Age, is more
a myth than a reality.

As a myth, it probably represents the wishful thinking of
those who, for their own designs, want America to become
uniform. Actually America is not yet uniform; very likely it
is less uniform than it was and far more Balkanized than
Mr. Stallings dreams. The unreconstructed Southerners have
done their part in keeping it Balkan; but there are unreconstructed Yankees, too, and other unreconstructed Americans
of all imaginable sorts, everywhere engaged in preserving their
local originality and independence.

The only people who do not know this are certain experts
who do most of the current talking about American society.
They live in a sociological pickle of statistics and progress.
They are eternally looking for what they call "social values,"

but they strangely confine their research to libraries and graduate "projects" at the larger universities. They avoid the places where social values may be encountered in the flesh. If they stumble upon a living social value, walking visibly about some spot of earth and drawing its nutriment from a tradition embodied in the houses, speech, crafts, music, folk-lore, and wisdom of an actual people, their rule is to denounce it as an anachronism and to call for its extermination. For them, nothing must grow according to its nature, but things "develop" by laboratory formulas, which are obtained by inspecting the reactions of the most abnormal and depressed specimens of humankind, too weak to protest against sociological vivisection.

Those of us who still believe in the map of the United States know that it marks the residence of some diverse Americans who had better not go unacknowledged. In Vermont, for instance, are people who are still Yankees; and in Georgia, and elsewhere, there are still Rebels. I remember talking with a certain Virginian who watched a Vermont sunset with me, one summer evening. As the sun passed below the distant Adirondacks, we looked at the Green Mountains around us, and at the trim Vermont fields where all the weeds were flowers and all the grass was hay. In the clear detail of the afterglow we saw the forests of spruce and balsam and maple, and spoke of how the very wilderness, in this New England state, had uprightness and order. The woods were as snug and precise as a Yankee kitchen—no ragged edges, no sprawling, nothing out of place. In the clearings the farmhouses were all painted; and the barns were painted, too. The streams were orthodox streams, almost model streams, with water always translucent and stones rounded and picturesquely placed among moss and ferns. They were often called "brooks"—a word that for Southerners existed only on the printed page.

On this land, the Virginian said, the Yankees had looked so intimately and long that, like the man in Hawthorne's story of the Great Stone Face, they had become the image of what they contemplated. The Yankee genius of Vermont was upright, vertical, and no doubt Puritan. Where the landscape itself enforced consistency and order, how could the people concede much virtue to inconsistency and irregularity? The forebears of the Vermont Yankee had once failed to understand how Southerners could be devoted both to slavery *and* to democracy. That old failure of understanding did not seem queer, or worth more than a passing sigh, to two Southerners who stood looking at sunset upon a land whose gentled wildness suggested the urgent possibility of a well-ordered universe, cut to a discreet Yankee pattern. But the human geography of America had now become a parti-colored thing, sprawling across the continent in a crazy quilt of provinces, or sections, each with its private notion of a universe. No longer, as in the sixties, could the Yankee make bold to set up a general pattern for the entire Union. He had enough to do if he would defend and preserve what was peculiarly his own—his very own, surely, in upper New England. In such a purpose of preservation the two Southerners at last could make bold to sympathize, even to help if possible. But preservation could not be achieved without recognizing a principle of diversity in American life. Only by such means could one make any sense out of Lamar's famous epigram in his eulogy on Sumner, "My countrymen, know one another and you will love one another." It ceased to have meaning if America was to be subjugated to the ideal of uniformity, or to the ideal universe that some one section might generate.

But how could the principle of diversity be inculcated? On the negative side, certain false images, the product of legend or propaganda, must somehow be counterbalanced. To the Virginian I recalled the horror of a good lady from the Middle West, who was motoring from Washington to Richmond. Mount Vernon was all right, she thought; there the legend was safely frozen. But beyond, on the road to Richmond, what had become of all the great manisons she had read about, the cotton fields with Negroes caroling,

the old gentlemen in goatees and white vests, sipping mint
juleps in the shade? They were not visible. There were only
a few scattered shacks and tumbledown barns in miles of impenetrable wilderness that looked for all the world as it must
have looked when John Smith first invaded it. If she could
have encountered the legend, the lady would have been content. But not seeing it or knowing how to locate it, she was
smitten with a housewifely desire to get at this ragged land
with a good broom and whisk it into seemliness.

Other sojourners had been anxious to do a far more drastic
tidying-up. The Harlan County visitors, the Scottsboro at-
torneys, the shock troops of Dayton and Gastonia asked no
questions about the genius of place. Wherever they went on
their missions of social justice, they carried with them a
legend of the future, more dangerously abstract than the
legend of the past, and sternly demanded that the local arrangements be made to correspond with it, at whatever cost. The
local arrangements, indeed, might bear mending. And yet
the only America that the visitors offered as a model was an
overgrown urban America, forever in process of becoming one
laboratory experiment after another.

What could be done about all this? Our answers were
shrouded in darkness as we walked back to the log fires and
good company of a New England inn. The Virginian, after
the fashion of good Southerners who do not want to let anybody know the incertainty of their minds under modern
conditions, did not propose any answer. Instead, he told several good stories. They were his courteous and delightful
way of saying that he was being pounded between his own
unyielding loyalty and the howling respectability of the great
world.

II

If any answer is to be found, if anything positive is to be
done, it must surely be through a laborious process of discovering America all over again. When one looks at America,

not to see how it does or does not fit the synthetic ideals proposed for its future, but only with the modest purpose of detecting the realities—let us say the social values—that persist in local habitations, he soon realizes that comparisons are more fruitful than condemnations. More specifically, when one has had the good fortune to go directly from a summer in Vermont to an autumn and winter in Middle Georgia, he forms a clear picture of sectional differences. This picture is not in the least favorable to the notion that the diverse America of the Rebels and Yankees is in any immediate danger of being submerged.

If on coming to Vermont I had consulted the modern legend of New England that vaguely haunted my mind, I would have received the iconoclastic shock which our advanced thinkers argue is the first step toward salvation. Had not a New England migrant to the South assured me that his ancestral acres were now inhabited by Montenegrins, who had turned them into a goat farm? Had not the sepulchral Eugene O'Neill and others told tales of the poverty and decadence of New England life? The farms were deserted, it was said; the immigrants and mill-towns had come; the Yankees had left for parts unknown, or, remaining, had become degenerate. Even the loyalty of Robert Frost gave no comfortable assurance, if one accepted the New York alec's criticism of *North of Boston;* though there were many wistful asides in which Frost put forth the guarded wisdom of a not yet daunted soul. The New England of Whittier and Webster was supposed to be extinct; it had been replaced by Puritan-baiters and F. Scott Fitzgeraldites who drank cocktails and read Proust when not conducting the insurance business of the United States.

But if the Vermont that I saw was in the least representative of New England, this composite picture was a wild detraction. In Vermont, if nowhere else, a New England like that of Whittier and Webster miraculously persisted, a reality capable of reducing a Southerner almost to despairing envy. I could understand what led Walter Hines Page, a quarter of a century ago, to disparage his native North Carolina and fall in love with New England. But the time was past when one needed to disparage or praise in the interest of the America Page dreamed about, for in the nineteen-thirties it seemed impossible of realization, or, where realized, already past saving. To one who did not accept Lincoln's quaint idea that the United States must become "all one thing or all the other," it seemed more than ever true that the unity of America must rest, first of all, on a decent respect for sectional differences.

If Vermont and Georgia could be taken in a broad way to stand for New England and the Deep South, one could easily trace out the most general differences. The Vermont towns, like the Vermont landscape, were swept and garnished, as if the Day of Judgment might at any moment summon them into the presence of the celestial inspector. They looked as if Vermonters lived by the adage "Handsome is as handsome does," and one could reflect that this proverb might well have issued from some collaborative effort of Poor Richard and Jonathan Edwards. The most delightful of Southern towns was almost certain to mix a little squalor with its grandeurs. Here, what a Southerner most particularly noticed was the neatly painted aspect of everything, the absence of ramshackle buildings and litter, the white steeples of churches, the shipshapeness of streets, yards, garages, barber shops, and public buildings. By some special benison of God and the New England conscience, not a billboard had been allowed to sprout between Bennington and the Canadian border. Perhaps by the same double grace, not a weed sprouted either. All the weeds had turned into ferns and buttercups. Vermont farms were Currier and Ives prints of what good farms ought to look like, with orchards and brooks in exactly the right places and gates that did not need mending. In the background were lakes and mountains where one would put them if he were Aladdin or Wordsworth. It was not surprising to be told that hardly a poison snake, and little or no poison ivy, existed in the state of Vermont; or to find that there were excellent trails running the whole length of the Green Mountains, with finger-posts at every wilderness crossroads, and tin huts, with beds, firewood, and caretaker, atop of the highest peaks. A few nagging irregularities of nature, like blackflies and mosquitoes, seemed really blasphemous in a land to which God had given a monopoly of all things good and precise. No wonder, with all this beneficence around them, that the Yankees remembered the *Mayflower* and forgot John Smith, honored Bunker Hill and neglected King's Mountain. If they could claim such priority in the beneficence of God, their proprietary feeling toward the Revolutionary War and their once almost hereditary claim to the direction of the United States government were by comparison insignificant appurtenances, theirs as a matter of course and by general presumption.

Although I did not hold very devotedly to the economic determinism of modern historians, it was a temptation to say that the people were a great deal like the land. There was the climate, which put keenness into a Southerner's veins. Summer was short, and one had to make the most of it; winter was severe, and one had to keep shield and buckler perpetually ready against it—in that matter was God benevolent or ruthless? Short summers and cold winters made the Vermont Yankee frugal and careful. He must watch his corners. If he were caught napping, he would perish. So much and no more was the gift of his seasons; so much and no more was the rule of his nature. And one had to watch over his neighbor as well as work with him if the general security were not to be imperiled by some outrageous letting down of bars. Very likely, the New England civic conscience derived as much from the imperatives of climate as from the Puritan tradition: the one egged on the other.

No great check had ever been put upon the development of qualities that the Southerner recognized as ineradicably Yankee. History had been as kind to the Yankee as God had been kind. Since Revolutionary times no great sudden change had ever swept over these peaceful towns and this quiet land-scape. Industrialism had come slowly and somewhat agreeably upon a people who had the ingenuity to use it and the moral force to make it behave. How could they who thought they knew how to tame the monster realize that he might walk unshackled and ravening elsewhere? The Yankees, indeed, had never tasted defeat. Since Burgoyne's expedition no in-vader had come upon them to ravage and destroy. They had freed the Negroes, replying "I can" to duty's "Thou must"; but they were fortunately exempt from the results of emanci-pation, for no Negroes lived among them to acquaint them with the disorder of unashamed and happy dirt. One knew that a slum in New England would be a well-managed slum, and that New Englanders would comprehend Secretary Per-kins' horror at the lack of plumbing in unreformed America and her notion of saving the barefoot South by building shoe factories. For in New England humanitarianism was the natu-ral flower of good sense. In a land where everything was so right, it was hard to imagine a perverse land where so much could be so wrong without disturbing either a people's com-posure or their happiness.

But in the plantation country of Middle Georgia the social values required a different yardstick. The genius of Georgia was stretched out, relaxed, and easy, in keeping with the land-scape, which required a large and horizontal view of mundane affairs. The Georgian assumed that God would have sense and heart enough to take into consideration, when Judgment Day came around, a good deal besides external and man-made appearances. God was a gentleman, indeed, who would cer-tainly know, without being told, that one was a person, a somebody, doing his best among some rather amazing ar-rangements that had better not be talked about too much. The climate might or might not predispose the Georgia Rebel to laziness; the fact was, he worked and fretted more than the Yankee knew. But the Rebel idea was never to *seem* to work and fret. You must not let your work ride you, was the saying. In plain truth, you did not need to. The land was bountiful, and the Lord would provide, and in event of the Lord's failure or displeasure you could always fall back on your kinfolks.

Where the seasons were all mixed up, so that autumn merged into spring without any sharp demarcation, and you might have a dubious summer in the middle of winter, it became almost a point of honor not to worry too much about provision. There was no need to watch corners when something was growing all the time. Almost anything would grow in Middle Georgia, and almost everything did grow, including weeds whose invasions could not possibly be repelled from every roadside and ditch if they were to be kept out of cotton and corn.

The Georgia landscape had a serene repose that lulled a man out of all need of conscience. It was anything but swept and garnished. It could be either mild or majestic or genial or savage depending on what view you got of pines against red earth, or Negro cabins underneath their chinaberry trees, or sedge grass running into gullies and thence to impenetrable swamps, or deserted mansions lost in oak groves and magnolias. Rivers were muddy and at times unrestrained; they got out of bounds, as all things natural did here. In the pine barrens you might get an impression of desolation and melancholy; but things could grow lushly too, with the overpowering vegetable passion that harrowed the Puritan soul of Amy Lowell, when she visited the Magnolia Gardens at Charleston. But finally, it was a well-tilled country, where you were forever seeing the Negro and his mule against the far horizon, or the peach orchards bursting into an intoxicating pink.

The seasons were full of charms and intimidations. Spring, with its dogwood blossoms and soft airs, might deliver a tornado or a flood; summer, full of grown corn and harvest ease, might turn into dusty drouth. The woods that lured you to enter and gave nuts and flowers for the taking were full of hidden terrors. Sit on a mossy bank without precaution, and in a few hours you might be on fire with chigoe bites. Stoop to pick a flower, and you might find a rattlesnake. Indoors the housewife had to fight cockroaches and flies; outdoors were hawks, weasels, possums, coons, and such varmints to harry the henhouse. Precision, for the Georgian, must rank among the Utopian virtues. If New England encouraged man to believe in an ordered universe, Georgia—and a good deal of the South besides—compelled him to remember that there were snakes in Eden. Nature, so ingratiating and beautiful, which bound the Georgian to his land with a love both possessive and fearful, was a fair but dreadful mistress, unpredictable and uncontrollable as God. The New Englander knew exactly where to find nature harsh and nature yielding, and he could make his arrangements accordingly. But the Georgian never knew. His safest policy was to relax, and he readily developed a great degree of tolerance for irregularity in nature and man. At his lowest level, this quality made him lackadaisical and trifling. In this he differed from the New England Yankee, who became a perfectionist, and then at his worst might turn into a zealot, strangely intolerant even while, as idealist, he argued for tolerance.

History, like God and nature, had been both generous and unkind to Georgia and the South. The Georgia Rebel must approach his early history through a bloody link of war and reconstruction that was hazy and bygone to the Vermont Yankee. Defeat had possessed him and had rubbed deep into his wounds. Around him were the visible reminders of destruction and humiliation. His land had been ravaged and rebuilt, and he had been told to forget. But he would not and could not forget, and was therefore torn between his loyalty and his awareness that the great world was bored with his not forgetting. He had been rebuked for seeming inept at administering a newfangled government that he did not understand or like any too well, and in which he had been allowed to participate only by a kind of negligent afterthought. Turning desperately to the industrial civilization against which he had once taken arms, he had played it as a hedge against the problematic future. Though agrarian at heart, he had been forced to wonder whether the ingenious Yankee might not be right after all.

Thus he remembered the faith and hankered after the flesh-pots at the same time. But industrialism, declining to be treated as a mere hedge, began Sherman's march to the sea all over again. It piled ugliness upon wreckage and threw the old arrangements out of kilter. The United Daughters of the Confederacy and the Kiwanis Club flourished side by side. Mule wagon and automobile, fundamentalism and liberalism, education and illiteracy, aristocratic pride and backwoods independence disproved the axiom that two bodies cannot occupy the same space. Cities that preserved the finest flavor of the old regime had to be approached over brand-new roads where billboards, filling stations, and factories broke out in a modernistic rash among the water oaks and Spanish moss. And everywhere was the Negro, a cheerful grinning barnacle tucked away in all the tender spots of Southern life, not to be removed without pain, not to be cherished without tragedy. The Georgian, when reproached for his intolerance, told himself that actually nobody outdid him in fond tolerance of the Negro. Lynchings, the work of hotheads and roustabouts, were regrettable; but what did a few lynchings count in the balance against the continual forbearance and solicitude that the Georgian felt he exercised toward the amiable children of cannibals, whose skins by no conceivable act of Congress or educational program could be changed from black to white. The presence of the Negro, which had its advantages in agriculture and domestic service, made the Georgian's life both comfortable and ramshackle. It gave him devoted servants and social problems, cheap labor and hideous slums, an endless flow of folklore and anecdote, and eternal apprehension for the future. But in his own way the Georgian respected the Negro, as another irregularity, taking a human and personal form, that had somehow to be lived with. He distrusted all ready-made prescriptions for bringing about regularity. In Georgia, life went along horizontally. You never crossed a bridge until you came to it—and maybe not then.

III

But sociologists not only cross bridges; they build all imaginable kinds of new ones. The picture of America, as sociologically reformed, does not contemplate any great concessions to Yankee uprightness or Rebel relaxation. Indeed, the sociologist, armed with science, is ready to follow reformation with transformation. In the vast inevitable working of the social forces, sectional differences become irrelevant. With a cold smile, the sociologist pronounces a death sentence upon Rebel and Yankee alike. Not that they matter very much— but they will have to yield!

When he talks like this, I am perversely compelled to remember the individuals I have seen, Brother Jonathan of Vermont and Cousin Roderick of Georgia, whom I cannot imagine as yielding to the puny weapons flourished by our social philosophers. They are local incarnations of the Old Adam. They are the immovable bodies that can furnish the irresistible social forces with an incalculable meeting. They are human beings, undebatably alive; and they are different.

Brother Jonathan lives in Yankeetown—for a place name is often a "town" in New England, and less often a "ville" or a "burg," as in the South. He is a wizened little chip of a man, with blue eyes and a bald head, and he looks frail enough for any northwest wind to blow away. But there is not a wind on this planet strong enough to blow Brother Jonathan off his mountain farm. If any wind contrived to do so, he would climb right back again in the matter-of-fact way that Robert Frost describes in "Brown's Descent." He would

> *Bow with grace to natural law*
> *And then go round it on his feet.*

Brother Jonathan is past seventy years, and his wife Priscilla is well over sixty, but between them they still manage to do most of the daily work, in house and field, for a two-hundred-acre farm, most of which is in woodland and meadow. Nathaniel, their adopted son, helps some now and then; but Nathaniel, who is carpenter, mechanic, cabinet-maker, mountain guide, and tax collector combined, is busy putting up the new house into which he and Sophronia, his wife, will soon move. They are building it extra large, to take in summer boarders. Sophronia helps Priscilla as much as she can, but she has her own small children to look after. Later on, Brother Jonathan hopes to get a twelve-year-old boy from the orphanage, who will do the chores for his keep. But now, Brother Jonathan must be up at daylight to start the kitchen fire and milk the cows. If it is haying-time, he is out in the meadow early with the mowing-machine, which he has sharpened and greased with his own hands, or repaired at his own smithy if it needs repairing. The mower bumps and clicks through the rough meadow, tossing the little man to and fro as he warily skirts the outcrops of stone that will have to be circled with a scythe to get the last wisps of hay.

Later, he changes the patient old horses from mower to wagon and starts in with a pitchfork. It is a sight to see him navigating the loaded wagon from the upper field to the barn, past jutting boulders and through deep ruts. But his pace is easy. He keeps it up all day without undue perspiration or agony, and after supper cuts his wood and milks his cows again in unruffled calm. He does not seem tired or bored. As he milks, he philosophizes to the listening stranger. Yes, times are not what they were, but a man can get along if he will be careful and honest. Foolish people, of course, never know how to manage. The harm all comes from people of no character that do things without regard to common decency. The stars are shining when he takes the pails of milk into the kitchen. Under the hanging oil lamp he reads the Burlington *Free Press* or the *Pathfinder* until he begins to nod.

All the arrangements on Brother Jonathan's farm are neat and ingenious—the arrangements of a man who has had to depend largely on his own wit and strength. The barn is cleverly arranged in two stories, with a ramp entering the upper story for the convenience of Brother Jonathan and his hay wagon, and running water on the lower story for the convenience of the animals. One well, near the barn, is operated by a windmill; it supplies the stock. Another well, higher up, supplies the house, for Brother Jonathan has a bathroom in the upper hall and faucets in the kitchen. He has no telephone or electric lights. A man can dig and pipe his own wells, and they are finished; but telephone and electric lights, not being home contrivances, require a never-ending tribute to Mammon. He has his own sawmill and his own workshop, where he can mend things without losing time and money on a trip to the village. His garage, occupied at present by Nathaniel's four-year-old car (which is not being used), contains a carpenter's bench and a small gas engine rigged to do sawing and turning. There are pelts drying on the walls.

The house is built to economize space and retain heat. For all its modest proportions, it is convenient and comfortable. The kitchen is spacious and well equipped. The pantry and cellar are stored with vegetables, fruits, and meats that Priscilla has put up with her own hands. The dining-room, with its long table covered with spotless oilcloth, is eating-room, living-room, and children's playground combined. Here all gather after supper: the women with their tatting and embroidery; the lively dark-eyed boy from the village with his homemade fiddle; a summer boarder or two, or a visiting relative; and always Brother Jonathan with his newspaper. In one corner is a reed organ, on which Brother Jonathan occasionally plays hymns. In another corner is a desk, filled with miscellaneous papers, books, and old magazines. On the walls hang a glass frame containing butterflies, the gift of a wandering entomologist; an 1876 engraving of General Washington being welcomed at New York, with the pictures of all the

Presidents, up to Hayes, around the border; and a faded photograph of a more youthful Brother Jonathan with his fellow baggage-clerks, taken in the days when he went west and got a job in Chicago. Brother Jonathan talks of Chicago sometimes, but he never reveals why he, unlike many other Yankees, came back to Vermont.

The temper of the household is a subdued and even pleasantness, which the loud alarms and excursions of the world do not penetrate very far. The progress of Nathaniel's new house; the next morning's arrangements for gathering vegetables and canning; what Brother Jonathan shall say in the speech he is to make at the approaching celebration of the Timothys' gold wedding—such topics take precedence over the epic contentions of Mr. Hoover and Mr. Roosevelt. Priscilla may go so far as to marvel that anybody can doubt the goodness of Mr. Hoover. (She does not add, as she well might, that Mr. Roosevelt, as a "Yorker," inherits the distrust of Vermont.) Or Brother Jonathan may warm up to politics enough to announce his everlasting distrust of liquorish Al Smith and to confess that, out of firm disapproval for vice, he has once or twice bolted the Republican ticket and voted for the Prohibition party's candidate. But in the South, he supposes, he would be as good a Democrat as the next one. They are all curious about the South—about Negroes—and whether the Southern people still have hard feelings against the North (on this point they seem a little anxious and plaintive). But the talk soon shifts to the Green Mountain Boys, from one of whom Brother Jonathan is descended, or to stories of his childhood, when bears were as thick as porcupines are now— he tells of how seven bears were once killed in the same tree. Into these stories Brother Jonathan may put a dry quip or two by way of garnishment. He has a store of homely jokes and extended metaphors, to which he frequently adds a humorous gloss to be sure the stranger gets the point. Then maybe there is a game of anagrams—or on another evening a corn-roast, with a few cronies and kinfolks from the village, who talk

the clipped Yankee talk that seems, to Southern ears, as pure
an English as can be, with only a little of the twang that dialect
stories have taught one to expect.

Brother Jonathan is not dogmatic to the point of testiness,
but he is firmly rationalistic on many points. He declares it
incredible, for instance, that Catholics can believe in tran-
substantiation—how can bread and wine *actually* turn into
the blood and body of Jesus Christ? Yet oddly enough, Brother
Jonathan is neither Congregationalist nor Unitarian, but
Methodist, and does not mind repeating the Apostles' Creed,
with its formidable references to the Trinity and the Resur-
rection. I am led to suspect that it is not the doctrine but the
authority to which Brother Jonathan is temperamentally hostile. He is used to depending on himself; he does not like to
be told things. And his independence is of a piece with the
whole conduct of his life. Years ago, when a famous local character eccentrically bought up all the surrounding woodland
and farm land and turned it into a forest reserve which he
bequeathed to a neighboring college, Brother Jonathan did
not sell out. He held on then, he holds on now, with a pos-
sessiveness that would be the despair of Communists. He
will continue to hold on, as long as trees yield maple syrup—
which he will never, never basely dilute with cane syrup—and
boarders return summer after summer.

For Brother Jonathan belongs in spirit to the old republic
of independent farmers that Jefferson wanted to see flourish
as the foundation of liberty in the United States. To conserve
that liberty he has his own Yankee arrangements: the "town,"
which the Southerner had to learn consisted of a village and
a great deal of contiguous territory up to the next "town-
line"; and the town meeting, at which Brother Jonathan can
stand up and tell the government what he thinks about it.
Of the uses of town meetings Priscilla has something to say,
which comes, I reflect, with a little feminine sauciness. A certain individual, she relates, was criticized for not painting
the "community house," as he had been employed to do; and

when he excused himself on the ground that the paint was
lacking, his own wife sprang up in the town meeting and
cried: "Don't believe a word he says. That paint's setting in
the cellar this minute!"

But the Southerner could reflect that such family intimacy
might have civic advantages. Brother Jonathan's local government is composed of nobody more Olympic or corrupt than
his own neighbors and relations. For him it is not something
off yonder, and he visualizes the national government (though
a little too innocently) as simply an enlarged town meeting,
where good management ought to be a matter of course. In
Yankeetown, good management is a matter of course; it maintains a library, it looks after roads, it sees that taxes are paid
and well spent. If the state government does not behave, Nathaniel himself will run for the legislature and see that it does
behave.

In all this there was much for a Southerner to savor curi-
ously and learn about—as he savored and learned about the
strange food that appeared on Brother Jonathan's table—
doughnuts for breakfast, maple syrup on pie and cereal, the
New England boiled dinner, the roasting ears that were really
roasted in the old Indian fashion. Just as Brother Jonathan's
menu suited the soil and the people, so his tidiness and responsibility suited the unobtrusive integrity of his character.
With emphasis, one could say: Vermont is upright, vertical,
and, even yet, Puritan—why not?

IV

And almost two thousand miles away, with an unconcern
about the state of the world that parallels but differs from
Brother Jonathan's, Cousin Roderick of Rebelville is achieving another salvation somehow not recorded in the auguries
of socialistic planning. Autumn is beginning, the scuppernongs are ripe, and he invites everybody to come over and
join him in the scuppernong arbor. In the late afternoon a
merry crew gather around the great vine, laughing and banter-

ing as they pick the luscious grapes and crush them against
their palates. Sister Caroline is there, with a figure as trim
and a wit as lively at eighty as it must have been at twenty.
Young Cousin Hector and his wife are there—they are "ref-
ugeeing" from the industrial calamity that overtook them in
a Northern city. And there are numerous other vague cousins
and sisters and children, all munching and passing family
gossip back and forth between bites. Cousin Roderick's
Dionysian laughter goes up heartiest of all among the leaves,
as he moves to and fro, rapidly gathering grapes and pressing
them upon the visitors. "Oh, you are not going to quit on us,"
he says. "You must eat more than *that*. Scuppernongs never
hurt a soul." The scuppernong vine, he declares, is a hundred
years old and nearly always fruitful. But not so old, never so
fruitful, puts in Sister Caroline, as the scuppernong vine at
the old place, that as barefoot children they used to clamber
over.

Then the meeting is adjourned to Cousin Roderick's great
front porch, where one looks out between white columns
at sunset clouds piling up into the deep blues and yellows
of a Maxfield Parrish sky. Down the long street of Rebelville,
between the mighty water oaks set out by Cousin Roderick's
kin, after the Confederate War, the cotton wagons are passing,
heaped high with the white mass of cotton and a Negro or
two atop; and the talk goes on, to the jingle of trace chains and
the clop of mule hoofs on the almost brand-new state highway, which is so much better for rubber tires than for mule
hoofs. Over yonder lives Cousin Roderick's Aunt Cecily, a
widow, the single indomitable inhabitant of a stately mansion
where economics has not yet prevailed against sentiment. Next
door is Uncle Burke Roderick, a Confederate veteran who at
ninety still drives his horse and buggy to the plantation each
morning. He is the last survivor of three brothers who were
named Pitt, Fox, and Burke, after their father's eighteenth-
century heroes. All around, indeed, are the Roderick kin, for
Cousin Roderick, whose mother married a Bertram, bears the

family name of his mother's people, a numerous clan who, by dint of sundry alliances and ancient understandings, attend to whatever little matters need attention in the community affairs of Rebelville, where Jefferson's "least government" principle is a matter of course. Before supper, or after, some of the kinfolks may drop in, for there is always a vast deal of coming and going and dropping in at Cousin Roderick's.

As he takes his ease on the porch, Cousin Roderick looks to be neither the elegant dandy nor the out-at-elbows dribbler of tobacco juice that partisans have accredited to the Southern tradition. He is a fairly tall, vigorous man, plainly dressed, with the ruddiness of Georgia sun and good living on his face. His eyes are a-wrinkle at the corners, ready to catch the humor of whatever is abroad. His hand fumbles his pipe as he tells one anecdote after another in the country drawl that has about as much of Mark Twain and Sut Lovingood in it as it has of the elisions and flattenings supposed to belong to Southern patrician speech. In fact, though he really is patrician, as the female members of his family can assure you, he does not look anything like the Old Colonel of legend, and in spirit he, too, belongs to the Jeffersonian constituency. He has something of the bearing of an English squire, and a good deal of the frontier heartiness that Augustus Baldwin Longstreet depicted in *Georgia Scenes*. He assumes that the world is good-humored and friendly until it proves itself otherwise. If it does prove itself otherwise . . . there is a glint in his eye that tells you he will fight.

Cousin Roderick is the opposite of Chaucer's Man of Law, who ever seemed busier than he was. Cousin Roderick is busier than he seems. His air of negligence, like his good humor, is a philosophical defense against the dangerous surprises that life may turn up. Really he is not negligent. He does not work with his own hands, like Brother Jonathan, or his Southern brothers of upcountry and bluegrass; but in the past he has worked a-plenty with his hands and knows how it should be done. On his several tracts of land, the gatherings of inheritance and purchase, are some one hundred and fifty Negroes whom he furnishes housing, food, and a little money; they do his labor—men, women, children together—they are his "hands." He is expected to call them by name, to get them out of jail, to doctor them, even sometimes to bury them, when "lodge dues" may have lapsed. They are no longer his slaves; but though they do not now utter the word, they do not allow him to forget that he has the obligations of a master.

As Cousin Roderick makes the "rounds" of his fields— no more on horseback, as of old, but in a battered Chevrolet —he sets forth his notions of economy. As for the depression, that is no new thing in Rebelville. People here have got used to ruination. After the Confederate War came Reconstruction; after Reconstruction, Tom Watson and the Populist turmoil of the nineties; a while later, the peach boom, and its collapse; then the Florida boom, with its devastations; and now, this new depression. Like most of his kin, Cousin Roderick has simply retreated into the old plantation economy. He tells how, when he was a young fellow, just beginning to take charge, his father came out to the plantation one day and asked for a ham. Cousin Roderick explained that hogs were up to a good price. He had sold the entire lot, on the hoof, and had good money in the bank.

"Sir," said the old man, "let me never again catch you without hams in your smokehouse and corn in your crib. You've got to make this land take care of itself!"

"And that," says Cousin Roderick, "is what I aim to do."

From the land he feeds his own family, the hundred and fifty Negroes, and the stock. Whatever is left, when taxes and upkeep are deducted, is the profit. Anything that grows, he will plant: asparagus, peaches, pecans, onions, peppers, to- matoes, and of course the great staple crops, grain, hay, and cotton. Especially cotton, for no matter how low the price, cot- ton is money. It is ridiculous, he thinks, to talk of getting people who are hard up for money to reduce cotton acreage.

For his part, Cousin Roerick intends to make every bale his land will produce. But if cotton fails, he still can sell cattle, or cabbage, or timber from his baronial holdings. Land is the only abiding thing, the only assurance of happiness and comfort. He wants more land, not less.

One suspects that Cousin Roderick, however hard pressed he may be at the bank, is fundamentally right. If he is not right, how does he manage, in these times, to send a daughter to college, and entertain his friends, and keep a cheerful face before the world? The portraits of his ancestors, looking down from their frames above great-grandfather's sideboard or his wife's new grand piano, eternally assure Cousin Roderick that he is right. They won this Eden of sandy earth and red clay, where all things grow with a vigor that neither winter nor drouth can abate. Not soon, not soon will their son give it up.

To the designs of experts who want to plan people's lives for them, Cousin Roderick gives no more than the indulgent attention of a naturally kindhearted man. He reads the anxious thunderings of the young men who reproduce, in the Macon *Telegraph,* the remote dynamitical poppings of the *New Republic,* and is unmoved. The young men are like the mockingbird who sat on the cupola of the courthouse while court was in session and so learned to sing: *Prisoner-look-upon-the-jury! Jury-look-upon-the-prisoner!* GUILTY! GUILTY! GUILTY! It is a little incredible that so much planning should need to be done. Don't people know how they want to live? As for politics, long since it became tawdry and uncertain. Politics is for lawyers. Cousin Roderick would no more think of running for the legislature than he would think of moving to China. In that, perhaps he lamentably differs from his ancestors. But in Rebelville political action is generally no more than a confirmation of what has been talked around among the clans. If you really want things done, you speak quietly to Cousin So-and-So and others that pass the word to everybody that counts. And then something is done.

In Rebelville the politics and economics of the bustling

world become a faint whisper. All that matters is to see one's friends and relatives and pass from house to house, from field to field, under Georgia skies; to gather at a simple family dinner where only three kinds of bread and four kinds of meat are flanked by collards, sweet potatoes, corn, pickles, fruits, salads, jams, and cakes; or at a barbecue for fifty or more, for which whole herds are slaughtered, it would seem, and entire pantries and gardens desolated; or to sit with the wise men in front of the store, swapping jokes and telling tales, hour after hour; or to hunt for fox, possum, coon, and quail, in swamp and field; or (for the ladies) to attend meetings of U.D.C.'s, D.A.R.'s, and Missionary Societies; or church service, or district conference, or the tender ceremonies of Confederate Memorial Day, or the high school entertainment; or to hear the voices of Negroes, sifting through the dusk, or the mockingbird in moonlight; or to see the dark pines against sunset, and the old house lifting its columns far away, calling the wanderer home. The scuppernongs are gone, and cotton is picked. But already the pecans are falling. And planting begins again while late roses and chrysanthemums are showing, and, even in the first frosts, the camellias are budding, against their December flowering. What though newspapers be loud, and wars and rumors threaten—it is only an academic buzzing, that one must tolerate for manners' sake. Sowing and harvest go together, and summer runs into winter, and in Georgia one is persuaded to take the horizontal view.

By some it may be said that dark clouds hang over Yankeetown and Rebelville—clouds of menace, maybe of destruction. I do not deny their presence, but my story is not of such clouds. In this strange modern world it may be observed that men talk continually of the good life without producing a specimen of it, to convince an inquirer. Brother Jonathan and Cousin Roderick do not talk about the good life. They lead it. If government is intended to serve human interests, what does it propose to do about them? If science is really intelligent, what does it mean by conniving to put a stigma upon them or to destroy them? I cannot believe that a government or a science which ignores or depreciates them is very trustworthy. I believe that government and science will fail unless they are taken into account. They, and others, are the incarnations of the principle of diversity through which the United States have become something better than Balkan, and without which the phrase "my country" is but a sorry and almost meaningless abstraction.

NEW YORK AND THE HINTERLAND

IN THE LOUD nineteen-twenties, when a Younger Generation could still hope to save the nation by disillusioning it, hardly anything American seemed destined to escape the scorn of the debunkers. A backward look, however, reveals a principle of selection that in former days was less apparent. Upon the Eastern metropolitan regions to which the Young Intellectuals were fleeing, the blows fell lightly and good-humoredly when they fell at all; this region, with Europe beyond, was their refuge. Regions of the South Atlantic Coast, though in the past they had greatly offended, were treated with some indulgence. Cities like Baltimore and Charleston, even parts of Virginia and North Carolina, were spared rough treatment; they were conceded a lingering modicum of civilization. But upon a region that came to be known as the hinterland, lying vaguely somewhere to the west and south, the blows fell ceaselessly, without quarter to persons, institutions, or localities.

Innocent of history as they were, the young scorners—many of whom were actually on the ragged edge of middle age—could hardly have been expected to know that their lament was so familiar in American annals as to be antique. The hinterland about which they complained was the Old West that long before this had annoyed the dynasties of Virginia and Massachusetts: it began then, as in the nineteen-twenties, with Kentucky and Tennessee, and extended through the enormous regions south and west to Texas and the Great Plains; and it covered the country north of the Ohio River and westward, athwart the upper reaches of the Mississippi Valley. The complaint of the nineteen-twenties was almost

identical, in some respects, with that of an earlier day: the
Eastern metropolitans were distressed by the uncouth manners
of the Western folk—in this case, their impudent disrespect
for the patterns of modernity that many of the critics were just
in the act of putting on for the first time.

The legend, thus renewed under peculiar circumstances,
of the barbarism of the South, especially in its southwestern
parts, and of the vulgarity and dullness of the Middle West,
for a good many years has governed the approach of the metropolitan East to the phenomena of life in the so-called hinterland. Whether the approach be literary, or sociological, or
merely journalistic, the assumptions have been always the
same, and the ensuing generalizations have been uniformly
tagged with shocked protest and pious exhortation. The South
—so the tale runs—is a region full of little else but lynchings,
shootings, chain gangs, poor whites, Ku Kluxers, hookworm,
pellagra, and a few decayed patricians whose chief intent is
to deprive the uncontaminated spiritual-singing Negro of his
life and liberty. But what is more shocking, it is inhabited by
believers in God, who pass anti-evolution laws; and more
shocking still, it is in thought and deed studiously backward
and antiprogressive. The Middle West—the tale says—is a
land of morons, boobs, and shoulder-smacking Babbitts, in
which, despite a plethora of schools and modern conveniences,
an artist soul feels cramped and misunderstood; or a land of
lonely farms where men and women drudge away their sterile
lives; or of repressions and shams, where tender little Clyde
Griffiths who start out as bellboys must perforce end up as
murderers. Over such pictures the East stormed, or shed
crocodile tears, in the clever nineteen-twenties.

The familiar condescension of the East for the West, of
course, may be viewed in part as the condescension of the
capital toward the provinces, or of the home country toward
the colonial dependencies. The American of the Atlantic coast
has been prone to cherish precisely the attitude of superiority
toward the outlying regions that the Englishman has assumed

toward the United States. The old New Yorker or New Englander, when not suppressing his real sentiments in order to
achieve a commercial or political bargain, has often spoken
of the manners of Westerners in the language of Mrs. Trol-
lope. But in the nineteen-twenties his condescension became
for the first time the source of an aesthetic theory which professed to explain the sterility of American art, and of a literary
fashion which produced a stream of "realistic" novels that
repeated over and over Mr. Van Wyck Brooks's strictures on
Puritanism and its fatal extension on the American continent,
or Mr. Mencken's volatile dissatisfaction with most things
indigenously American.

Although the aesthetic theory has lingered on rather per-
sistently, now and then fitfully reappearing in books like Ludwig Lewisohn's *Expression in America* or V. F. Calverton's
The Liberation of American Literature, the literary fashion
now seems to be falling on evil days. That the vitality has
gone out of it may be safely hazarded from the fact that the
Pulitzer judges, who are generally careful to stay at least five
or six years behind the times, have given an award to Mr.
T. S. Stribling's *The Store,* as the novel of the year that best
depicts American life. Since Mr. Stribling's theme is the old
theme of the backwardness of his native Southern region, we
are fairly well justified, under the circumstances, in labeling
that theme as dead. Furthermore, Mr. Mencken has left *The
American Mercury.* Mr. Bernard De Voto has demolished Mr.
Brooks's theory of Puritanism in frontier life. And Mr. Malcolm Cowley has sung a requiem over the home-coming remains of the Little Magazines and the expatriates of yesterday.
Now only a Pulitzer award for Mr. Erskine Caldwell is needed
to fill up the charnel house with bones of the long-since dead,
and to close one of the strangest, but one of the most ominous,
chapters in American literary history.

If there had not been a renaissance among historians, which
quietly began at almost the same time as the famous literary

renaissance, but produced its effects later, the literary fashion would doubtless have lasted longer and begotten more monstrous creations. It is strange—or perhaps it is not strange at all—that the historical movement has received little attention in comparison with the literary movement which it paralleled. The circumstances of its origin have not been recorded; its course has nowhere been charted. The genuine history of American life so quickly succeeded the debunking efforts of the rebel aesthetes that it must have been under way, as spadework and exploration, for a long time. Perhaps the rousing argument over American culture helped to give occasion for its appearance in a definitive and apprehensible form.

Now, at any rate, we can see that the years when Mr. Mencken and Mr. Lewis were blasting the hinterland with their negative excoriations were years of studied accumulation, in the hinterland itself, of the particular items of an American culture, or cultures, that the critics argued did not exist. Doubtless it was the slow drive of the historical movement that at last, somewhat to the surprise of Eastern publishers, swung popular taste away from realistic fiction to biography and history and ultimately forced even the intellectuals to reconsider the historical and cultural data which they had too blithely dismissed. In these years Claude Bowers' political studies of Jefferson and Hamilton and of the Reconstruction period swept the country; and a little later came James Truslow Adams with *The Epic of America* and *The Adams Family*. Although some of these books and others like them were in a popular or semipopular vein, they could not be passed by as insignificant, for they rested upon the solid foundation that the professional historians, unknown to the general public, had long been busy in erecting. From the semipopular books it was an easy step to the works of professional historians that were slowly but surely tipping the balance of American consideration. Of these works, many of which were of revolutionary importance, I shall name but two examples, for the general principles that they supply: the works of Frederick J. Turner, beginning with his study of the frontier and ending with his *Significance of the Sections in United States History;* and on the literary side, Vernon Parrington's *Main Currents in American Thought.*

A great many of the more notable histories were written by Southerners and Westerners—men from the regions that had been most severely attacked. Parrington was a man of the Far Northwest; Turner came from the Middle West; Ulrich B. Phillips, author of *Life and Labor in the Old South,* was a native of Georgia who had taught history at the University of Chicago; Beveridge and Bowers were Middle Westerners. Their account of the American past, and, by implication, their interpretation of the present, stood out in bold contradiction to *The Ordeal of Mark Twain* or *The Education of Henry Adams,* which had worked like a sweet poison in the veins of Eastern aesthetes. The new historical movement to a large extent denied the facts upon which the earlier critical statement had been based. But what was more important, the historians found the life of the hinterland rich, abundant, diverse, where the critics reported only barrenness. That it had serious blemishes, all admitted. But the Eastern explanations were not always the right explanations, and defects were not to be removed by the short cuts that were being prescribed. Eastern criticism implied that there was a sovereign national culture, still originating in the East and destined to rule the hinterland as its subject territory. But in the works of Turner and Parrington, the fundamental thesis read otherwise. The lands that were golden and had caught the westward spill of an Eastern population were no longer tributary. Now they were divided into the self-conscious and mature sections or regions into which the tendencies of their past and their physiographic environment had shaped them. There was no sovereign national culture for them to bow to, or none, at least, that was the private function of a region all too recognizable as an Eastern region.

In the historical movement, therefore, were not only the

facts for a rebuttal of metropolitan criticism, but the foundations of a self-assertive counterattack. The new regional movement at once built upon those foundations, adding to the work of the historians the researches of folklorists who were probing into the song, legends, and crafts that constituted the living and growing substratum of a native American culture.

The upshot was a counterstroke of a kind new in American history. The contention between East and West was not new. But the old quarrels had dealt with matters economic and political. In matters cultural the hinterland had in general previously aspired to possess the terms of civilization approved in the East from which it had lately come. Now the old economic and political feud was to reach into a new field. There was to be a battle of cultures as well. The quarrel was as to how people ought to live.

It is neither possible nor sensible to wave aside the metropolitan attack as completely futile or completely mistaken. It was often brilliant and sometimes pointed. But when one begins to ask what way of life the critics wanted the hinterland to adopt, one must pass by whatever undeniable merit the criticism may have had for its no less undeniable, and now startling, weaknesses. The works of the critics were anathemas, not credos. It is not easy to disentangle from their utterances any positive scheme to which they would give allegiance. Occasionally Mr. Mencken talked about "decency" or "intelligence." The advocates of "creative criticism" wanted personal taste to overrule aesthetic or historical standards. Mr. Van Wyck Brooks and others were anti-Puritan; but many of this school were so ill-informed historically that they thought Puritanism, Methodism, and Victorianism were precisely the same thing. Nearly all the critics were antireligious; nearly all preferred an aesthetic judgment to a moral one. All were anti-Victorian, and talked a lot about Freud and sex. If they had any strong positive belief, it was in the power of science to determine the conditions of human life, and in the power of

art to soothe and make genteel. Politics, economics, world affairs were at the moment beneath their notice. They did not
believe very firmly in anything; but they disbelieved stoutly
in a very great deal. They were sceptics or cynics. They had
cast off loyalties to place or kin, or they had none to begin
with. Though their ranks numbered a few men of native
Eastern stock, the greater number were of two sorts: migrants
to New York from some region of the hinterland, from which
they had escaped in search of a career; or scions of the newer
immigrant stock—the expatriated nationals from a medley of
European countries—who had no intimate share in the historic experience of any American place. Their temper was
cosmopolitan in a way; but the intensity of their dissociation
gives point to Chesterton's remark that New York, though a
cosmopolitan city, is not a city of cosmopolitans. The essence
of the doctrine that they sought to convey to outlying America
may be stated in one word: Decadence.

But at the moment when the Younger Generation were
making a choice for Decadence, the great regions of the South
and West had put their stormy youth behind them and were
ready for the counsels of vigorous maturity. In contrast with
the states of the Northeast and the Middle Atlantic, in which
the old American stock had become a minority, the population of the South was almost wholly native, and, if the Negroes
were excepted, it was still basically of the old colonial breed.
In the Middle West the same stock was still a dominant ma-
jority, which was far more successful than the East had been
in attracting and assimilating its later immigrants—largely
Scandinavians and Germans who were racially akin to the
older stock. The regions—physiographically linked as one by
conditions of life in the Mississippi Valley, but sectionally
split into a north and south by deep historic causes—were the
Old West of American story, the seat, for more than a hundred
years, of the "self-conscious American democracy" of Turner's
phrase. There were many reasons why the regions should examine their life in order to understand its strength or correct

its abuses. But within themselves there was no reason whatever for seeking salvation in Decadence.

It is one of the tragedies of American history that the intellectual leadership of the United States at this time should have been even temporarily in the hands of a group of artists and thinkers who were more impressed by the economic and artistic defeatism of postwar Europe than by the living and diverse traditions of their native America. But there they were, in New York. From old habit the regions looked naturally to the East, as one source from which to derive cultural guides and examples. Besides, New York had accumulated not only the prestige but all the material appointments of an intellectual capital. New York had a vigorous press, able critical journals, thriving publishing houses. It had wealth and power with which to influence or control opinion so far as opinion could be reached through urban agencies.

What the regions of the hinterland did not see at the time was that New York was beginning a spiritual secession from the America of which it had been an organic part. In its population it was already a foreign city, with an amazing preponderance of heterogeneous new racial stocks. Yet the mixed population mattered far less than the ideas which its peculiar sensitivity to the European postwar situation predisposed its intellectual leaders to transmit. For one reason or another these ideas had little to do with the fundamental European tradition which in times past had been valuable to American thought. What came across the Atlantic in the nineteen-twenties was the rationalized despair of European groups that felt vitality and power slipping from them or the rationalized aspiration of other groups, some of which were not essentially European at all, that were clutching after power. They were ideas born of political and economic situations that did not apply in the United States.

Thus it happened that New York transmitted, to the one people on earth who were freest of class-consciousness, the Marxian theory of the war of the classes. To the least neurotic and most energetic of races it offered the Freudian doctrine of repressions and complexes. To a people the greater part of whom were schooled in Protestant religion and morality New York presented, with a knowing leer, under the guise of literary classics, the works of voluptuaries and perverts, the teeming pages of *Psychopathia Sexualis,* and all the choicest remains of the literary bordellos of the ancient and modern world. German Expressionism, French Dadaism, the erotic primitivism of D. H. Lawrence, the gigantic *fin de siècle* pedantries and experimentalisms of James Joyce, the infantilism of Gertrude Stein and various Parisian coteries—these furnished most of the catchwords for all the clever people.

While all this was happening, the New Poetry movement was captured by Amy Lowell and the *emigrés* and given so thoroughly cosmopolitan a turn that it lost all root in America. Its aesthetics, always a little cloudy, became so tenuous that the reaction, when it set in, leaned over backward in excessive zeal for the scholarly, the learned, the exact. Poets like Frost, Robinson, or Lindsay, who wrote out of a frankly American experience, had to be looked at through a thick haze of French symbolist verse. Their traditionalism was as little understood as the more self-conscious and entirely different traditionalism of T. S. Eliot, which came a little later. Prohibition was iniquitous; the Versailles Treaty was iniquitous; politics, God, the Ohio Gang, the Old South, the New Middle West—all were iniquitous somehow or other, and were denounced in the tipsy medley that went on and on. It was the fashion, in fact, to be very pessimistic and a little drunk most of the time. While New York read *The Decline of the West,* Joseph Wood Krutch defined the modern temper as an artistic acceptance of coming doom, and quoted the "Hail, horrors!" speech of Milton's Rebel Angel in the accents of a toper who begins to recall snatches of poetry at 2 A.M.

To offer this farrago to the hinterland of America as representing what was worth thinking about in all fields of thought and was worth using as *exempla* of the good life was like

giving a man in ordinary health the perfected hypodermic
needle with which the complaisant quack furnishes the drug
addict. To the sections rebuked as lacking in civilization the
critics recommended, it would seem, the diseases of civilization rather than the true urbanity and high thinking that
would be expected to emanate from a civilized metropolis.
To the most powerful nation on the globe, unravaged by war
and anything but disheartened by circumstance, the spokesmen of New York found nothing better to offer than a gospel
of impotence and defeat.

Out of the various results of this process, three stand out as
important. First, the life of the outlying regions and the art
which they were now ready to produce—for the first time
abundantly, and consistently with their own traditions—were
judged in New York in the light of the weak cosmopolitanism
or decayed Europeanism in which the critical spokesmen were
interested. This judgment, once made and reported, was dis-
seminated in two directions. Since New York is the main chan-
nel of communication between America and Europe, it was
the New York account of the estate of the hinterland that
went abroad. And in telling foreign capitals what New York
thought of the hinterland, New York gave it the meaning that
Europe was only too eager to accept as correct. The black
reputation of America in Europe, though brought about in
part by political and economic causes, has clearly been moti-
vated and sustained by damaging evidence furnished from
New York. It was a strange disproportion that allowed a single
city, in a far eastern corner of America, a practical monopoly
in reporting the life of a continental area that it did not pre-
tend to understand. It is painful to recall how often that report
has been partial, how rarely it has been catholic. From one
point of view, such reporting looks almost like a betrayal of
the country from which New York draws its wealth, its power,
its life. But more likely it is only a blind presumption, which
a dweller in the hinterland can observe with incredulity and
growing irritation.

But New York views, New York standards, New York criticism of the nineteen-twenties also passed readily by domestic
channels into the hinterland itself. Far from being illiterate,
as the critics were charging, the regions of the hinterland now
seem to have been almost too literate for their own good. As
New York never failed to read British criticisms of America,
so the hinterland did not fail to read the books of its Eastern
castigators, and often made them best-sellers in the regions
most fiercely castigated. The younger generation of the hinterland, pouring from the crowded high schools and colleges, almost pathetically eager to keep up with the swift pace of the
times, were often enough persuaded to hail the literature of
disillusionment as the flag of their emancipation. In part, we
cannot doubt that the metropolitan onslaught made decided
progress within the hinterland; it captured, it perverted, it
inspired or deflated. But in part it also angered. As the historical movements gathered force, and as old political and
economic issues again came to the front, regional anger was
gradually fortified by deliberate cultural resistance of a kind
less easily routed than Fundamentalism or Ku Kluxism. A
still younger generation has arisen to succeed the younger
generation that was half persuaded to deny itself. To this
youngest generation Decadence makes little appeal, and the
metropolitan promise of New York is sterile. This generation
is ready, perhaps, to make the reply which the oldest generation, angered by metropolitan attacks, could frame only in
antiquated terms. That reply is regionalism, a doctrine of self-
determination which renews, in different terms, the old cleav-
age between the lands of the East and those of the South and
West.

This yielding and this resistance will serve to explain some
of the damaging confusions that the student of regionalism
will find today in whatever regions he attempts to explore. To
the onslaught of dissociated New York and to the mixed reaction of the hinterland are due the contradictory phenomena

that flourish side by side. In any given region one is sure to find warring schools of thought, opposing groups of writers, clashing social tendencies. Among the writers there are always regionalists, conscious or unconscious, old or young, who are loyal, and metropolitans who repeat the critical strictures of a decade ago. In Georgia, for example, are John Donald Wade and Erskine Caldwell, and what Wade loves the other hates; in Mississippi, Stark Young and William Faulkner; in Tennessee, T. S. Stribling and Allen Tate; in the Middle West, Willa Cather and Theodore Dreiser, Vachel Lindsay and Ben Hecht. The same confusion puts skyscrapers in cities whose chief resource is plenitude of land; Hollywood manners in mountain cabins; French eroticism in Puritan households; the urban wisecrack in the mouths of Sut Lovingood's grandchildren. But deeper than this conflict, which from day to day changes its terms, is a constant element: the inertia of the regions, which is also their unself-conscious life, their differentiating vitality. This constant element, which may be veiled but can never be obliterated, is likely to prove the deciding element.

But, lastly, the consequences of the situation are no less important for New York and the East than for the hinterland. If New York is to be an intellectual capital, New York ought to consider realistically what kind of relation to the hinterland will make its position secure and its function good. Obviously, New York cannot endure the impoverishment within itself which would be the result of too severe a dissociation. But that is exactly the result which its past tendencies have seemed to invite. Habituated to a conception of itself as metropolitan arbiter of taste and ideas, New York has erred in thinking that it can impose as freely as it can judge. America is not, as New York thinks, so nearly uniform, or so closely approaching the metropolitan image as to accept without demur any image proposed from New York. It would be more in point to contemplate the other possibility—that eventually New

York might no more be able to determine the life of regions around Chicago, New Orleans, San Francisco than it can now determine Rome or Vienna.

New York has generally refused to contemplate such a possibility. This refusal, when combined with the aesthetic preferences and forms of life that it has been prone to cultivate, threatens to make New York almost as much a center of repulsion as of attraction, and tends to deprive it of the continual refreshment from provincial sources that a capital might normally expect. Without too great temerity, one might find in this situation a partial explanation of the decay of its critical thought, or of the rapid transformation of many of its periodicals from "national" journals to sectional and propagandistic organs. Through a like consideration one can begin to understand books that are otherwise meaningless: the labored attempts of Waldo Frank, Granville Hicks, Ludwig Lewisohn, V. F. Calverton to camouflage American traditions with their own peculiar obsessions about sex, Zionism, and the downtrodden proletariat. One can also understand why New York journalists and critics so often essay by sheer noise to howl down any dissidence within their own metropolitan neighborhood, or the more ominous dissidence of Old New England, to which the turn of affairs in the nineteen-twenties was far from pleasing. But none of these attempts, understandable though they may be, will make New York a good capital, for they do not check the process of dissociation that has already set in. It cannot be checked unless New York will recognize that the hinterland of America is no longer New York's hinterland. But it is, as it has always been, the West, or the Southwest, where lands were golden once; and for dwellers there, self-reliant and not without a power of their own, they are golden still.

REGIONALISM AND NATIONALISM

IN AMERICAN LITERATURE

LIKE MANY other terms appropriated from the language of science, the words *region* and *regionalism* lose all exactness when they enter the literary vocabulary. But the resulting errors and confusions might well have been expected. The advent of the new terms is in itself the fact of prime importance, suggesting as it does that American criticism has recently encountered a problem it was not prepared to face or even to name. In desperation, the critics have made shift to borrow a name, but hardly as yet have they been willing to get down to the business of definition. For one group of critics regionalism is a catchword which they use almost as a formula of dismissal for tendencies that they do not bother to take seriously. For another group regionalism is a battle cry, the symbol of all they feel is worth fighting for in the reconstruction of American literature.

The first group are largely metropolitan critics. Their seat is the seat of power, in the great cities of the East. They enjoy a strategic advantage in that they have the means of conveying the impression that they themselves stand for what is forward-looking and alive; and they are content that the soft word *regional* should come to represent what the opposite party stand for: something, they would like to think, harmless and insignificant enough. But the opposite party refuse to let the soft word remain soft. They are not metropolitans. They are scattered in groups throughout the United States, now in a city of the West, now in a town or some country district of the South. They belong to the provinces, or, they often prefer to say, the regions. There is war between them and the metropolitans. It is probably only the beginning of a debate which may turn out to be the most important critical discussion in American history, for the issue is: What are the conditions under which American literature can achieve its full maturity?

This question is the central theme of Granville Hicks's book *The Great Tradition*. Though the major question is painfully narrowed to fit Mr. Hicks's Marxian economics and prejudices, here we may find, incidentally, the typical metropolitan idea of what regionalism is. To Mr. Hicks, regionalism is simply an evasion of the problems that touch the artist as one who ought to contemplate "the fundamental unity of the nation." It is an "escape," which may be merely "antiquarian," or it may be "a sentimental expression of sectional pride." Even when writers deal with "life in a particular region simply because it was the material experience gave them" (like Elizabeth Madox Roberts), they are doomed to sterility if they cannot surpass the narrow regional bounds. The regional approach, Mr. Hicks admits, may be valuable in the early part of a writer's career. "If he knows the manners and speech of a particular region, all well and good. But he cannot stop there; any honest attempt to understand the region quickly takes him outside its borders."

The errors of this view of regionalism are common, even among critics who do not, like Mr. Hicks, hold that a national American literature must take the class struggle as its central theme. The error is, first, in assuming that the character of a regional art is determined principally by its subject matter, which must be local and special, and next by its manner, which must be romantic and retrospective. The second error, which grows out of the first, consists in passing to the conclusion that regional art is necessarily at odds with national art, or is at best subordinate, minor and petty.

This is a kind of reasoning that seems to accompany adherence to the Marxian cause. It has nothing at all to do with the actual phenomena of American literature, past and present. If the regional work of art is to be distinguished by its "regional" subject matter, then what is the subject matter of the national work of art? Must it include the whole vast complex of our regional areas, or is it a magic elixir that can be extracted from them? It is not easy to discover an American work of art that meets either of these requirements. Where is the novel, poem, or play that deals with an experience of life common to all Americans, as Americans? I can think of a book that attempts to interpret the "typical" American: it is Henry James's novel *The American*. But the instance is embarrassing and inconclusive, for it suggests that a novelist must forsake America and become an exile if he is going to purify the American type from all the clinging alloys of local circumstance. And is James's *The American* a national work of art because of its generalized subject, and Hawthorne's *The Scarlet Letter* less than national because of its highly specialized subject matter? Is Poe, who wrote about no particular place, a clearer representative of the national genius than Mark Twain? Do *An American Tragedy* and *Strange Interlude* embody some national tradition not found in *The Sheltered Life, The Time of Man, Winesburg, Ohio, My Antonia, North of Boston,* or *Uncle Remus*?

It is clearly impossible to put on one side the works that are national by reason of their general subject matter and on the other side works that are regional because of their limited subject matter. The instinct of our writers, in fact, has consistently led them away from any such false distinctions. Writers who have attempted the great national theme are rare. Whitman is perhaps the single important instance, and the nature of his deliberate attempt to formulate a national theme is in itself very instructive. On page after page Whitman assures us that the national American poem must be written, and he is always telling us in what terms it will have to be written; but he himself does not write it. Instead, in every passage where he wishes to be quite clearly national, slighting no special interest and neglecting no peculiarity, he resorts to the catalogue, and gives us a list of all species and subspecies of Americana. The important aesthetic feature of the Whitman catalogue is its formlessness; the heterogeneous materials do not fuse into a splendid unity; they remain heterogeneous. They may be accepted intellectually, but they do not always persuade emotionally. The really persuasive parts of Whitman are those poems, like "Crossing Brooklyn Ferry," that touch Whitman's own special locale; and these, too, have as much form as Whitman ever achieves.

The test of manner is quite as unreliable as the test of subject matter. We could get up a highly miscellaneous list of works and authors that might be considered romantic, retrospective, or even antiquarian: most of Hawthorne, Cooper, and Irving; *Moby Dick, The Vision of Sir Launfal, Life on the Mississippi;* a good deal of Edith Wharton, James Branch Cabell, E. A. Robinson, Lindsay, Masters, Jack London. Are these to be excluded from the properly national shelf, upon the complaint that Mr. Hicks brings against regionalists; and are we to put there, instead, only works that are realistic and topical? There could be no more damning illustration of the low intellectual level to which our criticism has sunk than Mr. Hicks's notion that good art is in the present tense or possibly the future tense. The artists are not so meek as Mr. Hicks seems to think, and they will inevitably claim the privilege of writing in the past tense if they feel like it. It is not the time element that constitutes the weakness of merely retrospective or antiquarian books; nor is there here any unerring means of distinguishing works that are regional, not national.

What we have in the United States is a group of regions, and writers in them who exhibit diverse and conflicting tendencies even when they are identifiable as regional by the misleading tests that I have mentioned. It is a kind of special pleading to pick out one writer, Miss Roberts, and say: "This is a regionalist," and then to say of another writer of the same region, who might be Mr. Faulkner: "But this is a nationalist." We must deal with them all together, in their regions, if we are to talk sense.

We cannot define regionalism unless at the same time we

define nationalism. The two are supplementary aspects of the same thing. Regionalism is a name for a condition under which the national American literature exists as a literature: that is, its constant tendency to decentralize rather than to centralize; or to correct overcentralization by conscious decentralization. Or it describes the conditions and attitudes under which it is possible for literature to be a normal artistic outgrowth of the life of a region.

A regional literature, so-called, may thus very well be, among other things, a self-conscious expression of the life of a region. It may exploit intimate and local aspects of its scene, thus recovering the "usable past" so much referred to; but it does not narrow itself to mere picturesqueness and antiquarianism except as a reaction to an overdose of metropolitan nationalism. The overdose and the reaction are both regrettable. But the pettiness or belligerency that they produce are not the inevitable features of a good regional literature, for a good regional literature needs only (to quote Allen Tate) "the immediate, organic sense of life in which a fine artist works."

The national literature is the compound of the regional impulses, not antithetical to them, but embracing them and living in them as the roots, branch, and flower of its being. But I must here note that the relation between the national and the regional has an importance peculiar to American literature alone among the literatures of Western peoples. We are obliged to face problems that arise out of our fairly late arrival at the critical concept of a national American literature as the logical accompaniment of our achievement of political nationality; and out of the slowly dawning recognition that our political unity has to be very imperfectly accommodated to a real cultural diversity.

The concept of a national literature is a modern phenomenon, produced by the rise of the European nations to self-consciousness during the later states of the Renaissance. Before the Renaissance there were critical philosophies of literature, but not of national literature. The European idea of a national literature comes well after such literatures have taken definite shape. It is an attempt to rationalize a cultural tradition which it became almost a point of honor to label as a distinctive possession. The rationalization, furthermore, was made in the great days of the theory of evolution. If the modern Englishman had evolved from a one-cell organism up to the state of Victorian complexity represented in Mr. Gladstone, then English literature had to be exhibited as mounting nobly up the evolutionary ladder from amoebic verse to the lofty periods of Alfred, Lord Tennyson. The scientific analogy was probably a doubtful one, but in other respects the historians of national literatures in nineteenth-century Europe had a plausible case. They could define the nation's literature as the expression, attained by slow accretion and ingrained habit, of a character that might be described as national.

The existence of such a literature depended, however, upon certain conditions: one language, one race, a definite cultural homogeneity—or at least no heterogeneity fixed by inner geographic divisions; a definite intellectual leadership associated with the centralizing presence of a capital like Paris or London; and besides, a long period of growth under aristocratic and learned guidance, and a second period, no less important from the modern standpoint, of critical and retrospective exploration of the cultural tradition. Whatever critical questions might confront a literature thus formed, no Englishman ever needed to ask of a given work in his own language: "But is it really English?"

Yet in America for a hundred years we have continually felt obliged to ask of this or that American work: "But is it really American? Does it represent the nation?" And we have never ceased to be embarrassed at our inablility to produce a really satisfactory answer.

Our embarrassment is caused, not by the impossibility of making an answer, but by a wrong application of the European analogy. We can have, we do have, a national American literature, but not in the European sense, because we have not fulfilled the European conditions. One language we do have, and the rough cultural homogeneity that originates in our basic racial stock. Upon such a foundation, if we had remained a nation of the Atlantic seaboard, without a westward expansion or a great access of immigration, we might have recapitulated European conditions. But in the midst of our nation-making we both expanded into the West and received mixed population-elements that are still far from perfectly fused. Thus we cut ourselves off from all immediate prospect of achieving the kind of unity that in Europe has produced national literatures. Our literature, as an American literature, has no long tradition of unself-conscious growth. The nearest related tradition of that order, the English tradition, however precious it may be, does not come to us hallowed by associations of place and folk-way. It is not a part of our atmosphere, and to apprehend it requires an effort of the will that Englishmen do not have to make. We are a heterogeneous people, who in sheer consistency of democratic principle have learned to tolerate a mixture of religions and races, and not even the leveling power of an industrial system has been able to efface the resulting diversities. But to increase the difficulty, these diversities have shown a tendency to concentrate within geographic areas, which we call sections or regions. Finally, we have no center. No one city, for us, combines the functions of an economic and political capital with those of an intellectual capital. But in our literary history we have had a series of regional capitals—Philadelphia, Boston, Charleston, New York, Chicago—which have made their successive bids for attention.

Never have we been of one mind nationally; never have we experienced the "national glow of thought and feeling" that Arnold found characteristic of the great literary periods. Instead we have had a series of glows, appearing now in New England alone, now in the Middle States, now in the South or West. The literary tendencies that emerge from this complex of regional aspirations, as they interweave and form general movements. furnish us with the only kind of literary his-

tory that we can call national. So long as we speak of it as
American literature, we are safe; but when we insist upon its
performance as a national American literature, without the
qualifications indicated, we fall into error. It is hard to discover the typically American features shared by Mark Twain
and Hawthorne, Whitman and Poe, Dreiser and Cabell; it is
easier to discover the common traits possessed by members of
a New England, a Southern, a Western group.

For some time to come our literature will not represent a
uniform culture, but will be conditioned by the diverse regional cultures upon which it depends for its vitality. We
should welcome this tendency rather than rebel against it.
For out of this complexity we may draw a strength that will
allow us to escape the doom that seems to hang over national
cultures as soon as they pass their peak of self-conscious unification. No other great literature has ever enjoyed the prospect open to us, of an almost indefinite enrichment from
provincial sources that are not, in the usual sense of the
word, provincial at all, for our provinces are more like nations than provinces. To use the opportunity well, we have
need of a kind of Federal principle in our national criticism;
and we ought to be suspicious of any contrary principle which
would lay upon us the obligation to imitate the decadent
stages of the kind of national literature we have never had.

Throughout our history, however, the question of whether
or not to imitate has been a compulsive ghost, haunting all
our moments of earnest self-analysis with shadowy European
analogies that in the sacred name of civilization we are urged
to follow, or that in the still more sacred name of American
civilization we are besought to reject. We ought to shun both
alternatives as irrelevant. Our problems are in the domestic
field, and ought never to be settled in the light of foreign
relations, inescapable though these may be. The domestic
problem is, not how shall we achieve a unity that may be
spurious and deceptive, but how shall we secure the artistic

and cultural equilibrium that will give free play to our diverse regional geniuses.

That equilibrium is endangered whenever, in an excess of critical self-consciousness, we turn either regionalism or nationalism into a shibboleth, making either one or the other an "ism" of the dogmatic kind, with followers emitting aesthetic credos and rigid literary programs. We then enter the field of vituperation and combat, where the controversial parties are encumbered with the vices of oversimplification.

From Emerson and Whitman down to Messrs. Calverton, Hicks, and Lewisohn, the national shibboleth or "ism" has taken on various simplifications. When Emerson urged that we walk on our own feet and work with our own hands, the grandeur of his rhetoric obscured, for the moment, the insufficiency of the principle upon which he hoped to base the independence and unity of American letters. In that admirable peroration of "The American Scholar" in which he deplored our division into a North and a South, Emerson had no better principle of union to offer than the Yankee transcendentalism which, even at that moment, in another aspect than the literary, was about to attack and all but destroy the very foundations of Southern culture. His voice was not the voice of America, but of New England, and his plan of salvation was to result not in peaceful unification but in bloody disunion.

In our own time, the metropolitan critics are making national prescriptions that are equally partial, though somewhat more confused. In one sentence they assure us that the industrial unification of America is desirable and inevitable; but in the next sentence they declare that the civilization thus produced puts upon us an intolerable spiritual bondage from which the artist cannot escape save through the shibboleths of Marxism and Freudianism. Wearily, they proclaim that America is standardized; but angrily they scorn the rural backwardness of regions that prove to be, after all, less urban than New

York. Confidently they announce that America must be industrialized; but they sneer at Mr. Babbitt of the Middle West, the creature of industrialism. They urge the provinces to adopt the intellectual sophistication of the Eastern metropolis; but among themselves they bewail the poverty of the modern temper, which in its sophistication has left them nothing to enjoy.

Their error is precisely like Emerson's and has far less nobility in it. As a basis for national unity they offer the apologetic mechanisms that the metropolis sets up to explain away and palliate its own diseases. The impact of their arguments on American thought has been on the whole confusing and corrupting; but it is now clear that they cannot win out completely over the regions, except at the cost of a dangerous struggle.

For already the reaction has set in. Regionalism, so far as it is an actual literary movement, is in large measure a protest, sometimes angry and intense, but more often calm and assured, against the false nationalism that the metropolitans have been disseminating. No one who has studied American history intelligently could doubt that such a protest had to come. It is the American means of restoring our lost balance.

But the regionalists, in the extremity of their natural reaction, have also not been guiltless of oversimplification. The dangers of regionalism, if in its turn it becomes a shibboleth, begin at the point where aesthetic rationalization magnifies means into ends. Consider, for example, the new "regional" consciousness of folk art. The immense research into folk-ways that has characterized the regional movement is of enormous instrumental value. For critical and historical purposes we need to know a great deal about American ballads, songs, stories, myths. But there is some doubt whether in recovering these critically we can also recover them creatively, except by simulating a naïveté which, the critics assure us, the modern principle of sincerity will never permit. The regionalist may

well retort that naïveté in literature does have a value, but
only when it is assumed or simulated. The danger is, however,
that the regionalist, in attempting through folklore to express
the genius of place, will be content merely to dwell among
the artifacts he has dug up, and will thus narrow his expression almost to documentary limits. We shall have to wait on
performance to see what the function of a folk-pattern is in
American literature; but meanwhile the regionalist should
be warned against retiring into folklore as into an ivory tower.
Folklore is good, but alone it is not good enough, it is only
one feature of a regional literature. And the modernist critics
are right in their claim that modern issues cannot be evaded.
The writer of a given region cannot shut himself away under
the name "regionalist"; but he must, from his region, confront
the total and moving world.

Such calamitous retirements, however, are not implied in
the organic relation of regional and national elements that I
have tried to describe. When the two become warring "isms,"
they have the common defect of anaesthetizing the artist
against reality. Of the two, considered as "isms," nationalism
is the more vicious, in its present aspect at least, for it is harsh,
oppressive, and swaggering. Regionalism proposes to live and
let live, and its narrow or belligerent features will fall away
quickly enough when the repressive force is softened or removed.

I return to my central point. Regionalism is not an end in
itself, not a literary affectation, not an aesthetic credo, but a
condition of literary realization. The function of a region is
to endow the American artist with character and purpose. He
is born of a region. He will deny its parenthood to his own
hurt. Without its background he is a homeless exile in the
wilderness of modern life. That self which he is, if not ig-
nobly impugned, will readily be a modern self; and what he
creates, if he can resist the perversions of our time, will be
the expression of both the region and himself, no matter what

the subject or what the style. It is the office of the nation to conserve and cherish this free effort, and surely never by precept or example to delude us into thinking that a novel about a plowboy is only a regional curiosity, but a novel about a bellboy, a national masterpiece.

INDEX